William Carlos Williams

AN AMERICAN ARTIST

James E. B. Breslin

WITH A NEW PREFACE

D0873646

The University of Chicago Press
Chicago and London

The University of Chicago Press, Chicago 60637
The University of Chicago Press, Ltd., London

© 1970, 1985 by James E. Breslin
All rights reserved. Published 1970
University of Chicago Press edition 1985
Printed in the United States of America

94 93 92 91 90 89 88 87 86 85   5 4 3 2 1

Library of Congress Cataloging-in-Publication Data

Breslin, James E. B., 1935–
    William Carlos Williams, an American artist.

    Includes index.
    1. Williams, William Carlos, 1883–1963—Criticism and
interpretation.   I. Title.
PS3545.I544Z577   1985   811'.52   85–16343
ISBN 0–226–07407–2 (paper)

To the memory of

James T. Breslin
Marion M. Breslin
John F. Breslin

01226 2047

Grateful acknowledgment is given to the following publishers for permission to reprint from their publications:

Beacon Press for *I Wanted To Write a Poem* by William Carlos Williams, edited by Edith Heal. Copyright © 1958 by William Carlos Williams.

City Lights Books for *Kora in Hell* by William Carlos Williams. Copyright 1920 and © 1957 by The Four Seas Company, Boston.

New Directions Publishing Corporation for letter to his brother (1908), including poem about Isadora Duncan, copyright © 1970 by Florence H. Williams; *Collected Earlier Poems*, copyright 1938, 1951 by William Carlos Williams; *Paterson*, copyright 1946, 1948, 1949, 1951, © 1958 by William Carlos Williams; *Paterson*, Book VI, copyright © 1963 by Florence H. Williams; *Pictures from Brueghel and Other Poems*, copyright 1954 by William Carlos Williams; *Poems*, all rights reserved; *In the American Grain*, copyright 1925 by James Laughlin, copyright 1933 by William Carlos Williams; *The Great American Novel*, copyright 1923 by William Carlos Williams; *The Farmers' Daughters*, copyright 1932 by William Carlos Williams, copyright © 1957 by Florence H. Williams; *White Mule*, copyright 1937 by New Directions Publishing Corporation; *Personae* by Ezra Pound, copyright 1926 by Ezra Pound.

Contents

Preface, 1985

When I told my wife that my Williams book was going to be reissued, she said, "It's like Lazarus come back from the dead." Sylvia Plath has written a poem exploring what it would feel like to be Lazarus. But what would it be like to be Lazarus' father? At fifteen *William Carlos Williams, An American Artist*, having several years ago been remaindered and then expired, was now stirring in his grave clothes. Would we have him for Sunday dinner? Would anybody else?

Perhaps with a few organ transplants, a blood transfusion and a new suit, he could be made vital and even presentable. But surgery and shopping take time, more than I'm now willing to give. The solution, then, is to deal with the book as with any other possibly disappointing adolescent: the damage has all been done; lead him to the door and send him off—but not without a few parting recriminations.

Recently I found in my University office a photograph of myself taken just as I was finishing this book: thin hair slicked down across my forehead, tweed jacket, striped shirt, thin tie, slightly fleshy and slightly worn (darkened areas under the eyes), a mournful and apprehensive look to the eyes, an upward curl of the mouth giving a hostile edge. The author at thirty-two, constrained and surly. One of the constraints was the Berkeley tenure system: a book in six years or it's back on the job market. In fact, during my first week in Berkeley I had lunch with the senior professor who had read my dissertation for the department. At the faculty club we sat underneath an enormous moose head and I lunged around desperately looking for an area of mutual agreement. Afterward, on the way back to our offices, he confided to me that it was really impossible to write about Williams: it was like explaining jokes. The thought flashed through my mind, would the tenure faculty go for three hundred blank pages? Flaubert had imagined a novel about nothing; how about a critical work that would *be* nothing? No; better risk violating Williams than my career. But my prospects seemed dim.

At the time Williams was a marginal figure (from New Jersey) in the canon of English and American literature. At the time I was a marginal figure (from Brooklyn) in a department of Ivy League graduates. Surly but constrained, I admired Williams as a belligerent rebel. My job, however, was to please authority: to take two marginal figures and install them both within the academy. In my case at least, it worked. I grew a beard and began wearing Mexican wedding shirts to class.

My identification with Williams gave my book an enthusiastic sympathy for his work, but it also created an idealization of Williams that now strikes me as false and limiting. The book's tone is too serious, its substance too identified with Williams; heroizing him as someone who refused constraints created its own kind of constraint—eliminating the playfulness and skepticism that would create a fuller and more human picture of him.

At the time, moreover, I was a "lapsed" Catholic, as we were called in those days before they started serving whole wheat for the communion service; my anticlericalism made me eager to find Williams a *secular* authority. But a sacred principle clearly resides at the center of Williams' poetics. He gives it many different names—the "filthy Passaic" of "The Wanderer," Kora of *Kora in Hell* and *Spring and All*, the "She" of the DeSoto chapter of *In the American Grain*, the "Beautiful Thing" of *Paterson*, the "secret core" of the self in the *Autobiography*, the "light" in "Of Asphodel"—and he gives it so many names because no name, no words, can ever fully capture this elusive, hidden "presence." Williams stresses its manifestation in physicality—the body or the earth—and he does not imagine it as existing separately from matter and so it is hard to call it transcendent. Yet this principle is eternal, universal (the "all" of *Spring and All*) and sacred, and so it is hard not to call it transcendent. Acknowledging this sacred presence would have

enabled me to see Williams, like so many of the modernist generation, as a poet whose anti-romanticism is a cover for his latent
romanticism; it also would have strengthened, and complicated,
my argument for his connection to Whitman.

Williams's sacred principle always turns out to be female—an
equation that points to another (by me) unquestioned element of
his thinking, his idealization of women. In the *Autobiography* he
recalls that "men have given the direction to my life and women
have always supplied the energy." Combative with many of the
males of his own generation, Williams mythologized the female as
the creative "source" or "core" (Kora). This view limited in proportion as it elevated women in Williams's imagination. In "The pure
products of America," Elsie expresses the truth about "us" with
her "broken // brain"; she is "voluptuous water"—sensuous
fluidity, unconscious physicality. That Williams admires these
qualities makes his conception no less narrow. For what's lacking
in the female is mind, direction. Williams heroizes Madame Curie
in Book IV of *Paterson*, but he physicalizes her mental achieve-
ments by imagining her scientific quest as a pregnancy.

Williams similarly mythologizes the lower classes. Through his
medical practice he knew the poor as no other modern writer did,
and his stories often explore his mixed feelings toward his patients.
Yet much of the writing of this advocate of particularity is premised on a very simple and abstract social mythology. The well-to-
do are brutal, as in "The Yachts"; the members of the middle class,
like the suburban "us" of "The pure products," are bland, lacking
in color, force, or hard-edged particularity. "It is only in isolate
flecks that / something / is given off"; it is only among socially
marginal figures, like Elsie, that a "crazy" but vital energy can be
found. For Williams, dreams of upward mobility, of "cheap /
jewelry / and rich young men with fine eyes," only alienate the
poor from the sacred ground, "the earth under our feet." Of
course, this view is more likely to be held in the suburbs than in the
inner city; its romanticizing of the poor implicitly argues against
social change. In his well-known letter to Marianne Moore, Williams spoke of his "sudden resignation to existence, a despair"; he
wanted contact with things *as they are* and so he was a fierce

antagonist of all—be it social, historical, economic or linguistic—
that mediated between him and "existence." Yet he was also a
fatalist who "resigned" himself to some sort of mediation as inevitable; this inevitability explains why the creative principle can never
be caught and made fully present. Williams, then, was a cultural
radical whose deepest instincts led to political quiescence.

William Carlos Williams, An American Artist was written in Berkeley between 1964 and 1969—that is to say, it was begun during
the Free Speech Movement, worked on during the Third World
Strike and the anti-war protests, and completed during the People's Park "riots." In 1968 there was a major fire in the English
Department building on the Berkeley campus and for a few pan-
icked hours that night I believed that all copies of the then-existing
manuscript had been destroyed. As it turned out, many of its pages
had been singed along their edges, but all had survived. Yet in spite
of its literal marking by the history of the sixties, the book's text
had been purified of all contaminating personal and political origins. In this respect it now seems to me less a creation of the sixties
than of the fifties, heyday of the New Criticism.

My own experience of New Critical aestheticism had been
belated but enthusiastic—a secular conversion. I had grown up in
the Flatbush section of Brooklyn, then an Irish-Italian ghetto
adjacent to Brooklyn College, reviled in the neighborhood as a
dangerous enclave of Jewish radicalism. My father died, however,
two weeks after I graduated from high school; that fall I enrolled at
Brooklyn College, my anti-Marxist family having accepted that
economic realities must outweigh political fears or religious ideals.
The College was free; besides, "it's in the neighborhood." Many of
the adults I knew viewed my attending the College as the beginning of a cunning project in ethnic subversion: "We ought to send
more of our own kind there." They, of course, sent their own sons
to Georgetown or Fordham and their daughters to secretarial
school. As lone Papist infiltrator I soon discovered the College to
be nothing so twentieth century as the red menace; it was strictly
Stone Age—both politically and intellectually.

Politics certainly came up, regardless of the ostensible subject.
Two of my teachers bragged, in class, that they had testified

against old Communist Party cohorts before HUAC; one, with whom I had studied Horace, refused to testify and was fired. No doubt his translations of Horatian Odes had subtly inculcated Marxist doctrine. In other classes, time was spent in weepy denunciations of the tenure system; in fond strolls down memory lane; in gossip and sexual innuendo against other members of the faculty. I doubt that in the four years I spent there I attended more than twenty classes that had been prepared. In English courses, when the conversation faltered and we lurched back to the assigned works, comment usually took the form of historical or biographical annotation. I studied Shakespeare with a woman who read us the notes she had taken in a course given by George Lyman Kittridge. Nevertheless, I doubt I would have been receptive to a more up-to-date or even a better faculty; my main interests at the time were playing basketball, playing my saxophone, and reading James Joyce—in exactly that order. Still, *something* happened during those four years in which I never left the neighborhood or even the house I had grown up in. I entered college as an engineering major who thought that Joe McCarthy was on to something; I graduated as an English major who was politically liberal—a combination that aggravated my family almost as much as it was intended to. Fathers of the Catholic girls I was still dating questioned me suspiciously and spoke at length, and ominously, of their son, the priest.

My list of sacred texts had generously expanded to include several twentieth-century authors besides Joyce; I was now a former altar boy in search of a critical faith to bring to my canonical authors. Graduate school was the seminary of choice, but it wasn't free and I didn't have the money. So I worked for a year. I became the reader in the course taught, at one remove, by George Lyman Kittridge; I wrote stories on literary events for *The Village Voice;* and I worked as an insurance adjustor. I tailed allegedly disabled accident victims to their secret jobs; I read the complete writings of Thomas Wolfe; I interviewed Ayn Rand. At the end of a year I packed my bags and made Thomas Wolfe's journey in reverse— from Brooklyn to North Carolina. His home turned out to be no better than mine; I soon discovered that my carefully hoarded money was being spent on a faculty that was just as stodgy, and in some cases just as sluggardly, as my undergraduate teachers. My Shakespeare instructor (I seemed to be on a roll with Shakespeare) would come to class with a large pile of critical studies of Shakespeare, read out each author and title, commenting in a rolling baritone, "Now, this is one of the *really* great books about Shakespeare"; he spent the rest of the term doing readings from the plays, in which he performed all parts.

At the University of North Carolina in 1959 the New Criticism was at least enough of a presence in the academic world to be attacked. What my teachers feared, I concluded, couldn't be all bad. I transferred to the University of Minnesota, which had two things in its favor: it was even further away from my old neighborhood and it had Allen Tate, the most theologically pure and critically severe of the fugitive group. I enrolled in his seminar on "Critical Theory." For three weeks I walked through frozen streets and 30 degree below zero temperatures to listen to Tate read Aristotle's *Poetics* aloud to the class. I then dropped the course and considered a return to the insurance business. Fortunately for me, the Minnesota department also contained younger faculty—J. C. Levenson, G. Robert Stange, Sarah Youngblood—who were actually interested in talking about poems and novels. They combined New Critical close reading with historical and cultural concerns; they adopted a much less narrow canon of English and American writing than Tate did. I was converted, even educated and certified as a Ph.D. I came to Berkeley, still further away from my old neighborhood; I wrote my book on Williams, a book which, I've been suggesting, combines hostility to authority, deference to authority, and a desire to be an authority.

In 1985 I'm less constrained and even less surly than I was in 1969. My name has changed: from James E. Breslin to James E. B. Breslin when I adopted my second wife's maiden name (Bell) as my second middle name. If I were writing the narrative of all these changes, the story would begin and end with her. Still, when I look back at my old photograph or at the text of the Williams book I feel as though I'm in touch with someone who both is and is not me. My critical faith is still one that could be accused of fetishizing texts—and one that looks at those texts in their human, historical context. Now, I'd simply push those principles much further than I was willing or able to do fifteen years ago, particularly toward a fuller psychological understanding of Williams that would work against my simple idealization of him. In fact there are moments when, rereading the text and thinking of my 1969 photograph, I think, "You wrote better than you looked."

WILLIAM CARLOS WILLIAMS

I

The Quest for Roots:
Williams's Early Development

> "The place of my birth is the place where the word
> begins."   *A Voyage to Pagany*

"Everything exists from the beginning," writes William Carlos
Williams in his *The Great American Novel* (p. 9). The implications of this remark are vast; the consequences of believing
them are radical. From this point of view, all conventional
ways of ordering experience are abstract and empty—dried
husks. Conceptions of time as a linear, historical progression are
false; only the moment is real. The present is the beginning,
and it contains everything: the seed of all life. Williams's career
was a series of attempts to enter this moment; his art, a continuous search for the new forms required for its expression.
Yet, his espousal of the momentary did not send Williams on a
rushed quest across the American continent for novel sensations. He spent all but a few years of his life in Rutherford,
New Jersey, where he worked as a physician. Poetry, he
believed, could only thrive in a landscape familiar to the poet.
In spatial terms, too, everything exists from the beginning;
"the place of my birth is the place where the word begins."

Still, Williams's acceptance of his own origins came only
after a long and arduous struggle. At first, his family inhibited
his strong sensuality, creating an agonizing division in the boy.
While the opening sections of his *Autobiography* stress the

3

physical exuberance of childhood, there is an undercurrent of terror throughout. "Terror dominated my youth, not fear," Williams says (p. 3). "I was not afraid. I had the normal fears, naturally, but they could be condoned, not the terror that flared from the hidden places and all 'heaven.'" In a real sense the terror he felt did come from heaven—from the rigid idealism and moral perfectionism his parents tried to instill in him. The mature Williams was to emphasize the physical as the source of all life; but the idealism of his parents at first made his earthy instincts frightening to him and, through adolescence and even into early manhood, Williams obediently sought to distance himself from the corporeal.

These self-divisions were particularly evident at the awakening of his interest in poetry. In 1902, while a student at Horace Mann High School in New York City, Williams read Whitman's *Leaves of Grass*. In the fall of that year, when he entered the Medical School at the University of Pennsylvania, "I brought that book with me and I absorbed it with enthusiasm. I loved to read the poems to myself." [1] He was inspired to fill a set of notebooks with "quick spontaneous poems" in the manner of Whitman (*IW*, p. 5). Yet, as he was enthusiastically absorbing Whitman, he was also reading Keats with a submissive reverence: "Keats, during the years at medical school, was my God" (*Auto*, p. 53). The result was that at the same time he was writing rough, free poems after Whitman, he was also writing what he thought to be suave, polished sonnets after Keats. The Keatsian poems, in deference to the respectable literary opinion of the time, were those intended for public view. Granted an interview with his brother's English teacher, Arlo Bates of M.I.T., the young medical student brought a Keatsian imitation rather than the notebook poems (*Auto*, pp. 54–55).

"It is curious," Williams later remarked, "that I was so preoccupied with the studied elegance of Keats on the one hand and with the raw vigor of Whitman on the other" (*IW*, p. 8). His divided allegiance is not so curious, however, when we look at it in the context of the tensions of his adolescence. The Whitmanesque poems he called "my secret life," suggesting that what was most alive in him was feared and hidden at this point (*IW*, p. 8). It may be, as Eric Erikson argues, that a prolonged period of restraint is necessary to generate revolutionary energy.[2] But between 1902 and 1914, as Williams became the earnest, upright, and remote young man his parents encouraged him to be, he became increasingly impatient with their constraints—from which he dramatically delivered himself by his identification with the physical locality, the "filthy Passaic," announced in "The Wanderer" (1914).

Both of them immigrants—the father an Englishman and the mother a Puerto Rican—Williams's parents had great expectations for their first son. They sent him to Horace Mann and then to medical school at Penn, so that he could achieve acceptance via professional success—the classic pattern of immigrant hopes. At the same time, while the parents were by no means fervently religious, they did impose on the boy a strong sense of propriety and a rigid moral code. Their teachings here were reinforced by the boy's English grandmother, in whose care he was often left and who insisted that he be a "gentleman" (*Auto*, p. 4). At one point, Williams dutifully formulated a project, after Benjamin Franklin, to become morally perfect, and even after he had left home for college, he earnestly assured his mother

> that I never did and never will do a premeditated bad deed in my life. Also that I never have had and never will have anything but the purest and highest and best thoughts about you and Papa, and that if anybody ever says a word contrary to your wishes or high ideals I never fail to fight them to a standstill. . . . I have always tried to do all that you and Papa wished me to do and many times I have done things against my own feelings and convictions because you wanted me to. (*SL*, p. 7)

Both parents, success-minded aliens in the New World, seem in different ways to have been personally remote. The father was often physically absent, away on business trips to Central and South America (*Auto*, p. 14), and the mother, a dreamy individual, was a "medium" who often had hallucinatory fits—heavenly visitations that terrified the young Williams (*Auto*, pp. 15–17). Later, Williams viewed his father as the man Williams himself might have become—as a man who had sacrificed his own feelings and convictions to a rigid sense of duty. In the poem "Adam" the father's fear of the physical banishes him from paradise, converting the lush Caribbean island on which he grew up into a hellish world, filled with terrifying sensual seductions. Behind all of Williams's later animus against the Puritan lies this tough, cold, aloof figure of his father. "He was typically English," Williams, who later became an Anglophobe, said: "too English ever for me to be able to talk with animal to animal" (*YMW*, p. 3; *SL*, p. 127). The mature Williams was even more fascinated with the complex character of his mother, dealing with it in "Eve," "All the Fancy Things," and a brief biography, *Yes, Mrs. Williams;* but the most illuminating statement of what she meant to him in early manhood appears in *I Wanted To Write a Poem:*

> I was conscious of my mother's influence all through this time of writing, her ordeal as a woman and as a foreigner in this country. I've always held her as a mythical figure, remote from me, detached, looking down on an area in which I happened to live, a fantastic world where she was moving as a more or less pathetic figure. Remote, not only because of her Puerto Rican background, but also because of her bewilderment at life in a small town in New Jersey after her years in Paris where she had been an art student. Her interest in art became my interest in art. I was personifying her, her detachment from the world of Rutherford. She seemed an heroic figure, a poetic ideal. I didn't especially admire her; I was attached to her. I had not yet established any sort of independent spirit. (*IW*, p. 16)

Into a largely sterile environment, Mrs. Williams introduced an early and important impetus toward artistic activity. Because of her, Williams was at first interested in painting. But the direction of her influence was not immediately creative, since it inspired a sense of beauty that was dreamily nostalgic; it was she who led him to Keats. Behind all of Williams's later attraction to the elegant, his frequent squeamish distaste for the common, lies the refined and remote figure of his mother. A woman of violent temper, Mrs. Williams was more passionately alive than her husband; but she, too, dreaming of her aristocratic past in Puerto Rico and in Paris, was detached from the ordinary life around her in Rutherford.

Had Williams succumbed to his parents, he might have built a lucrative practice, contributed polite, nostalgic verses to *The New Yorker*, and become a neat, orderly, prosperous physician who would "never think anything / but a white thought" (*CEP*, p. 36). But the frustration created by the seeming acceptance of these ideals was evident not just from the poems it produced, as we shall see shortly, but from the very existence of the Whitman notebooks. They worked, he tells us, as a "sort of purgation and confessional, to clear my head and my heart from turgid obsessions" (*Auto*, p. 53). As Williams prepared a face to meet the faces that he met, these notebooks provided expression for the buried life of the body that he always associated with Whitman. Ultimately, the high aspirations, strict morality, and personal aloofness of his parents worked to reinforce his rebelliousness. Their detachment he later equated with constraint and consequently he felt an intense desire to possess the here and now. "Of mixed ancestry," he once wrote, "I felt from earliest childhood that America was the only home I could ever possibly call my own. I felt that it was expressly founded for me, personally, and that it must be my first business in life to possess it" (*SL*, p. 185). Williams later liked to think of himself as combining his father's tenacity of purpose with his mother's passionate feeling; but to be fully awake and creative, he felt, he had to purge their remote idealism and enter the ordinary life, crude as it might be, of the New Jersey town in which he had been born.

As a step toward liberty, the decision to attend medical school at Penn turned out to be an important one. The journey of the young man from the New Jersey provinces to the city of Philadelphia slowly intensified the conflict between his impulses and the high ideals of his family. In Philadelphia, moreover, Williams discovered such people as Ezra Pound,

H. D., and Charles Demuth, who shared the kinds of feelings that in Rutherford had made him frightened and isolated. They shared his desire to create and manifested "a provocative indifference to rule and order which I liked" (*Auto*, p. 68). So encouraged was Williams that he dared to show the Whitman notebooks to Pound, who promptly denounced them (*IW*, p. 5). As incidents like this must have shown, meeting other artists was also conducive to more precise and more vigorous self-definition. He sensed a precocity and remoteness about both H. D. and Pound that made him keep to himself. From the flamboyant Pound he had a direct perception of the romantic artist as bohemian, about which he had immediate reservations:

> What I could never tolerate in Pound or seek for myself was the "side" that went with all his posturings as the poet. To me that was the emptiest sort of old hat. Any simpleton, I believed, should see at once what that came from; the conflict between an aristocracy of birth and that of mind and spirit— a silly and unnecessary thing. The poet scorning the other made himself ridiculous by imitating that which he despised. My upbringing assumed rather the humility and caution of the scientist. One was or was not *there*. And if one was there, it behooved one to be at one's superlative best, and, apart from the achievement, a thing in itself, to live inconspicuously, as best it might be possible, and to work single-mindedly for the task. Not so sweet Ezra. (*Auto*, p. 58)

Here, as throughout the *Autobiography*, the theatrical egotism of Pound is set against the innocent humility of the author. Like all announcements of humility, this one carries its own egotism. Yet his ambivalent friendship with Pound did eventually help Williams to define his own kind of aspiration—to define the artist as an inconspicuous citizen who, immersing himself in the life of his community, dedicates himself to his artistic tasks with the impersonality of a scientist.

The only "higher" education he had, Williams's scientific training was basic in shaping his style of life and art. In the *Autobiography* Williams says of his motives as a medical student:

> I would continue medicine, for I was determined to be a poet; only medicine, a job I enjoyed, would make it possible for me to live and write as I wanted to. . . . My furious wish was to be normal, undrunk, balanced in everything. I would marry (but not yet!) have children and still write, in fact, therefore to write. I would not court disease, live in the slums for the sake of art, give lice a holiday. I would not "die for art," but live for it, grimly! and work, work, work (like Pop), beat the game and be free (like Mom, poor soul!) to write, write as I alone should write, for the sheer drunkenness of it, I might have added. (*Auto*, p. 51)

These remarks no doubt project the intentions of the mature on the younger Williams, but they also reveal how important medicine became in moving Williams away from aestheticism. The practice of medicine clearly deepened his involvement in the life of his locality, offering the writer intimate contact with the lives of its inhabitants and eventually opening up a new world for literary exploration. Parental ambitions had sent him to medical school in the first place; but what he learned there was a way to creativity rather than success.

For medicine was not just a way Williams had of extending his experience; it profoundly affected the point of view from which he absorbed experience. To the young man who dreamed of moral perfection, the study of medicine suggested the radical imperfection of the flesh and taught him that no human organism is ever finally cured.

> We recover from some somatic, some bodily "fever" [he writes] where as observers we have seen various engagements between our battalions of cells playing at this or that lethal maneuver with other natural elements. It has been interesting. Various sewers or feed-mains have given way here or there under pressure: various new patterns have been thrown up for us upon the screen of our knowledge. But a cure is absurd, as absurd as calling these deployments "diseases." (*Auto*, p. 286)

This passage shows how medicine finally shaped Williams's basic sense that life, once genteel illusions have been stripped away, is a fierce contest for survival; the body is a dark and violent place. But the pressures of battle throw up new patterns, he adds; the arduous struggle to adjust to the physical, terrifying as it may be, does not brutalize—it generates. How perceptions like these might become the source of poetry Williams did not yet know; but meanwhile the study of medicine clearly supported him in his struggle against the moral idealism of his parents.[3]

Separation from home and family, the discovery of fellow artists, the science of medicine itself—all these helped to stir the independent spirit of the young Williams. But the full liberation of his passionate, physical nature was slow to come about —as the highly derivative and artificial poems of his first collection make plain. In 1909, when *Poems* first appeared, Williams had just completed three years of internship in New York City; part of the time had been spent in a children's hospital in the violent Hell's Kitchen district of the city. But the gross actuality of his everyday life—the children, women, doctors, and nurses—could not yet, in Williams's view, generate poetry. Knowing what we do about this period from the *Autobiography* (pp. 71–105), we get the feeling reading the 1909 *Poems* that at this time Williams, as he says of the citizens of Paterson, walked outside of his own body, unroused. In 1908 the sources of poetry for Williams were clearly in earlier poetry—mainly Keats and the Elizabethans. The results were correctly assessed in a letter by Pound: "Individual, original [the book] is not. Great art it is not. Poetic it is . . . but nowhere I think do you add anything to the poets you have used as models." [4] Straining after the opulence of Keats or the grace of the Elizabethans, Williams seems merely awkward and flat. What is most obviously missing is a unique point of view which might generate a fresh, inventive use of the language.

Still, certain of the poet's attitudes, especially his conception of himself, are significant, since they are the very opposite of the attitudes in his mature work. Williams's first book opens with characteristic affirmations of Innocence and Simplicity; but at this point in his career he thinks of them as transcendent qualities, of "heavenly birth," preserved by a precious remoteness from the here and now (*Poems*, p. 7). For the most part the poems either praise abstractions, personified as goddesses, or they pay court to a distant, lovely lady. In either case, the attitude of the poet before the female—the "poetic ideal" he identified with his mother—is reverential, while he views mundane reality with a superior disdain. Implicitly, female or poetic beauty is defined as something rare and distant, ethereal and indistinct. Desire and creativity, which torment as they delight, are activities of the mind, not the "foul and gritty" body (*Poems*, p. 13). "True having lives but only in the mind," the sententious young aesthete declares in "The Quest of Happiness" and in an exhausted idiom which undermines the request as it is made, he prays, "Then loose ye all, ye earthly bonds which cling / About my heart, and—life's new song, begin!"

In accordance with such Platonic aspirations, the poet looks upon himself as an outcast and wanderer; he constantly yearns for "everlasting peace" in some far-off, unobtainable realm (*Poems*, p. 14). Plainly, the melancholy author of this volume is not an ordinary mortal, but one whose vision of the ideal makes him A Man Set Apart. But in spite of the insistence upon the uniqueness of the author, the poet who emerges from this collection is one who is entirely dependent—dependent emotionally upon the remote and lofty figure of his mother as a mythical female ideal and dependent artistically upon Keats and the Elizabethans.

These tendencies are all illustrated in "The Uses of Poetry," a sonnet dedicated to H. D. (whom Williams later recalled as an airy creature whose feet never seemed to touch the ground). The poem's language is flat and awkward; but it is worth looking at closely to establish Williams's personal and poetic identity at this point in his development.

> I've fond anticipation of a day
> O'erfilled with pure diversion presently,
> For I must read a lady poesy
> The while we glide by many a leafy bay,

Hid deep in rushes, where at random play
The glossy black winged May-flies, or whence flee
Hush-throated nestlings in alarm,
Whom we have idly frightened with our boat's long sway.

For, lest o'ersaddened by such woes as spring
To rural peace from our meek onward trend,
What else more fit? We'll draw the light latch-string

And close the door of sense; then satiate wend,
On Poesy's transforming giant wing,
To worlds afar whose fruits all anguish mend.

Very simply, the poet yearns to "close the door of sense"—to
transcend the flesh—and drift off into some sheltered domain of
"rural peace" and "pure diversion." In a similar way, the poem
itself lifts us away from sense experience. Williams's later
poems attempt to put us inside immediate experience, but he
here tries to enclose and formalize the moment. There is the
closed, conventional form of the sonnet. Moreover, with the
use of epithets such as "leafy bay," "rural peace" and
"hush-throated nestlings," and of inversions such as "whose
fruits all anguish mend," Williams deliberately adopts a language that is artificial and literary. The sentence structure—especially the elaborate subordination of the first sentence—
shows too that the speaker is not rendering the process of
experience but is stepping back, to achieve a polished, finished
mode of artistic expression. This distant relation to subject,
along with the identification of the beautiful with the remote
and the artificial, suggest a use of poetry antithetical to that
advocated by the later Williams, who renounced all established
forms like the sonnet and argued for a new poetry in the spoken idiom—both as part of his program to jolt his readers out
of their yearnings for dreamy tranquility, unlock the doors of
their senses, and place them in loving contact with the actual.

    Four years after his first volume of poems—in March 1913—
Williams was outraged by Harriet Monroe's suggested revi-
sions of two metrically irregular poems. "The poet," he wrote
to her,

comes forward assailing the trite and the established, while the editor is to sheer off all roughness and extravagance. . . . Now life is above all things else at any moment subversive of life as it was the moment before—always new, irregular. Verse to be alive must have infused into it something of the same order, some tincture of disestablishment, something in the nature of an impalpable revolution, an ethereal reversal, let me say. . . . *Poetry* I saw accepting verse of this kind: that is, verse with perhaps nothing else in it but life—this alone, regardless of possible imperfections, for no new thing comes through perfect. (*SL*, pp. 23–24)

The assertive tone of this letter from an unrecognized poet to the editor of *Poetry* reveals a new spirit of confidence in the writer; Williams has now envisioned the creative act as a process in which constricting conventions are broken apart in order to release the instincts of the individual artist. Independence, revolution, chaos are now all part of his program for life and art. Still, the poems of this period, most of them collected in *The Tempers* (1913), remain largely derivative, with Ezra Pound replacing John Keats as the chief model. If Williams was moving toward an abstract definition of art as an experimental process, he continued to write poems that sought to provide conventional subjects with new verbal finish. His practice, while often deliberately rougher than in 1909, still equated art with rhetorical polish rather than self-expression.

The feeling that generates much of Pound's work in this period is the melancholy of the outcast. Characteristically, he sees himself as an urbane, weary courtier oppressed by the vulgarities of his bourgeois age. Similarly fatigued by the wintry environment of the modern world, Williams expresses *tristitia post coitum* in "Postlude," a mournful persistence in the face of futility in "Ad Infinitum," a feeling of impotence in "Crude Lament," and the stylized weariness of "An After Song":

> So art thou broken in upon me, Apollo,
> Through a splendor of purple garments—
> Held by the yellow-haired Clymene
> To clothe the white of thy shoulders—

Bare from the day's leaping of horses.
This is strange to me, here in the modern twilight.

As in the 1909 poems, the beautiful is identified with the remote, here the lost world of the past. The immediate experience, the observation of the sunset, will not suffice for poetry.
Such a commonplace occurrence is infused with poetic significance only by lifting it into the rare world of classical myth.
Contemporary experience, neatly shaped into the form of the
classical epigram, is rendered by a deliberately archaic language and imagery. Lyric nostalgia, although now mixed with
irony, remains the dominant mood. The myth informing this
poem, contrasting the radiant past with the "modern twilight,"
is not the myth of growth but of decline.

Still, there were signs of progress. Williams's observation
that "certain poems in *The Tempers*, or perhaps just certain
lines in some of the poems, show that I was beginning to turn
away from the romantic" is true enough if we understand "romantic" to mean the remote (*IW*, p. 17). On the whole, these
poems do show a greater range and vigor of feeling than the
1909 volume. In "Mezzo Forte" a dramatic lyric which begins
"Take that, damn you; and that!" we have a strong feeling expressed in strong speech, although the angry defiance is a literary convention as old as the Petrarchanism it mocks. "The
Death of Franco of Cologne: His Prophecy of Beethoven," a
dramatic monologue after Browning, is declamatory in style
but its argument prefigures the mature Williams. Williams
praises Franco of Cologne, who invented our system of musical
notation, over Beethoven, who worked to mastery within it;
this adumbrates Williams's later insistence upon rough inven-
tiveness over formal perfection. "Con Brio" works out some of
the more radical implications in this shift. There, for the first
time in his work, Williams denounces repression and calls for
an emotional spontaneity and openness. In these last two poems
the young poet is asserting an expressive rather than a rhetorical view of art. To this extent, he had become more, not less,
romantic. But except for the use of the colloquial voice in a

few poems, there is little sense that poetry can be generated out of contact with the immediate. Invention, experiment, release are, importantly, advocated; but it is still, in the language of the letter to Miss Monroe, in the nature of an *impalpable* revolution, an *ethereal* reversal.

By imitating Pound, Williams learned he could not with conviction write the kind of smooth, concentrated, highly finished song his friend had mastered. He also learned, it appears, what he did not want to be: he was no courtier, but a plain, inconspicuous inhabitant of the ordinary world. "Contemporania," the most direct poetic tribute to Pound in *The Tempers*, also asserts Williams's awareness of the fundamental difference between Pound and himself.

>   Contemporania
> The corner of a great rain
> Steamy with the country
> Has fallen upon my garden.
>
> I go back and forth now
> And the little leaves follow me
> Talking of the great rain,
> Of branches broken,
> And the farmer's curses!
>
> But I go back and forth
> In this corner of a garden
> And the green shoots follow
> Praising the great rain.
>
> We are not curst together,
> The leaves and I,
> Framing devices, flower devices
> And other ways of peopling
> The barren country.
> Truly it was a very great rain
> That makes the little leaves follow me.

This somewhat enigmatic poem becomes clearer once we remember that "Contemporania" was the general title for a group of eleven poems which Pound published in *Poetry*,

April 1913. Williams's "great rain" from the "country" and his "flower devices" allude to one of these poems by Pound, "Salutation the Second" :

> You were praised, my books,
>   because I had just come from the country;
> I was twenty years behind the times
>   so you found an audience ready.
> I do not disown you,
>   do not disown your progeny.
>
> Here they stand without quaint devices,
> Here they are with nothing archaic about them.

As he goes on, Pound makes clear he is announcing his own liberation from the genteel tradition; he enjoins his new irreverent songs to defy the oppressive propriety of his audience:

> Ruffle the skirts of prudes,
>   speak of their knees and ankles,
> But, above all, go to practical people—
>   go! jangle their door-bells!
> Say that you do no work
>   and that you will live forever.

Dissatisfied with the genteel mask of the courtier, Pound here proclaims a reversal of aim and method from his earlier work. His new songs, he says, are to be rough and exuberant—"impudent and naked"—not smoothly fashioned in "quaint devices." Thus, in "Salutation the Second" we encounter not the urbane control of the aristocrat but the scornful defiance of the bohemian and expatriate. Still, the assumptions are elitist: Pound is not so much trying to jolt the Philistine awake as he is sharing his scorn with an audience of those who are already saved.

In his own "Contemporania" Williams is acknowledging an important debt to this new Pound. While the "great rain" in his poem can mean any violent innovation, the literary allusions indicate that Williams is specifically praising Pound for his role in breaking up established human and literary orders. Unlike the practical farmer who curses the disruption of routine, the Williams of "Contemporania" rejoices in chaos. In fact, the liberating shift from a fixed, constraining order to a fertile chaos was shortly to become a major subject of Williams's verse and Pound clearly helped him to find it. But if Williams here declares an affinity with Pound the revolutionary, he also expresses the reservations he had felt about the egotistical bohemian from their first encounters in Philadelphia. Williams's "Contemporania" acknowledges a debt, but it also defines a basic difference.

Both Pound and Williams want to move away from the artificial "quaint devices" of their earlier work. But Williams's desire to frame "flower devices" suggests a conception of himself as quite different from Pound. In "Salutation the Second" Pound speaks derisively, as the expatriate; in "Contemporania" Williams speaks in the familiar voice of a townsman. The gardener of his poem, a humble and amiable citizen, seeks not to provoke the wrath of his audience but to nurture growth in his "barren country." The poet is thus a modest and commonplace figure—with prophetic ambitions: he enters the ordinary world in order to regenerate it, to release the creative powers buried in his fellow citizens. Such an act of release requires the violent breaking apart of fixed modes of thought and feeling; it requires self-reliance. But this liberation is only the beginning of the process of renewal. "Only he is lost who has been cut off from his fellows," Williams believed (*SE*, p. 186). But the repressed bodily forces that Williams wants to release are shared by all men, and so their liberation draws men together, by asserting what is common. The aesthete impoverishes himself by cutting himself off from his fellows and becomes a mirror image of their isolation and impotence. The democratic poet, by the very act which accomplishes his independence, achieves communion with his fellows; self-reliance leads to fraternal contact.

The radical shift evident in just a few of *The Tempers* poems had already been acted out in Williams's life. In 1909 Williams had returned briefly to Rutherford, where his first book was published and where he met Florence Herman, later his wife. The couple were engaged for three years—"I had to do a lot of readjusting to come out softened down for marriage," he later said (*Auto*, p. 129)—and before settling down he left, in early 1910, for a year in Europe. Most of this time was spent studying medicine in Leipzig, but the high point of the trip was a visit with Pound in Kensington. There, he was exposed to an "intense literary atmosphere" which he found "thrilling, every minute of it," but "fatiguing in the extreme" (*Auto*, p. 117). Importantly, he felt that the effect of his arduous duties as a physician was precisely the reverse. The writer could experience a profound regeneration through his medical practice—because in the very intensity of his identification with the patient's struggle, he could escape the turgid obsessions of his own life.

> I lost myself in the very properties of their minds [he says of his patients]: for the moment at least I actually became *them*, whoever they should be, so that when I detached myself from them at the end of a half-hour of intense concentration over some illness which was affecting them, it was as though I were reawakening from a sleep. For the moment I myself did not exist, nothing of myself affected me. As a consequence I came back to myself, as from any other sleep, refreshed. (*Auto*, p. 356)

Typically, Williams here conceives of integration as a movement in and out of the self in a continuous process of renewal —a process that is thwarted by the rarefied atmosphere of the literary world. And so when he returned here in 1911, he was purging himself of aestheticism and identifying himself with the common ground of his locality. Within a few years—by early 1913—he had been married, bought a large old house, set up medical practice and become a father. Life in these banal surroundings was certainly not without its tensions, but these pressures would, Williams hoped, generate authentic creativity.

Influencing these changes in Williams were a variety of forces. As we shall see, in addition to the direct impact of Pound, such matters as the Paterson silk strike of 1913 and the sense of a widespread insurgency in the arts generated by the

Armory Show and the arrival of the New Poetry must be taken
into account. But of deep importance for Williams was a new
reading of *Leaves of Grass*. On the first of March 1913, just
two weeks before he advocated "roughness and extravagance"
to Harriet Monroe, Williams received a copy of Whitman's
poetry from his wife. Now owned by the library at the University of Pennsylvania, this book, which falls open to the beginning of "Song of Myself," has obviously been read many
times, although it has not been marked in a way that would
suggest detailed study. What the condition of the book suggests is that Whitman exerted little stylistic influence on Williams, who later wrote that "the only way to be like Whitman
is to write *unlike* Whitman." [5] What Whitman helped Williams to do was to root himself in the here and now and release
those creative energies repressed by his family and society—so
that he could begin to learn to write like William Carlos Williams.

Throughout his career—in "America, Whitman, and the Art
of Poetry" (1917), in "An Essay on *Leaves of Grass*" (1955),
and in numerous comments in letters and essays—Williams asserted his debt to Whitman and made clear that what he had
derived was not a literary style, but a bold conception of his
poetic task.[6] Keats, whose style he had imitated, Williams remembered as a "God" (*Auto*, p. 53); Whitman, who helped
him to be himself, Williams remembered as a comrade with
whom he had "an instinctive drive to get in touch." [7] What
brought the two poets together was their self-reliant need to
break apart conventional poetic forms in order to release *their*
passions, and their belief that these secret passions were shared
by their audience. In the opening lines of "Song of Myself,"
we hear, Williams wrote, "the cry of a man breaking through
the barriers of constraint IN ORDER TO BE ABLE TO SAY
exactly what was in his mind." [8] In Williams's view, Whitman
was "tremendously important in the history of modern poetry" because he

broke through the deadness of copied forms which keep
shouting above everything that wants to get said today drown-

ing out one man with the accumulated weight of a thousand
voices in the past—re-establishing the tyrannies of the past, the
very tyrannies that we are seeking to diminish. The structure
of the old is active, it says no! to everything in propaganda and
poetry that wants to say yes. Whitman broke through that.
That was basic and good. (*SE,* p. 218)

Only occasionally, Williams believed, had Whitman been able
to recombine successfully the fragments he had freed. Whitman had "composed 'freely,' he followed his untrammeled necessity. What he did not do was to study what he had done, to
go over it, to select and reject, which is the making of the artist" (*SE,* p. 230). But Whitman's "barbaric yawp" did return
us to the simple, unformed elements of poetry and perception,
the place where we must begin. Pound, conceding in his famous "Pact" that Whitman had broken new wood, believed
that the modern task was to carve and polish; Williams wanted
to re-enact fully the process of release and re-formation that
Whitman had started. After his reading of Whitman in 1913,
Williams identified not the suave manipulation of conventional
attitudes but the passionate expression of feeling as the proper
business of poetry.

Whitman thus helped Williams both to discover and to affirm his creative powers; but in 1913 it was no longer quite
possible to assume a personal omnipotence and simply let go.
The poet who grew up in the expansive Age of Jackson could
easily leap free of oppressive conventions—as Whitman does in
the opening sections of "Song of Myself"; but for Williams,
who grew up after the closing of the frontier and during a period of savage industrial exploitation, the self no longer seemed
quite so omnipotent. His early poems, we have seen, assume
impotence and yearn for flight. But in the poems written after
1914 Williams's theme is the power of the marginal or embattled self to break through restrictions and generate new
growth: "Saxifrage," he said, "is my flower that splits / the
rocks" (*CLP,* p. 7). The new Williams is brought forth in
"The Wanderer," published in early 1914. In this poem, crucial to any study of his development, Williams examines his
personal and poetic development, renounces the dreamy ideal-

ity of the aesthete and identifies himself with the "filthy" but
generative reality of the here and now.

A "story of growing up," as Williams called it, "The Wanderer" describes the rebirth of a young poet: his evolution of
a new identity and his redefinition of such concepts as beauty
and the self (*IW*, p. 26). This initiation is conducted under the
guidance of a fierce old goddess, a dramatic contrast to the
lovely females of the earlier poems. "How shall I be a mirror
to this modernity?" is the Whitmanesque question he puts to
her, and constantly, she instructs the hero by undermining his
lofty aspirations; she humbles and awakens him by forcing him
to concentrate upon the immediate rather than the remote. In
the opening two sections of the poem, as in Williams's previous work, the poet's quest for beauty takes the form of a
flight from mundane reality. When, in the third episode, the
goddess abruptly returns the young aesthete to the ordinary
reality of the city, he is sickened by its ugly squalor and prays
to be liberated from this terrifying world. "Give me always /
A new marriage," he asks:

> May I be lifted still, up and out of terror,
> Up from before the death living around me—.

But in answer to this yearning for transcendence, the poet is
taken in "The Strike" out onto the streets of Paterson. For a
moment he enjoys the brute power of the battling workers,
but in the end he is terrified by it, lamenting to the goddess,
"Nowhere you! Everywhere the electric!" Hence, in the next
section, "Abroad," he is lifted from the terror of the city and
taken out onto the Jersey hills. There, the young poet urges
his degraded townspeople to release the creative powers within
them:

> "Waken! my people, to the boughs green
> With ripening fruit within you!
> Waken to the myriad cinquefoil
> In the waving grass of your minds!
> Waken to the silent phoebe nest
> Under the eaves of your spirit!"

This passage represents an important new phase of the artist's development. For as the figurative language here implies, creativity is not to be sought by an inward withdrawal but by a thrust outward, a process of organic growth. The capacity for such growth is common to all men, and so the point of view has become more democratic. At the same time, the tree and the flower, to become persistent metaphors for organic growth in Williams's work, suggest a democratic poetics, an identification of the beautiful with the commonplace.

The poet's prophetic call to awaken goes unheard. The self is no longer sovereign, as in early Whitman; but neither is it powerless, as in early Eliot. The embattled self here is most like that in Williams's later poems. In fact, the symbolic topography in "The Wanderer"—the city, the mountain, the river—anticipates the symbolism in *Paterson*. In both poems, the quest for creativity through attachment to a locality provides the central action, and the poet, constantly thwarted by oppressive social forces, is tempted to despair. This temptation is overcome in part by a vision of eventual triumph—a vision afforded the poet in "Soothsay," the sixth section of "The Wanderer."

So fortified is the poet's confidence by this vision that in the final episode, "St. James' Grove," he is able to humble himself and enter the violent present. Here the young man is granted that "new marriage" for which he had earlier prayed—not by being lifted up out of the terror, but by immersing himself in "the Passaic, that filthy river."

> Then the river began to enter my heart,
> Eddying back cool and limpid
> Into the crystal beginning of its days.
> But with the rebound it leaped forward:
> Muddy, then black and shrunken
> Till I felt the utter depth of its rottenness
> The vile breadth of its degradation
> And dropped down knowing this was me now.

Williams once described "The Wanderer" as a "reconstruction from memory of my early Keatsian *Endymion*"—a long, romantic poem he had been working on while an intern in New

York (*IW*, pp. 25–26). But if the influence of Keats is resurrected here, it is in order to be purged: the inhibiting "God" of Williams's formative years is slain and the poet is reconstituted through a *baptism in filth*, purged of his need to be clean, perfect. In Williams's mythology, we encounter our origins not by ascending a tower or mountain, but by descending to the stream of the present—not by transcendence but by immersion. The creative principle has been contaminated in modern industrial America, but it remains persistently alive, hidden in the here and now. As Williams suggested a few years later in *Kora in Hell*, the ancient mythical "giants" are buried in the "dirt," the "gods" are "smothered in filth and ignorance": immersion in the filth of the present is the only way we can get to the timeless (*Kora*, pp. 50–51). Everything exists from the beginning. Hence the poet must break loose from constricting conventions, open himself to the crude, violent energies of the present and find the sources of his art there.

By early 1914, then, the precious author of such poems as "An After Song" had already become the fiercely independent but humane figure we can identify in most of Williams's mature work. His later emphasis upon the laboriousness of the process of self-renewal surely derived in part from the difficulties he had in beginning. Yet "The Wanderer" does not, as J. Hillis Miller argues, describe an experience which, once and for all, freed Williams from the pull of conscious ego. Professor Miller's study of Williams in *Poets of Reality* brilliantly analyzes the structure of Williams's imaginary world, but I disagree with his main contention that in Williams's work all tension between subject and object disappears.[9] In fact, this tension is the starting point for most of his major work. Williams remained a self-divided man, alternately repelled by and drawn to the "filthy" present. But as an artist he learned how to use these tensions creatively; and to miss them is to miss the dynamic play of voice in his work. "Most of my life has been lived in hell, a hell of repression," says Williams, a hell of repression "lit by flashes of inspiration, when a poem such as this or that would appear" (*SA*, p. 43). What "The Wanderer" describes is not a final act of emancipation, but a process that Williams enacts again and again in his mature work. His life and art were a series of new beginnings—a process of constant renewal.

II

Williams and the Modern Revolt

"How shall I be a mirror to this modernity?"
"The Wanderer"

By identifying himself with Rutherford—as he does at the end of "The Wanderer"—Williams was not entirely isolating himself from other artists. He was placing himself at the periphery of the artistic center in New York City and, again, the geographical relation defines the spiritual one. With the salons, museums, galleries, theaters, and magazine offices of the metropolis only an hour's drive away, Williams had quick access to the pre-war ferment in poetry, painting, even the dance, and he was deeply stirred by it all. In fact, now confidently established in his own center, he was freed to take ideas and techniques from his contemporaries and convert them to his own ends. Williams thus remained at the edge of the modern movement; the impact of his own generation was real, but it was radically modified by his determination to become, like Whitman, a poet of the individual in his primary relation to place.

In 1911 Henry Adams noted that poetry had become a "suppressed instinct" in America.[1] Certainly, the young Williams had at first confined his instinct for poetry to a set of "secret" notebooks, while the rarefied verses he offered to public view strained to meet some externally imposed idea of beauty. But, as Adams's remark suggests, Williams was not alone in finding it difficult to articulate or even to respect his deepest instincts. The modern revolt in poetry that began around 1913 was the outgrowth of a prolonged and painful germination, not the swift invention of exuberant young men. In that year Pound was twenty-eight, Williams thirty, Stevens and Lindsay thirty-four, Sandburg thirty-five, Frost thirty-eight, and Masters forty-four. What they had to struggle with was almost half a century of genteel torpor and drift in American poetry. Almost every one of these writers began as imitator of Keats or Tennyson. Before they could finally identify themselves, each of them had to throw off an aspiration toward dreamy remoteness—a retreat from the seemingly anti-poetic world opened by late nineteenth-century science and industrialism. Poetry went dead at this time simply because it had lost all fertile contact with social reality—a dissociation we have seen in Williams's earliest verse. The sources of his early confusion are not to be found just in his "personal" biography; there were larger historical forces he had to contend with too.

To a young poet in the early years of the twentieth century, Whitman's career could have provided an instructive illustration of the dilemmas of American poetry. In America, transcendentalism, by affirming the metamorphic powers of the human mind, had liberated the creative energies of the generation that included Whitman. The gesture animating Emerson's *Nature* is one that transforms the cosmos into an ocean—as it was at the very beginning of the creation—so that we, godlike, can start building a world all over again. But the trouble with heeding Emerson's injunction to "build therefore your own world," as Whitman soon found out, was that you became its sole inhabitant. Only a few years after the first edition of *Leaves of Grass* Whitman, no longer chanting joyfully of his sovereignty but withdrawn and melancholy, found himself a solitary singer. Perhaps the chief task that T. S. Eliot performed for his contemporaries was to objectify this problem in such characters as Tiresias, Gerontion, and J. Alfred Prufrock. In the early work of Eliot, all objects and values have been psychologized and the individual left in an impenetrable isolation. An insurmountable gap opens between subject and object and the result is the disintegration of the individual consciousness. "The Waste Land" internalizes—and shatters—the action of the traditional epic poem. "The Love Song of J. Alfred Prufrock" shows that if the perceiving mind transforms everything, then a man can connect himself with nothing. If philosophic idealism began by asserting the unity of "each" with "all," it ended by leaving the individual isolated, abstracted, and fragmented.

But the world into which the modern poets were born was broken socially as well as metaphysically. Clearly, all subsequent poets have experienced great difficulty in believing, with Whitman, that "what I assume you shall assume"—thus adding to their sense of remoteness and sterility. In 1855 an American poet could still think of himself as the voice—or voices—of all his countrymen. Of course, even then there was a kind of tension between writer and audience; Whitman has to tell—in fact, to command—his audience to yield to his assumptions, and he clearly anticipates that his reader will be, superficially at least, a man who has prudently stifled his creative powers in the quest for economic gain and social status. Yet, when Whitman began writing seriously in the early 1850's, he was working in a country that still had a rolling frontier, an almost omnipresent mobility and an enthusiastic faith in the perfectibility of the common man. His culture—like the Emersonian cosmos —could be felt to be unformed and fluid, but homogeneous; it was not a terrifying chaos. Hence the split between the economic individualism that Whitman saw around him and the transcendental individualism he envisioned appeared not as an impassable gap but as an opening for creative activity. Into this opening Whitman boldly stepped, in 1855, seemingly out of nowhere. In the buoyant mood of his discovery of his own godlike powers, he hoped to liberate the divine powers buried in all of his countrymen. At once the companion of gods and the comrade of men, the poet of 1855 could still conceive of himself as a generative social force.

Yet, again, in just a few years Whitman's confident belief that his own aspirations were shared by his readers began to collapse; America did not absorb him as affectionately as he

had absorbed it. The characteristic gesture of the poems of his
1860 edition of *Leaves* is not an expansion but a contraction, as
the poet covertly seeks fulfillment, away from the "clank of
the world." [2] Along with this ebbing sense of power and compensating for its loss, there is a self-conscious straining after a
prophetic role, with Whitman now fussily arranging his poems
as a "Bible" for democracy. Private and public selves, joined in
the lovely scene on the grass in section 5 of "Song of Myself,"
are now split. And with the accelerating pace of industrial
growth after the Civil War—the more elaborate division of
labor, frequent waves of immigration, developing sense of class
stratification, and the closing of the frontier in the 1890's—no
American could think of himself as embodying a "common"
American identity.[3] No poet could blow the "communal
trumpet"—as Pound later put it—without sounding vulgar or
shrill.[4] The vast masses that Whitman had celebrated now became a crude mob, threatening artistic creativity. Gradually,
the beautiful harmony of Whitman's America was shattered.

In the Gilded Age most American poets, rather than confront these forces of disintegration, increasingly tended to ab-
dicate the public role and withdraw into a genteel aestheticism.
Dominating the literary scene in New York during the latter
decades of the nineteenth century was a group of poet-critics
that included Richard Henry Stoddard, George H. Barker,
Thomas Bailey Aldrich, and Edmund Clarence Stedman. These
men viewed themselves, correctly, as the last proponents of the
Ideal in poetry; but in their work the robust ardor of Emerson
had dwindled to a precious remoteness, a deliberate turning
away from such sordid vulgarities as materialism and science.
Idealism, no longer opening a total apprehension of experience,
had become exclusive and attenuated. Moreover, the dominance of these assumptions about poetry continued down
through the initial decade of the twentieth century; the kind
of poetry developed under these conditons can be fairly epitomized from the first poem—"Poetry" by Arthur Davison Ficke
—in the first issue of the new magazine *Poetry:*

It is a little isle amid bleak seas—
An isolate realm of garden, circled round
By importunity of stress and sound,
Devoid of empery to master these.
At most, the memory of its streams and bees,
Borne to the toiling mariner outward-bound,
Recalls his soul to that delightful ground;
But serves no beacon toward his destinies.

It is a refuge from the stormy days,
Breathing the peace of a remoter world
Where beauty, like the musking dusk of even,
Enfolds the spirit in its silver haze;
While far away, with glittering banners furled,
The west lights fade, and stars come out in heaven.[5]

It was poems like this one that Williams was imitating, as
much as Keats, when he wrote "The Uses of Poetry." And it
was poems like this that hung, like a thick fog, over the minds
of early twentieth-century poets and prompted them to de-
nounce the work of their immediate forerunners as genteel,
blurred. Yet it is crucial to see that what they were attacking
was not just a style that had gone stale, but the notions of ideality that were ultimately behind the style. Modern art starts
with the recognition that all transcendent sources of order and
value have broken down; the modern artist lives in a world
that is broken, neutral, indifferent to human feeling or purpose. "They enter a new world, naked / cold, uncertain of all
/ save that they enter" (CEP, p. 241). That is why Wallace
Stevens in "Modern Poetry" calls for

The poem of the mind in the act of finding
What will suffice. It has not always had
To find: the scene was set; it repeated what
Was in the script.
                    Then the theatre was changed
To something else. Its past is souvenir.

The crisis of belief, in turn, leads to a specifically literary crisis. All established literary forms, based on obsolete ideas of

order, must be abolished and replaced. And this is not just another moment of artistic revolt. Modern writers are required not just to develop new forms appropriate to a new idea of order, but to develop forms appropriate to an age in which all fixed ideas of order have been called into question. For the modern artist, nothing is given. The past is a souvenir; he must write an entirely new script.

It is in this context that we should view Williams's determination to go back and start the growth of poetry all over again, from the ground up. In this endeavor he was influenced by Walt Whitman, as we have seen. But Williams was also an admirer of such avant-garde artists as James Joyce, Ezra Pound, Gertrude Stein, Marcel Duchamp, and Juan Gris, and he was implicated in the modern movement from the first. In fact, his own awakening from attenuated idealism was roughly simultaneous with that of a great number of not-so-young young poets; and he was greatly stimulated in his own development by what he later called the "great surge of interest in the arts generally before the First World War" (*Auto*, p. 134). We have become so accustomed to thinking of poetic modernism as developing out of a reactionary horror at contemporary chaos that we forget that it began in a spirit of millennial expectation; the disintegration of all established forms was experienced at first as a liberation, a creative opening. In 1913, even Ezra Pound was speaking hopefully of an American Renaissance.[6] The spirit of the time has been sharply evoked by Meyer Schapiro in his study of the Armory Show:

> About 1913 painters, writers, musicians, and architects felt themselves to be at an epochal turning-point corresponding to an equally decisive transition in philosophic thought and social life. This sentiment of imminent change inspired a general insurgence, a readiness for great events. The years just before the first World War were rich in new associations of artists, vast projects, and daring manifestoes. The world of art had never known so keen an appetite for action, a kind of militancy that gave to cultural life the quality of a revolutionary movement or the beginnings of a new religion.[7]

Thwarted so long, poets in particular felt a deep and sudden sense of release. As Williams recalls those years, "there was a heat in us, a core and a drive that was gathering headway upon the theme of a rediscovery of a primary impetus, the elementary principle of all art, in the local conditions" (*Auto,* p. 146). Among the forces acting on Williams were the new developments in the dance, painting, and poetry.

No doubt the dance affected Williams less than other art forms, but as early as 1908 he had seen Isadora Duncan perform and became a participant in the widespread literary cult of Isadora. His excited account of the evening, set down in a letter to his brother, shows how an artist experimenting in one medium can inspire and encourage one working in another.

> Last night I went to see Isadora Duncan in her classical dances, really Bo it is the most chaste, most perfect, most absolutely inspiring exhibition I have ever seen. It fairly made my hair stand on end Bo and best of all she is an American, one of our own people and I tell you I felt doubly strengthened in my desire and my determination to accomplish my part in our wonderful picture. You Bo and I must be what we crave to see in those around us and what this great girl has shown is possible of accomplishment now. . . .

> Isadora Duncan, when I saw
> You dance, the interrupting years fell back,
> It seemed, with far intenser leave than lack
> Of your deft step hath e'er conferred. No flaw
> However slight lay 'tween me and the raw
> Heat thirsty Sythians craving wrack,
> Lithe Bacchanals or flushed, in roseate track,
> Athenian girls completing vict'ry's law.
> I breathed their olden virgin purity
> Their guileless clean abandon, in your fling
> Those truth refound which heavenly instincts bless
> Bare innocence withal, but most to me
> I saw, dear country-maid, how soon shall spring
> From this our native land great loveliness.[8]

The kind of loveliness Miss Duncan defined for Williams, whom she transported from a fallen present to an innocent past, was essentially refined and remote. But to the constricted young man who wrote this sonnet she at least affirmed the possibility of some kind of creativity in America—an important affirmation in 1908. Williams pursued the interest in modern dance aroused at this time. He came to know and admire Martha Graham, whose free, broken gestures were very different from the classic grace of Isadora; and he once considered writing a biography of Miss Graham.[9] The dance intrigued him as "the origin of our verse" and as a form of bodily speech; [10] in his own work—from the joyous eccentricity of "Danse Russe" (1917) to the "satyric dance" of *Paterson V* (1958)—it figured as a persistent metaphor for creativity.

At least one Continental influence must be counted among the forces converging on the Rutherford poet—modern painting. "As I look back I think it was the French painters rather than the writers who influenced us, and their influence was very great," Williams said.

> They created an atmosphere of release, color release, release from stereotyped forms, trite subjects. There was a lot of humor in French painting, and a kind of loose carelessness. Morals were down and so were a lot of other things. For which everybody was very happy, relieved.[11]

Relief, a word Williams uses again and again to describe his feeling in this liberating period, is now associated with defiant energy rather than the refined languor of the 1909 poems. Of course, as Williams remembers, "it came to a head for us in the famous 'Armory Show' of 1913" where he saw work by Cézanne, Gauguin, Renoir, Matisse, Picasso, Braque, Picabias, Gleizes, and Duchamp. The atmosphere of rebellious gaiety was epitomized for Williams in Duchamp's "Nude Descending a Staircase": "I laughed out loud when I first saw it, happily, with relief" (*Auto*, p. 134).

Clearly, lengthy study is needed to define precisely Williams's relation to modern painting.[12] He himself started out as a painter and maintained a lively and sophisticated interest in the medium throughout his lifetime. Later in 1913 Williams

met Walter Arensberg through his association with the magazine *The Globe*, and he began attending parties given at the
connoisseur's New York City apartment. There he came to
know a group that included Duchamp, Man Ray, Charles
Sheeler, Joseph Stella, Charles Demuth, Albert Picabias, and,
on one or two occasions, Isadora Duncan. He had access there
to Arensberg's extensive collection of contemporary art, and
by this time he certainly knew of Alfred Steiglitz and his
"291" gallery. The immediate effect of the painters was not
only to create an ethos of revolt, although they helped do that;
the severe, hard-edged lines of the Cubists opened a new world
to a young man accustomed to thinking of the beautiful as the
indistinct—as did the intense primary colors of an artist like
Matisse. Both of these preoccupations come together in the
work of Juan Gris, at one time Williams's favorite painter.
Perhaps most important, as we shall see, is that in the multiple
perspectives of certain modern paintings Williams saw a technique which, adapted to literary structures, would make the
demise of fixed truth a liberating thing.

Still, Williams was a literary artist and by this time a number of young writers were already moving toward a sharp rendering of the physical object as a way out of romantic subjectivity. The immediate result was Imagism, which had a
profound effect on Williams. As a friend of Pound, a contrib-
utor to *Poetry*, and a direct participant in the movement behind the little magazine *Others*, Williams was intimately related to the modern revolt in poetry from the start. At
Greenwich Village parties or at Grantwood, New Jersey,
where the *Others* crowd congregated on Sunday afternoons,
Williams got to know people like Wallace Stevens, Kenneth
Burke, Alfred Kreymborg, Malcolm Cowley, Amy Lowell, and
Maxwell Bodenheim. A distinct thrust within the broader phenomenon of the New Poetry, Imagism was given a credo in
Pound's "A Few Don'ts," published in *Poetry* in March 1913.

The central doctrine of Imagism was best stated by Pound:
"For it is not until poetry lives again 'close to the thing' that it
will be a vital part of contemporary life." [13] Thus in the criti-

cal polemics of the movement—mainly supplied by Pound himself and T. E. Hulme—late nineteenth-century work was dismissed as "fuzzy," "gummy," "wet," whereas good modern verse was praised as "clean," "sharp-edged," "dry." In a deliberate reversal of the romantic tendency to dissolve the object by looking through it, these poets emphasized the solid, independent existence of the thing and the need to perceive its surface with care and precision. Modern poetry thus began as a radical repudiation of the romantic ego and the idealistic philosophy that supported it. Any symbolic reading of the object is resisted; all moralizing about the object is avoided; these are subjective impositions, merely "personal." In Imagism, as in a great deal of the poetry that was to follow it, the artist insists that he is simply letting the objects speak for themselves—not transforming them to accord with his private moods. He is impersonal, self-effacing, more like a photographer than the dilating seer of romanticism.

In their efforts to arrive at an intimate knowledge of the solid, irreducible *thing*, modern painters and poets were working along with some of the advanced philosophic opinion of their day. The best account of the kind of speculative thought that was most influential among artists appears in an essay, "The Intellectual Temper of the Age," written by George Santayana in 1913.[14] As the "civilization characteristic of Christendom" disappears, Santayana begins, we observe "the slow upward filtration of a new spirit—that of an emancipated, atheistic, international democracy" (p. 1). In many ways skeptical of the age's animal vigor, the philosopher is chiefly concerned to refine and organize it; but even he is moved by the fluidity of the present circumstances and his essay, when not delivering lofty moral strictures, offers an accurate description of the contemporary scene.

It is Santayana's contention that in philosophy, as in the fine arts, we are "in full career toward disintegration" (p. 10). In the decline of abstract thought the main cause has been a new movement, exemplified in the work of William James and Henri Bergson, which "may be called irrationalism, vitalism, pragmatism, or pure empiricism" (p. 11). "An extreme expression of romantic anarchy" (p. 12), this movement, far from having an organizing instinct, makes all forms of mental organization arbitrary and subjective. Abstraction, a mutilation of the flow of experience for mere practical ends, becomes anathema, and truth, in Bergson's view, "is given only in intuitions which prolong experience just as it occurs, in its full immediacy" (p. 13). Now "what appears is the thing, not the mind to which the thing appears" (p. 15). Here we see the sources not just of Imagism, but of the hostility to abstract language that is pervasive in early twentieth-century literature. But, as Santayana argues, the important point is that this drive toward immediacy leads to a focus not just on the object but on the *flow* of experience: "change, growth, action, creation" are stressed (p. 15), in opposition to the sterility of any fixed position. There are clear affinities here with nineteenth-century forms of vitalism, the difference being that what is now vital is not divine spirit but pure matter. Once he has cut away the arbitrary constructions of the conscious mind, all the artist has left is matter in motion; it is the stuff of which Williams's art is made.

These trends in speculative thought, the insurgent activity in all the arts, his new reading of Whitman—all converged on Williams in the crucial year 1913. Without more biographical information than we now have, it is difficult to distinguish parallel developments from actual influences, or to determine which influences were prior; but together, these forces shaped the historical context in which Williams's self-identification took place. Yet, as affected as he was by the modern movement, Williams remained a stubbornly isolated figure within it. As time went on, fewer and fewer writers shared his belief that the bare, splintered contemporary world was a place in which to grip down and begin to awaken. Williams's work has the impersonality and objectivity of a great deal of modern art; but it is special in that self-effacement works for him as part of a process of maintaining intimacy with immediate experience and thus of evolving true individuality.

One way to formulate more precisely the distinctions between Williams and his contemporaries is by examining his
critical prose. But before doing that we need to raise two questions: How valuable a theorist is Williams? And how useful
are his essays as a way into his poetry? My own belief is that
Williams is a refreshing and sometimes original essayist whose
virtues are often hidden by a polemical spite and rigidity. He
did not really begin to write critical prose until he had developed an outraged sense of literary and popular neglect, and the
products of this frustration are frequently simple exercises in
polemical self-justification. The man who wrote the short stories and poems had a wonderful capacity to make himself vul-
nerable, but the figure that emerges from some of the essays is
an embittered and assertive prophet of rebellion—a figure close
to the one he himself discerned in the egotistical young Pound.
Loose, disjointed, oracular, defiant—often exhilarating and
often bombastic—Williams's essays look back stylistically to
the prose writings of Emerson and Whitman. Williams, however, is a liberating prophet who is tormented at times by his
position at the margin of his society. Less buoyantly confident
than the nineteenth-century seers, he is more often rancorous.

With their abrupt shifts of tone, their jolting epigrams and
their slangy defiance of critical decorum, the essays strike us at
first as immensely refreshing, particularly to readers accustomed to the severe, circumspect manner in which T. S. Eliot's
polemics are delivered. But Williams's position as embattled
Prometheus was hardly conducive to the equanimity out of
which accurate critical judgments are made. The famous "Prologue" to *Kora in Hell,* one of his first critical manifestoes, was
certainly one of his most spiteful and implacable. There, Williams starts by splitting modern poetry into two warring
camps—the stay-at-homes and the expatriates—and his infuriated need to destroy his exiled foes forces him to rank Marianne Moore, Alfred Kreymborg, and Maxwell Bodenheim
over H. D., Ezra Pound, and T. S. Eliot. Few have followed
him here. Moreover, Williams often lowers the attack to a personal level. In the "Prologue" Williams quotes from unpub-

lished letters by H. D., Pound, and Wallace Stevens in order to answer, deridingly, their criticisms of him. Pound's erudition, a quality which always annoyed the anti-intellectual Williams, is debunked with a simple anecdote—"It is not necessary to read everything in a book in order to speak intelligently of it. Don't tell everybody I said so," he quotes Pound as saying (*SE*, p. 7); the immaculate, dandified manner of Stevens is mocked— "Wallace Stevens is a fine gentleman whom Cannell likened to a Pennsylvania Dutchman who has suddenly become aware of his habits and taken to 'society' in self-defense" (*SE*, p. 12); and Eliot and Pound are swiftly dismissed as "men content with the connotations of their masters" (*SE*, p. 21). There can be little doubt about who is to arise out of the destructive antics of this essay as the major-domo of modern poetry. Here, the rebellious energy of a frustrated Williams hardens into a dogmatic vindictiveness.

Certainly, no contemporary writer has written more and said less about T. S. Eliot. The origin of Williams's wrathful treatment of Eliot was his correct sense that the magnitude of Eliot's talent would make him the dominant poet of his generation and that he would move that generation in a direction precisely opposite to that which Williams envisioned for it.

> I felt he had rejected America and I refused to be rejected and so my reaction was violent. I realized the responsibility I must accept. I knew he would influence all subsequent American poets and take them out of my sphere. I had envisaged a new form of poetic composition, a form for the future. It was a shock to me that he was so tremendously successful; my contemporaries flocked to him—away from what I wanted. It forced me to be successful. (*IW*, p. 30)

In his best moments, Williams knew that his own determination to seek new beginnings rather than formal perfection committed him to anonymity and "defeat." But he often regarded the poetic scene as a contest and whenever he contemplated the triumphant figure of Eliot, a fiercely messianic side emerged. No doubt the image of a successful foe with whom he had to contend answered a psychic need in Williams: "de-

struction and creation are simultaneous," he believed (*SE*, p.
121). But the candid acknowledgment of Eliot's formal excellence, the angry denunciations of his anonymous academic al-
lies, the hints of literary interlocking directorates, all suggest
that Williams's estimate of Eliot is properly accounted a contribution to demonology rather than literary criticism. The
differences between the two poets are real and profound; but
they often rendered the neglected Williams unable to speak of
his famous contemporary except in the language of invective.

The confident self-reliance and ardent fraternalism of the
pre-war years became difficult for Williams, a man of violent
moods, to sustain—particularly when, having committed himself to America and its renewal, he discovered that he was having little impact. As a release from frustration, essays and letters were necessary and even healthy; but one thing that
emerges from a reading of the *Selected Essays* is a sense of the
way the doctrine of rebellion tended increasingly to narrow
Williams. He was a man with extraordinarily alert senses, violent but profound moods and a ruminative quality of mind—
with the result that he arrived at ideas slowly and clung to
them tenaciously. Whereas Williams was able to generate a remarkably extended development as a writer, his critical ideas
underwent little growth or modification. The need for an organic relation to place, for a poetry growing out of the spoken
language, for new literary forms consonant with our day—
these interconnected notions are repeated again and again in
the essays, and in the final ten years of the author's life they
narrowed into an obsessive preoccupation with a new "variable" poetic foot, Dr. Williams's contribution to the age of relativity.* Williams's generosity is to be found in his creative
work; as a critic, while he became famous late in life for the
generous encouragement he often gave to younger writers, he
was really not relativistic enough. He correctly saw the need
to establish a center from which he could apprehend the chaos
of the contemporary world; but he could never admit the va-
lidity of any locus—such as Eliot's in tradition—that appeared
to threaten his own.

* For a full discussion of the "variable" foot see Chapter VII.

Still, when he is on his own ground—when he is developing the theoretical bases of his own work or when he is dealing with writers for whom he feels some basic affinity—Williams can work in a way that is startlingly original, yet solid and deep. At his best Williams can theorize in a plain, compact style that moves with a quick, broken, epigrammatic thrust:

> The true value is that peculiarity which gives an object a character by itself. The associational or sentimental value is the false. Its imposition is due to lack of imagination, to an easy lateral sliding. The attention has been held too rigid on one plane instead of following a more flexible, jagged resort. (*SE*, p. 11)

Like the poetry and fiction, the essays almost never follow a single line of logic but leap, jaggedly, from one insight to the next—a method that opens new possibilities in the form of the critical essay. The solidest results emerge when Williams concentrates on a limited subject, a single author, or a particular work. Here are some passages from an essay on the *Cantos:*

> Here is a theme: a closed mind which clings to its power— about which the intelligence beats seeking entrance. This is the basic theme of the XXX *Cantos*. (*SE*, p. 106)

> All the thought and implications of the thought are there in the words (in the minute character and relationships of the words—destroyed, avoided by . . .)—it is *that* I wish to say again and again—it is there in the technique and it is that that is the making or breaking of the work. It is that that one sees, feels. It is that that *is* the work of art—to be observed. (*SE*, pp. 107–8)

> How far has he succeeded? Generation, he says, as I interpret him, is analytical, it is not a mass fusion. Only superficially do the *Cantos* fuse the various temporal phases of the material Pound has chosen, into a synthesis. It is important to stress this for it is Pound's chief distinction in the *Cantos*—his personal point of departure from most that the modern is attempting. It is not by any means a synthesis, but a shot through all material—a true and somewhat old-fashioned analysis of his world. (*SE*, p. 110)

> It stands out from almost all other verse by a faceted quality
> that is not muzzy, painty, wet. It is a dry, clean use of words.
> Yet look at the words. They are themselves not dead. They
> have not been violated by "thinking." They have been used
> willingly by thought. (*SE*, p. 111)

A rapid-fire manner throughout jolts us along, alert, from one
flash of insight to the next; but the effect is not one of inco-
herence. Rather, it is of an object examined probingly from several angles of vision so that its basic qualities emerge. Seldom
does Williams "read" or even quote from a poem. What he
does do is to define forcefully the theoretical underpinnings
for the work of a "difficult" writer, as he does in the essays on
Pound, Joyce, Marianne Moore, and Gertrude Stein. Characteristically, he is not concerned with settling or civilizing the
poem; he opens new ways into obscure territories, like the explorers he celebrates in *In the American Grain*.

But Williams was at his critical best when developing the
theoretical bases for his own literary experiments, especially in
the prose commentary that originally accompanied the *Spring
and All* poems. The disjunctiveness of the critical prose, we
discover, is made possible by an underlying coherence of
thought. And while Williams's ideas about art often resemble
those of other modern poets and painters, they become his by
virtue of his unique center: his insistence on the ego-annihilat-
ing process that keeps taking us back to the sources of life and
art in the common ground. Thus, Williams often employs the
critical vocabulary of Hulme—words such as "dry," "hard,"
"clean"—but he uses it in a value system that is radically different. Williams is vitalistic; Hulme is self-consciously anti-vitalis-
tic. Trying to identify the special character of modern art,
Hulme chose an analogy which he knew would shock his lis-
teners. To an audience accustomed to hearing the work of art
compared to a living, organic thing—a flower or a tree—Hulme
proposed the comparison to a machine. In the new painting, he
argued, there is

> a desire to avoid those lines and surfaces which look pleasing
> and organic, and to use lines which are clean, clear-cut and

mechanical. You will find artists expressing admiration for engineer's drawings, where the lines are clean, the curves all geometrical, and the colour, laid on to show the shape of a cylinder, for example, graduated absolutely mechanically.[15]

Williams, too, compared the work of art to a machine:

> To make two bald statements: There's nothing sentimental about a machine, and: A poem is a small (or large) machine made of words. When I say there's nothing sentimental about a poem I mean that there can be no part, as in any other machine, that is redundant.
>
> Prose may carry a load of ill-defined matter like a ship. But poetry is the machine which drives it, pruned to a perfect economy. As in all machines its movement is intrinsic, undulant, a physical more than a literary character. (*SE*, p. 256)

Hulme and Williams are both reacting against the dreaminess of late nineteenth-century verse. Yet what is striking about the two passages is their very different assumptions about the way out of that impasse. Later in "Modern Art," Hulme speaks enthusiastically of Cézanne's "Women Bathing," in which "all the lines are ranged in a pyramidal shape, and the women are distorted to fit this shape." [16] For Hulme, what makes possible a clean presentation is an "abstraction" from ordinary experience and he accordingly stresses the formal or what Williams calls the "literary"; Hulme wants to distance us from the immediate. "The separation of the high heel and the powdered face," he writes elsewhere, "is essential to all emotions, in order to make a work of art." [17]

Williams, on the other hand, concerns himself with precisely the reverse: capturing a "physical" movement—not an abstract form, which mutilates, but an intimate one that is an organic extension of the immediate experience.* He uses the machine metaphor to suggest the clean efficiency and thus the force with which this physical thrust must be rendered. As Williams always stressed, it's not what a writer "*says* that counts as a

---

* As we shall see, there is a kind of abstraction in Williams's work, an abstraction from temporal and causal sequences, but its effect is to intensify our experience of the immediate.

work of art, it's what he makes, with such intensity of perception that it lives with an intrinsic movement of its own to verify its authenticity" (*SE*, p. 257). The form must be unfolded,
from the inside out—an *intrinsic* movement, invented, not imposed. And for the realization of such a form, neither the
generating experience nor the words of the poem can be violated by thinking. A poet is not a sayer, but a maker; this is
part of the impersonal ideal of modern art. In fact, Williams
often takes this position to its extreme by asserting that a poem
is not an argument or an expression of feeling or a representation of reality so much as it is an organization of sounds and
rhythms—a physical object. As J. Hillis Miller points out, Williams espouses "a subtle theory of poetry which rejects both
the mirror and the lamp, both the classical theory of art as imitation, and the romantic theory of art as transformation. In
their place is proposed a new objectivist art in which a poem is
'Not prophecy! NOT prophecy! / but the thing itself!' " (*P*, p.
242).[18] This stress on the poem as a made object puts Williams at one with a good deal of modern literary thought. But
it is important to see that Williams does not conceive of the
poem as a completely autonomous object with only aesthetic
value, only internal relations. The poem *is* the thing itself.
"The work of the imagination," he declares in *Spring and All,*
is "not 'like' anything but transfused with the same forces
which transfuse the earth" (*SA*, p. 50). The writer's problem
is to catch these forces in a language that will not tame, atten-
uate, or otherwise violate their physical character; he strives to
keep the poem down, "inside" experience. It is to keep it pure
in this sense that Williams emphasizes the poem's primary existence as a body, as sound and rhythm. He is not arguing that a
poem has merely existence, no meaning. What he does hold is
that its meaning will not be found at the surface, explicitly
stated, buoyed up by a pleasing rhetoric. It will be found, as
he says of Pound's work, hidden in the minute relationships of
the words. If in life there are no ideas but in things, then in art
there are no ideas but in style. In a world where shared ideas
of order are lacking, surface connections disappear from art;

the result is that, in objectivist art, ideas are not asserted but experienced, and they are experienced at a level below that of conscious activity.

To understand fully Williams's theory of the poem, we need to work out systematically the theory of consciousness implied by his critical prose. For Williams, mental activity in most people is conducted predominately at the level of the ordinary consciousness or the ego. The distinctive feature of such life is its tendency toward a rigid conservatism, a fear of new experience and a need to operate safely within established categories. Ordinary consciousness is governed by habitual and conventional associations—the "easy lateral sliding" from the "peculiarity" which is the "true value"—and thus constitutes a kind of veil cutting the individual off from otherness and from unique selfhood. Locked within a system, cut off from fresh experience by the desire for security, the ordinary man will be emotionally and sensually starved—walking outside of his own body, unroused, like the citizens of Paterson. In a real sense, such a man will not even exist. "The reader," Williams complains in *Spring and All*,

> knows himself as he was twenty years ago and he has also in mind a vision of what he would be, some day. Oh, some day! But the thing he never knows and never dares to know is what he is at the exact moment that he is. And this moment is the only thing in which I am at all interested. (*SA*, pp. 2–3)

Ironically, then, the person who seeks security in this way uproots himself from the present moment, the only thing that *is*, and so he becomes a perpetual drifter. Because he is impoverished, his activity will be incessant; but because he is dissociated from the sources of life, his restless activity will be futile. The ordinary American, in Williams's view, is a man whose swift-moving commitment to material ends has abstracted him from immediate experience—from the New World; his fear of the new, thwarting the creative process of renewal, is self-destructive.

Yet the restless dissatisfaction which drives such a man to

act is the expression of a deeper level of personality, a buried self, a rebellious force that Williams identifies with our physical nature. In the body we find the core of our being—to which we must constantly return. Against the fixity of ordinary consciousness, Williams sets the fluidity of consciousness at moments of intensity. "We speak of a man's 'mettle,'" he says.

> It might better be metal. It is as with other metals, when it is heated it melts. It is when the metal is fluid that the imagination can be said to become active; it is the melting, the rendering fluid of the imagination that describes the mind as entering upon creative work.
> It must be melted to create; fluid, unfettered by anything. (*SE*, p. 308)

At such moments a buried primitive power is released and we hear "the deeper, not 'lower' (in the usual silly sense) portions of the personality speaking, the middle brain, the nerves, the glands, the very muscles and bones of the body itself speaking." [19] The ego melts, the body speaks and we renew, momentarily at least, our participation in "the rhythmic ebb and flow of the mysterious life process." [20] Descent into the body takes us back to the primordial unity where distinctions between inner and outer, self and object, do not yet exist. Objects are perceived with a jolting distinctness and, freed of all conventional associations and fixed relationships, they can combine in startling ways. It is now the body thinking, speaking. And the work of art, refusing to dissociate form and meaning from physical experience, tries to draw us down into this intense consciousness; it is an act of descent. Still, this state of integration is only momentary: immediacy begins to slip away as soon as we grasp it, the ego reasserts itself—and the whole process must be enacted over again.

Implicit in the writings of Pound and Eliot is a conception of the artist as a cosmopolitan whose primary allegiance is given to the ancient tradition of his craft. Both authors apprehend the chaotic present through the perspective of past literature. To understand fully the translations of Pound or the allusive verse of Eliot, a great deal of acquired knowledge is needed—a requirement that deliberately narrows the audience to an alienated cultural elite. Pound's portrait of the modern artist in "Hugh Selwyn Mauberley" shows a lonely aesthete, thwarted by a vulgar and hostile society. When Eliot looks at the contemporary world in "The Waste Land," he does so from the lofty, ironic perspective of the seer Tiresias. Both poets characteristically attempt to extinguish the personality of their reader, distance him from the present and lift him into a "higher" perspective that is impersonal and timeless.

Williams, too, sought a mode of consciousness that would be impersonal; he found this, however, not in high culture but in the immediate physical environment. Tradition was the nightmare from which he was trying to awaken, in order to enter the New World and begin to build an organic culture. Like Whitman, Williams held a democratic idea of the artist as one who fulfills himself in intimate relation to his locality. Hence, while there was personal envy involved, his frequently acrimonious treatment of writers like Eliot and Pound came from his correct sense that they were trying to alienate readers from exactly that which he was trying to connect them with. In his "Letter to an Australian Editor" Williams defines calmly and precisely the split between himself and Pound.

> I wish only to say that for years we have been of opposite but friendly camps, touching the origin of poetic genius. We parted years ago, he to move among his intellectual equals in Europe, I to remain at home and struggle to discover here the impetus to my achievements, if I found myself able to write anything at all. . . . He left the States under the assumption that it was mind that fertilizes mind, that the mere environment is just putty and that—assuming one's self great [—] the thing to do in this world is, or was then, to go to Europe, which he did.

Against this view of creativity, Williams sets his own idea of constant return to our origins in the immediate physical world.

> A man may live for a time on a gathered hoard of skills, granted, but if he live his meat will run out unless replenished

about him. He will continue to produce only if his attachments to society continue adequate. If a man in his fatuous dreams cuts himself off from that supplying female, he dries up his sources—as Pound did in the end heading straight for literary sterility.

The ultimate effect, Williams adds, is "schizophrenic attitudes of final exhaustion": "The great creations, like those of the past in every case, arise from the close ties between the poet and the upsurging (or down surging) forms of his immediate world." [21] The expatriate finally becomes a mirror image of the world he rejects: isolated, uprooted, and sterile. As a way out of such impotence, Williams offers the generative powers hidden in the supplying female, the forces which transfuse the earth.

But Williams differs from Pound and Eliot not just about the origins but also about the ends of poetic genius. The ground is an impersonal source; but burial in the earth results for him, in an intensely individual identity. In men as well as objects, "peculiarity" is the "true value"—as against an "easy lateral sliding" into the crowd. With the confidence that comes of being rooted in the common, a poet is freed to follow "his own way of doing things"—a quality Williams constantly praises in the heroes of *In the American Grain*. As one of his characters proclaims, "Nobody / Nobody else / but me— / They can't copy it" (*CEP*, p. 269). Opposed to all finalities and decorums, breaking out of the fixed categories of ordinary consciousness, Williams adopts the stance of the self-reliant democrat.

For all his insistence on identification with place, Williams was a highly peculiar figure, a lonely and alienated individual, a man on the margin. The very need to distinguish between "ordinary" and a deeper, liberated consciousness reveals him as separate from the mass of men around him. His repudiation of established literary forms, the loose, broken manner of his writing, its frequently flat, literalistic rendering of "unpoetic" objects, even the peculiar appearance of the poem on the printed page, reveal a writer radically at odds with the ordinary reader's expectations about art. At first glance, his work may seem more like the product of a fastidious aesthete than a robust democrat. Moreover, Williams, who had violent moods of disgust with his townspeople, had his own longings for refined beauty; he was so fierce with Eliot because the expatriate represented a side of himself. Poems, stories, letters show Williams worried about wasting his creative energies on the banal; and in such moods he imagined himself as a giant surrounded by smaller men, who were tearing at him savagely, drawing him down into the anonymous crowd. The fear of a simple diffusion of his powers must have been always with him.

But if Williams, like all the moderns, assumes an initial separation between himself and his reader, his work attempts to dissolve that distance. The opening pages of the prose commentary in *Spring and All* exactly reveal Williams's sense of his relation to a reader. "If anything of moment results—so much the better. And so much the more likely will it be that no one will want to see it," he bitterly begins (*SA*, p.1). But after scornful condemnation of the hostile bewilderment he anticipates from his audience, Williams goes on to invite the reader to enter the world of the imagination, the deeper consciousness hidden in the body.

> In the imagination, we are henceforth (so long as you read) locked in a fraternal embrace, the classic caress of author and reader. We are one. Whenever I say "I" I also mean "you." And so, together, as one, we shall begin. (*SA*, pp. 3–4)

The tension between author and audience, a gap to be spanned, becomes a source of energy for the poet; their relation is finally one of mutual dependence. What begins in alienation ends in a comradely embrace.

The important point is that while Williams did see himself as a man apart, his perspective on society was from a point below rather than above. This does not mean that he was more humble than Pound or Eliot, only that he had a different kind of pretension. For the difference between adopting tradition or place as the creative source is that the ground is available to anyone who will look under his bootsoles. Williams speaks from a crude locus—in the earth and in the body—that is potentially, if not actually, common. It is by adopting this physical perspective that Williams deals with the modern breakdown of belief; he can now claim to be articulating a kind of consciousness that is buried in all of us. Thus he contends with the poetic expectations of his reader; but he does so in order to shatter egotistical distance, open the core of personality buried in the body and generate an acceptance of all things. What he says of the French missionary Rasles is true of his own work: "Nothing shall be ignored. All shall be included" (*IAG*, p. 120). The objects and people in his work are usually coarse in order to jolt the torpid reader awake—by showing him the beauty to be found in the ordinary. It is exactly this defiance of poetic decorum that Williams finds and praises in Whitman:

> Whitman's proposals are of the same piece with the modern trend toward imaginative understanding of life. The largeness which he interprets as his identity with the least and the greatest around him, his "democracy" represents the vigor of his imaginative life. (*SA*, p. 38)

Well aware of the way Whitman's expansiveness could become simply a kind of euphoria, Williams made his own work more concentrated and precise—to persuade us that his ardor has been awakened *now*, by *this object*. As we shall see, the formal oddities in his work derive from his need to include all things, but slowly, carefully, "one by one." In his broken poems objects are "well spaced"; there is freedom *and* concentration. In Williams's imaginative work we enter a world in which all the objects are common, but they have been lifted, by the intensity with which they have been perceived and rendered, into a sharp distinction. It is the familiar, seen *for the first time*—a new but solid world. If Williams was, in disgust, often tempted to drift off in fantasies of pure beauty, he consistently purged himself of such yearnings, again and again

showing his readers a way to uncover novelty in the banal, a
hard-edged beauty in the commonplace.

Williams looked at history as a cyclical process of growth.
"Whatever we see of worth in the world," he says, "the generation of it has been crude, corpor [sic] as the sexual itself.
Then that force begins to fan out, grows thinner, more fragile
as it gets further and further from the fountainhead" (*A Novelette*, p. 122). When he himself began to write, the poetic impulse had become so attenuated that Williams felt an impera-
tive need to take it back to its generative source in the
physical. He wanted to walk *inside* of his body, intensely
roused, through the familiar landscape of his native locality, as
crude and broken as that might be. This aim essentially isolated Williams from his contemporaries, although he remained
alert to what they were doing. But the advantage of his position was that, liberating him from the ideality of late nineteenth-century verse, it opened a hard, solid, common world
for exploration by the imagination. Rooted in this world, a
man, unlike the inhabitants of Eliot's "unreal city," fears neither birth nor death, but makes his life a continual process of
renewal.

III

Spring and All: A New Lyric Form

How easy to slip
into the old mode, how hard to
cling firmly to the advance—
"The Black Winds"

In its original version, published by an obscure expatriate press in France in 1923, *Spring and All* was a serial poem consisting of twenty-seven untitled but numbered poems, introduced and accompanied throughout by a sometimes fierce, sometimes flamboyant prose polemic.[1] The *Spring and All* poems, striking for their toughness and spontaneity, their abrupt and radical shifts of tone and direction, generate all the intensity and persistence of a pitched battle; and they get their extraordinary power from their proximity to chaos—from their capacity to bring together violently antagonistic forces and to leave them, suspended and unresolved, in a moment of agonizing tension. Individual poems, as we move through them, seem to fly off in several directions simultaneously and, by doing so, become the first in Williams's career to illustrate what he later called "the poem as a field of action." No argument, no narrative—no linear mode of organization—imposes a single direction on the full, rounded moment of experience. Instead of relations that are stated and therefore fixed, we get relations that are left open and therefore fluid and multiple. Instead of a designated *path* we can follow through the poem, we get the poem as a *field*—as a field of *action*. *Spring and All*, for its startling originality and tensed force, must be ranked as one of the major documents of modern literature.

Williams was slow in arriving at his new mode. His artistic development was in many ways an enactment of his myth of continuous renewal—a series of new beginnings. His practice was to bring some new mode in prose or verse to its fullest expression, then to break it apart and start all over again. He refused to live off a hoard of "gathered skills," but kept coming back to the sources of his art in the "supplying female." The result is that when we look across his entire career, we find long periods of dispersive experiment that culminate in brief phases of accomplished expression. Williams had more or less defined his position as a writer by early 1914; but it took him until 1923 to develop a literary medium that was an organic extension of his point of view. The volumes *Al Que Quiere!* (1917), *Kora in Hell* (1920), and *Sour Grapes* (1922) show him experimenting with a variety of technical means, groping toward his own style.

Of the transitional poems, those collected in *Al Que Quiere!* remain the most interesting. The book does have the quality of a "miscellany," as Wallace Stevens long ago remarked.[2] Some of the poems attempt to realize the effects of modern painting, particularly Cubism; others experiment with Imagistic technique; still others work in a public voice.[3] But the book's most authentic impulse lies in its acceptance of that literal, personal, local level of experience which was missing from the stilted romanticism of *The Tempers.* The first poem in *Al Que Quiere!,* "Sub Terra," calls for a "band," "with the earthy tastes I require; / the burrowing pride that rises / subtly as on a bush in May." The poet who comes forward in the ensuing poems deals with such low, earthy subjects as chicory and daisies, man and dog lime, sparrows, cluttered backyards, a young housewife, a woman in bed, his proletarian townspeople. The man who had praised the "clear radiance" of Elvira can now speak enthusiastically of Kathleen as an "exquisite chunk of mud" (*CEP,* pp. 18, 157). The language is generally cleaner, less affected than in *The Tempers.* At its best it renders prosaic subjects with a tough colloquial flatness—as in "The Young Housewife."

> At ten A.M. the young housewife
> moves about in negligee behind
> the wooden walls of her husband's house.
> I pass solitary in my car.

Rhyme, conventional meter, figurative language, literary associations have all been purged from this matter-of-fact verse; details do not combine into symbolic clusters but instead create a literal specificity. There is a clear resemblance to all of those poems in which the speaker yearns after the affections of a coy or distant lady; but Williams, stripping the poem of much conventional artifice, keeps it cleanly attendant upon its literal occasion.

Yet throughout *Al Que Quiere!* Williams, rather self-conscious about his earthy tastes, often does too much work for the reader. Many of the poems adopt a declamatory voice to offer public advice and instruction. "Gulls" and "Tract" are explicitly directed to "my townspeople." To his "solitary disciple" Williams instructs, "rather notice," "rather observe," "rather grasp" and in "Keller Gegen Dom" he takes a similar stance with "witness, would you," and "witness instead." Many questions are addressed to the general mind—especially as endings to poems— "Who shall say I am not / the happy genius of my household?" (*CEP*, p. 148) A great number of the poems, in short, proceed more from idea than from perception, although what they argue for is unmediated encounter with things. And even when he does confront objects more directly, Williams seems not entirely convinced of their intrinsic poetry. Often conventional figurative language is used to imbue commonplace objects with a poetic force. Williams goes on to compare the young housewife to a "fallen leaf"; the little girl in "The Ogre" becomes a flower, as does the moon in "To a Solitary Disciple." Elsewhere he heightens his material by closing poems with an enigmatic, oracular utterance. The first of the poems called "Pastoral" ends, "No one / will be-

lieve this / of vast import to the nation"; the second goes like
this:

> The little sparrows
> hop ingenuously
> about the pavement
> quarreling
> with sharp voices
> over those things
> that interest them.
> But we who are wiser
> shut ourselves in
> on either hand
> and no one knows
> whether we think good
> or evil.
>   Meanwhile
> the old man who goes about
> gathering dog-lime
> walks in the gutter
> without looking up
> and his tread
> is more majestic than
> that of the Episcopal minister
> approaching the pulpit
> of a Sunday.
>   These things
> astonish me beyond words.

The silent humility of the old man gathering dog-lime makes a
better sermon than what we hear from the pulpit on a Sunday
morning; but Williams himself sermonizes, telling us we have
"shut ourselves in" and that the old man is "more majestic"
than the minister. The last line attempts to cast an aura of profound and mysterious significance over what has preceded. Yet
the effect, as in so many of these poems, is that the poetry
seems imposed on rather than discovered in the objects described. "Bring him down—bring him down! / Low and inconspicuous"; what Williams asks for the hearse driver in "Tract,"
we demand of him in *Al Que Quiere!*; he is too conspicuously

present as teacher, artist, and personality. In the book's best poems he is trying to work with the familiar objects and people of his locality in an Imagistic mode—to take Imagism out of the "rare world" of H. D. and Pound and root it firmly in the ground.[4] But Williams is still not sure enough of the intrinsic poetry of his objects to disappear from the poem and let them speak for themselves.

Yet the power of the *Spring and All* poems frequently comes from the way they create an intense, ego-shattering concentration upon physical objects. Williams has here created a literary style that is uniquely his, but one from which he has entirely disappeared as a conscious personality. The voice of these poems, coming from far below the level of conscious will or reason, gives poetic speech to bodily consciousness. We enter a world where seemingly banal objects, carefully perceived, can generate ecstatic emotion—as in "The Red Wheelbarrow."

so much depends
upon

a red wheel
barrow

glazed with rain
water

beside the white
chickens

How can a poem about things as hopelessly ordinary as a wheelbarrow and white chickens be anything but flat? Again, Williams is deliberately seeking flatness—through banal objects and an impersonal manner. The personal element—the instructing, argumentative "I" of *Al Que Quiere!*—has disappeared; we get instead an impersonal assertion: "so much depends. . . ." With the disappearance of the poet comes a close focus upon the object: short, jagged lines and long vowels slow down our movement through the poem, breaking off each part of the scene for exact observation. Any symbolic reading of the

scene, a possible imposition by the observer, is carefully resisted; its hard, literal, objective reality is insisted upon.

But Williams risks banality in order to push through to startling discoveries. The scene is not entirely bare: the wheelbarrow is red and it has just been rained on, giving it a fresh,
"glazed" appearance. A spare, clinical manner, it is clear, asserts by relief the primary color and novelty that are there.
We are brought down, into a new world. Similarly, the effect
of the impersonal subject "so much" is not to empty the poem
of feeling but to fill it with the ecstatic emotion which these
particulars inspire. By its slow movement the poem not only
forces us to concentrate on the physical scene, but also renders
the intensity of the emotion; intensity means a stretching out.
Originally, there is the feeling of a laborious thrust downward,
away from all conscious activity and toward a heightened receptivity; but the final effect is the sense of a slow lifting, with
the discovery of a distinct beauty in the commonplace. The
poem *is* impersonal; its impersonality, however, is not that of
the indifferent God paring his fingernails, but one that comes
from the way the poet has yielded himself intimately to the
scene. The particulars in the poem, broken apart to be seen
clearly, are drawn together by the ecstatic feeling generated
by the poet's discovery. This kind of crisp, intense lyric, in
which self is dissolved into scene, is one way Williams had of
constantly renewing himself.

Significantly, Williams's next literary project after *Al Que
Quiere!* had been a series of exercises in the annihilation of the
conscious personality, the prose improvisations collected in
Kora in Hell. He had "no book in mind" when he began the
improvisations.

> For a year [evidently 1917–18] I used to come home and no
> matter how late it was before I went to bed I would write
> *something*. And I kept writing, writing, even if it were only a
> few words, and at the end of the year there were 365 entries.
> Even if I had nothing on my mind at all I put something down,
> and as may be expected, some of the entries were pure non-
> sense and were rejected when the time for publication came.

They were a reflection of the day's happenings more or less, and what I had had to do with them. Some were unintelligible to a stranger and I knew that I would have to interpret them. (*IW*, p. 27)

Of the original improvisations Williams chose eighty-four, arranged them in groups of three, provided "interpretations" for most of them, then wrote the "Prologue."

With its use of commonplace subjects, the artist's alternate affirmations of his eccentric individuality and his exhortations to the public mind, *Al Que Quiere!* was the most Whitmanesque of all Williams's books. *Kora in Hell* shows his awareness of the experiments in automatic writing by the Dadaists and early Surrealists, many of whom were in New York during the 'teens. The book, absorbing that influence, represents an important personal and stylistic breakthrough. "The attention has been held too rigid on the one plane instead of following a more flexible, jagged resort," Williams writes in the "Prologue." "It is to loosen the attention, my attention since I occupy part of the field, that I write these improvisations" (*SE*, p. 11). The attention, loosened, descends to "pre-logical" levels of consciousness. Composition itself becomes a leap, a swift recording of the free, jagged associations of the unconscious mind. Individual improvisations are printed unrevised; experience is not violated by any "higher" level of consciousness that might evaluate, omit, supply connectives, shift order —in short, make smooth and finished. The change from the style of *Al Que Quiere!* is radical; the language here is thick, densely metaphorical, flamboyantly broken in its rapid shifts of figure, tone, or mood. The author of *Kora in Hell* appears to be one who writes from "inside" his experiences rather than one who suavely possesses and contains them.

Starting all over again at thirty-four was no easy thing for Williams, as he makes clear in *Kora* itself. Several of the improvisations deal with the author's struggle against the pull toward artistic reputation and success. *"In middle life the mind passes to a variegated October. This is the time youth in its faulty aspirations has set for the achievement of great summits.*

But having attained the mountain top one is not snatched into a cloud but the descent proffers its blandishments quite as a matter of course" (Kora, p. 25). In this view a man's life does not proceed in linear fashion toward some final end; at the mountain top, as Williams put it in *Paterson,* "the descent beckons." Creative movement is cyclical, a wheel or a dance in two of the book's recurrent metaphors. All conventional moral categories, artistic neatness and finish, purposive activity of any kind must be repudiated to release bodily energy. This is the second of the first three improvisations:

> For what it's worth: Jacob Louslinger, white haired, stinking, dirty bearded, cross eyed, stammer tongued, broken voiced, bent backed, ball kneed, cave bellied, mucous faced—deathling —found lying in the weeds "up there by the cemetery." "Looks to me as if he'd been bumming around the meadows for a couple of weeks." Shoes twisted into incredible lilies: out at the toes, heels, tops, sides, soles. Meadow flower! ha, mallow! at last I have you. (Rot dead marigolds—an acre at a time! Gold, are you?) Ha, clouds will touch world's edge and the great pink mallow stand singly in the wet, topping reeds and— a closet full of clothes and good shoes and my thirty-year's-master's-daughter's two cows for me to care for and a winter room with a fire in it—. I would rather feed pigs in Moonachie and chew calamus root and break crab's claws at an open fire: age's lust loose! (*Kora,* p. 9)

Surrendering to instinctive life, bumming around in the meadow rather than sitting comfortably by the hearth, the old man is beautifully transformed in death into a meadow flower. Again and again the writer celebrates those who follow their passions in defiance of established moral codes. The tone, often missed by readers, is comic, since "laughter is the reverse of aspiration," a releasing rather than a tightening of the nerves and muscles (*SE,* p. 15). One effect of this breakthrough is to free man from the experience of time as a fixed cause and effect sequence. "*There is neither beginning nor end to the imagination but it delights in its own seasons reversing the usual order at will. Of the air of the coldest room it will seem to build the hottest passions*" (*Kora*, p. 15). There can be lust in old age, summer in October, dawn in sunset, illumination in the darkness, mythical giants in the squalor of a modern town—Kora in Hell. The wheel turns, the descent beckons: with the abdication of conscious direction we can enter the present moment where everything becomes possible.

When adopting a public role in his verse, Williams had done too much work for the reader; *Kora*, which he defensively regarded as an intensely private work, presents the reader with a set of radical challenges. "One must be a watchman to much secret arrogance before his ways are tuned to these measures," he early warns us (*Kora*, pp. 12–13). A prose of pure process, lacking explicit connectives, the writing here leaves many gaps for us to fill in. To do this, we are required to yield whatever fixed point of view we bring to the work; we must surrender *our* conscious personality and let ourselves be drawn in. To put it another way, the reader is forced to experience the work from the inside; aesthetic distance is disintegrated. With this kind of patient absorption, a basic coherence emerges, which can be defined through the myth which has given the book its title. While gathering flowers on Mount Etna, Kora (or Persephone) was abducted by Pluto and taken to the underworld; with her disappearance the earth became barren. Eventually, her mother Demeter had her freed, but only for nine months of the year; the other three she had to spend in the underworld. Kora is thus the generative principle, whose yearly round signifies the burial and sprouting of the seed. Internally, she is the dark, unknown region of the unconsciousness—a bodily force; she is the dark core of our being, the buried creative principle that Williams is striving to release by the jagged movement of these improvisations. Gradually, the reader discovers a series of recurrent metaphors—descent, darkness, winter, ascent, light, flower, meadow—which combine to recreate the cyclical movement of Kora.

Yet the important thing is not the fact of the book's coherence but the way the reader is forced to come upon it. Classical myth does not provide a graceful narrative surface, as it might have for an earlier writer; it appears fragmented, hidden, as creative forces are in the contemporary world, and it must be resurrected by the imaginative activity of the reader. To see how this works, we can look at the first and third parts of the first section, those coming just before and after the story of Jacob Louslinger.

(1)

Fools have big wombs. For the rest?—here is penny-royal if one knows to use it. But time is only another liar, so go along the wall a little further: if blackberries prove bitter there'll be mushrooms, fairy-ring mushrooms, in the grass, sweetest of all fungi.

(3)

Talk as you will, say: "No woman wants to bother with children in this country";—speak of your Amsterdam and the whitest aprons and brightest doorknobs in Christendom. And I'll answer you: "Gleaming doorknobs and scrubbed entries have heard the songs of the housemaids at sun-up and—housemaids are wishes. Whose? Ha! the dark canals are whistling, whistling for who will cross to the other side. If I remain with hands in pocket leaning upon my lamppost—why—I bring curses to a hag's lips and her daughter on her arm knows better than I can tell you—best to blush and out with it than back beaten after. (*Kora*, pp. 9–10)

Individual improvisations work contrapuntally: each of the first three shows life coming out of darkness and death, contrasting acceptance of this natural process with a need to control and exclude. The practical-minded use pennyroyal (for abortion), view Louslinger reductively ("Looks to me as if he'd been bumming around the meadows for a couple of weeks"), have a closet full of clothes and good shoes and a winter room with a fire in it, certainly don't want to bother with children, and efficiently maintain a house of "gleaming doorknobs and scrubbed entries." This daylight surface of order, practical and clean, is part of life, but so is the underworld "across the canal" where we find Kora (the daughter), darkness and passion—nature striving to perpetuate itself and cursing those who refuse to participate in the process. Hence the improvisations open a world of primitive abandon and life —big wombs, sweetness in fungi, shoes twisted into incredible lilies, chewing calamus root and breaking crab's claws at an open fire, nighttime invitations to lust. The reader is made, then, to circle around between voices of practicality and abandon. Similarly, with no explicit connections given between sections, he must turn back from 2 to 1, from 3 to 2 and 1 in order to discover recurrences. Williams's argument for cyclical movement—the natural process—is enacted structurally. It is this kind of reflexive movement that creates what Williams called, in comparing the improvisations to the superimposed planes of the frontispiece by Stuart Davis, "an impressionistic view of the simultaneous" (*IW*, p. 29). Just as recurrence in nature makes time a "liar" and brings life out of death, the reflexive movement of the prose subverts any linear advance and creates a living moment, filled with many perspectives and voices.

"The imagination transcends the thing itself," Williams declares at one point (*Kora*, p. 24). *Kora in Hell* represents a marked turn inward, the artist moving away from daylight down into the darker regions of the self, hitherto buried. The aim is not evocation of the Image but the release of a primitive force of imagination. The improvisations are a literary version of the defining gesture of the heroic figures in *In the American Grain*, who turn their backs on society and move single-mindedly into the wilderness. Part of the heroism of this gesture is in its acceptance of isolation and neglect. But Williams himself, always self-conscious and divided, kept looking back over his shoulder as he assembled the pieces into a book. First he added the interpretations, which move either toward the literal occasions of the improvisations or proclaim the timeless truths they illustrate. In either case they are written in a clear, detached, third-person style. The relation between comment and improvisation is not always simple; the reader is made to turn back through the material once again, and the dimension of the conscious mind is added; but the ultimate effect is most often to reduce or tame the raw experience. So, too, with the

"Prologue," which argues the significance of the improvisations in the contemporary scene but in doing so becomes a
heated expression of the very will-to-conquer which the author, inside the book, is struggling to quit. The pull between
the artist's desire simply to express himself and his sense of ob-
ligation to an audience is characteristic of Williams. But the
conflict here does not produce a dynamic integration.

It was in the actual improvisations that Williams came clos-
est to the new mode in verse he was to reveal in *Spring and
All.* But we need to mention at least one more major influence
on that remarkable volume—the publication of T. S. Eliot's
"The Waste Land" in 1922. To Williams, Eliot's poem was the
"great catastrophe to our letters" (*Auto*, p. 146). "I shall never
forget the impression created by 'The Waste Land,' " he later
wrote in "An Essay on *Leaves of Grass.*" "It was as if the bottom had dropped out of everything. I had not known how
much the spirit of Whitman animated us until it was withdrawn from us." [5] The extravagant spirit of Whitman had in-
deed been withdrawn from the main line of American poetry,
not to re-emerge until the mid-1950's. But as Williams here implies, the impact of Eliot's poem helped him to identify himself
at the same time that it angered and frustrated him. Williams
now had a role, at once humble and messianic, to play in
American poetry and culture. In Whitman he had a revolutionary predecessor whose acceptance of the New World Williams hoped to generate among his own contemporaries, while
in Eliot he had a feudal contemporary who provided an exact
focus for all of his poetic and social repudiations. In this context, Williams himself became a kind of anonymous figure in
modern poetry, but one who carried within himself the seeds
of a New World consciousness.

Sour Grapes (1921) had been filled with images of a vital
force buried but persisting in winter or old age; the book
seems to have derived from Williams's own experience of
post-war disillusionment. As he writes in the *Autobiography,*

> the freshness, the newness of a springtime which I had sensed
> among the others, a reawakening of letters, all that delight
> which in making a world to match the supremacies of the past

could mean was being blotted out by the war. The stupidity,
the calculated viciousness of a money-grubbing society such
as I knew and violently wrote against; everything I wanted
to see live and thrive was being deliberately murdered in the
name of church and state. (*Auto*, p. 158)

The feeling in the poems of this period is more like oppression
than despair: there is a sense of life buried in a kind of hell of
repression, but powerless to revive itself. But in *Spring and All*
we find a new power of affirmation and acceptance. Whitman
had opened Williams to the myth of plenitude; Eliot had
confronted him with the myth of sterility. Together, they
prompted Williams to identify his own informing myth—the
discovery of plenty lodged, as it must be in the contemporary
landscape, amid barrenness. Characteristic of the poems in this
volume, "The Eyeglasses" begins with descriptions of the flowers that grow near the edges of garbage heaps and of the delicate beauty of the farmer's daughter issuing from the crude
strength of her father:

> The universality of things
> draws me toward the candy
> with melon flowers that open
>
> about the edge of refuse
> proclaiming without accent
> the quality of the farmer's
>
> shoulders and his daughter's
> accidental skin, so sweet
> with clover and the small
>
> yellow cinquefoil in the
> parched places.

The constant subject of the *Spring and All* poems is the
emergence of life out of death, ecstasy out of despair, poetry
unexpectedly blossoming in a parched industrial landscape.
Once again the presiding mythic figure is Persephone, whose
savage force is hidden but still alive in our world. Her power
is evident in the roots that "grip down and begin to awaken"

in the first poem and in the wildflower ("Arab / Indian / dark woman") of the last. Persephone is explicitly named in "At the Faucet of June"; she appears as a gypsy woman in "Quietness" and "The Avenue of Poplars," the farmer's daughter in "The Eyeglasses," Kiki in "Young Love" and Elsie in "To Elsie." Persephone is always embattled, surrounded by "white" "crowds" as she is in "The Wildflower"; but she is fierce as well as beautiful, "rich / in savagery," and she persists along with the mechanical and industrial realities of modern life.

Like so many works of the 'twenties, *Spring and All* is often apocalyptic in tone; the prose commentary, which opens the book, moves toward a vision of cataclysmic destruction. Yet Williams, who believed that "destruction and creation / are simultaneous" (*CEP*, p. 266), celebrates the "end." The root sense of apocalypse is "uncover" and what excites him is that the upheaval will uncover Persephone, the buried creative principle. In fact, what Williams imagines is the release of the imagination from the "rock" (*SA*, p. 14), the very place where Eliot was attempting to secure it. At the moment of release, the rigid forms of the old order are shattered and we are forced to enter a new world. Everything exists from the beginning. "It is spring," Williams asserts after the catastrophe, "THE WORLD IS NEW" (*SA*, pp. 10-11). The major impetus behind *Spring and All* is the reaffirmation of a creative power which is often thwarted, repressed, surrounded by blankness, but which ardent pursuit can still uncover.

All of the books of poetry Williams had written since "The Wanderer" had begun with a spring poem. But in 1923, as the poet of birth in a seemingly sterile environment—as the poet of spring *and all*—Williams invented a new spring for poetry. The poem that follows the cataclysm, genuinely new, does not take us into the traditional spring song world of bounding lambs, gamboling children, gentle breezes and universal fecundity. We are moved down, from a literary to an actual landscape. And instead of jocund song, Williams gives us a rough, harsh music, broken rhythms that jolt us into an awakened perception of the scene.

By the road to the contagious hospital
under the surge of the blue
mottled clouds driven from the
northeast—a cold wind. Beyond, the
waste of broad, muddy fields
brown with dried weeds, standing and fallen

patches of standing water
the scattering of tall trees

All along the road the reddish
purplish, forked, upstanding, twiggy
stuff of bushes and small trees
with dead, brown leaves under them
leafless vines—

Lifeless in appearance, sluggish
dazed spring approaches—

They enter the new world naked,
cold, uncertain of all
save that they enter. All about them
the cold, familiar wind—

Now the grass, tomorrow
the stiff curl of wildcarrot leaf
One by one objects are defined—
It quickens: clarity, outline of leaf

But now the stark dignity of
entrance—Still, the profound change
has come upon them: rooted, they
grip down and begin to awaken

This poem does not simply describe the physical qualities in a
landscape; its center is an *act* of perception, "the stark dignity
of / entrance," the slow penetration of a desolate landscape by
an awakening observer. We follow the thrust of his imagination downward, through obstacles, to a new union with the
physical environment. The progression in the poem is literally
downward: the observer goes from "the blue / mottled
clouds," across a distant view of "broad, muddy fields," to the
quickening plant life right before him—and then penetrates

even further downward, into the dark earth, as he imagines the roots taking hold again. The panoramic view, with its prospect of "muddy fields," dried weeds, "patches of standing water," offers nothing with which the imagination might joyously connect itself. At first an apparently blank and "lifeless" nature invites the observer to passivity and despair; but Williams pushes through vacancy to uncover dormant life.

Implicitly, "By the road" argues that Eliot's despair derives from his cosmopolitanism, his detachment from a locality. What the tenacious observer here finally perceives is no "waste" land but a "new world" and he makes his discovery by narrowing and focusing Whitman's panoramic vision upon the near and the ordinary. In the torpor of ordinary consciousness, what we find by the road to the contagious hospital is a desolate landscape. But the awakened consciousness, focused sharply and including everything in the scene, discovers novelty and life, the first "sluggish / dazed" stirrings of spring. Hence poet and landscape are gradually identified—as he too grips down and begins to awaken.

In Eliot's early poetry, spoken by "voices dying with a dying fall," the characteristic movement is the fall of anti-climax; for instance, Prufrock's romantic "visions" of communion are continually undercut by his fear of self-exposure. In Williams's verse, movement is typically through a slow, downward thrust toward an ecstatic lift. The poems move us down into the physical world, back to our origins, to release creative power. In "By the road," even after he has discovered the burgeoning life in the amorphous "stuff" around him, Williams slips forward into a dream of April definition: "tomorrow / the stiff curl of wildcarrot leaf." The abrupt shift back to the "now" in the last stanza partly accounts for its great force. At the beginning, a plain diction, use of short, disconnected phrases, loose, flat rhythms create a sense of stasis; but the poem tightens at the end with the pounding stresses, heavy pauses, and epigrammatic force of its final stanza. We get a final, compact moment of illumination.

As Williams asserts in one of the commentaries in *Kora,*

*"Between two contending forces there may at all times arrive
that moment when the stress is equal on both sides so that with
a great pushing a great stability results giving a picture of perfect rest"* (p. 11). Each of the poems in *Spring and All* gives us
such a moment when contending forces, pushing and pulling in
opposite directions simultaneously, achieve a dynamic equilib-
rium. "By the road" grows out of the elemental contest between winter and spring, death and life; so does "The Black
Winds." "The Eyeglasses" brings together gross strength and
delicate beauty; "Shoot It Jimmy!" plays off classical and jazz
language: "Our orchestra / is the cat's nuts"; "Rigamarole"
shows "the *veritable* night" (my emphasis) which now contains "wires" as well as "stars." At the end of that poem Williams says that "moonlight // is the perfect / human touch":
its scene includes both light *and* darkness. "At the Faucet of
June" creates a modern June morning in which we hear the
sound of the motor car as well as the more delicate music of
nature.

> The sunlight in a
> yellow plaque upon the
> varnished floor
>
> is full of a song
> inflated to
> fifty pounds pressure
>
> at the faucet of
> June that rings
> the triangle of the air
>
> pulling at the
> anemones in
> Persephone's cow pasture—
>
> When from among
> the steel rocks leaps
> J.P.M.
>
> who enjoyed
> extraordinary privileges
> among virginity

to solve the core
of whirling flywheels
by cutting

the Gordian knot
with a Veronese or
perhaps a Rubens—

whose cars are about
the finest on
the market today—

And so it comes
to motor cars—
which is the son

leaving off the g
of sunlight and grass
Impossible

to say, impossible
to underestimate—
wind, earthquakes in

Manchuria, a
partridge
from dry leaves.

Williams comically conceives of the financier J.P.M. as a modern Pluto, the rapist of Persephone—a man who plunders the natural landscape, becomes a hero of mechanical civilization and then turns for relief to the lush, heavily ornamental beauty of old world art. But if J.P.M. represents the drive to dominate and exclude, Williams himself exhibits a creative acceptance of what is immediately before him; he enters the New World. The poem does have an "argument" which urges the acceptance of the machine as part of the contemporary world and therefore part of its poetry. Yet this argument is never explicitly stated; it is advanced by the way the poem keeps circling around between natural and mechanical images. In the first four stanzas, the lines "the sunlight in a," "is full of a song," "June that rings," "the anemones in" could all appear in any romantic celebration of the summer; but these soft images appear along with their opposites here. The sunlight doesn't fall on the grass; it shines in a "plaque"—an artifact—on the "varnished floor." The day is not filled with melodious birdsong but with the noise of motor cars, whose tires are "inflated to / fifty pounds pressure." June is a "faucet," the air a "triangle," Persephone's meadow not Mt. Etna but a "cow pasture." The music of the poem itself is by no means conventionally songful; typical is the use of harsh, explosive sounds (p,f) and long vowels in "full of a song / inflated to / fifty pounds pressure" to create the poem's feeling of tight fullness. In the "Prologue" to *Kora in Hell*, Williams had written that "the stream of things having composed itself into wiry strands that move in one fixed direction, the poet in desperation turns at right angles and cuts across current with startling results to his hangdog mood" (*SE*, p. 15). "At the Faucet of June" works in precisely this way, the poem fluid, open, unpredictable in its reversals. These reversals are not, it is important to see, ironic. The circling between natural and mechanical images subverts any "one fixed direction" or mood, builds energy, achieves a totality—creates the poem's tensed force.

Thus, for Williams, any energy which is directed, in a straight line, toward some preconceived goal is energy that denies itself and dissolves; man as a conscious agent is hard, fixed, closed, or, to take a recurrent metaphor from the poems, an empty shell. "The perfect type of the man of action is the suicide," as Williams asserts in an essay (*SE*, p. 68). The possibilities for action may seem "infinite," he writes in "To Have Done Nothing," but they all involve the "moral / physical / and religious // codes." Thus, "everything / I have done / is the same"; all those infinite possible actions, because they can only occur within a pre-existing code, have the same quality. To do "everything" is to do "nothing"; but to do "nothing" is to experience "everything":

> for everything
> and nothing
> are synonymous
> when

    energy *in vacuo*
    has the power
    of confusion

    which only to
    have done nothing
    can make
    perfect

The poem begins with an allusion to "The Love Song of
J. Alfred Prufrock": "No that is not it." Prufrock is tormented
by his inability to act, but Williams's acceptance of inaction
puts him into a creative confusion where *everything* can be experienced.

Yet Williams found himself in a culture devoted to success
via purposive action; and it is toward the devastating consequences of that idealization of ascendency that he turns in the
well-known "To Elsie." A pure product of America, one of
the famous Jackson Whites of northern New Jersey, Williams's hulking half-mad maid Elsie expresses with her "broken / brain the truth about us." Addressing herself "to cheap /
jewelry / and rich young men with fine eyes," she embodies
the national desire for quick, easy wealth. The myth of success,
with which Williams had been imbued in his youth, has now
become part of his mature demonology. For Elsie expresses
the truth about a culture in which aspirations are not fed by
an organic relation to the physical environment. As Williams
argues, most Americans, like the original settlers of the continent, believe that this world is a dunghill. We act

    as if the earth under our feet
    were
    an excrement of some sky

    and we degraded prisoners
    destined
    to hunger until we eat filth

    while the imagination strains
    after deer
    going by fields of goldenrod in

    the stifling heat of September

Our dreams of heavenly tranquility, our straining after a paradise above, separate us from the real sources of life under our bootsoles; the result is dehumanization. At the end of "To Elsie," Williams delineates his culture with the image of a driverless car.

> No one
> to witness
> and adjust, no one to drive the car

The pure products of America *have* gone crazy: abstracted, swift-moving, brutal. The driverless car is another modern version of Pluto, god of avarice and rape, the mythic embodiment of man's dream of dominion. It is from this narcissistic dream that Williams's poems attempt to jolt us awake.

To act is to choose; and to choose is to adopt some "code," some system of preferences. But in Williams's verse, as in *Kora in Hell*, the reader is forced to experience a radical shift of perspective—down to a mode of consciousness, anterior to all conscious acts of choice, in which oppositions exist but hierarchies do not; that is why the poems leave tensions unresolved rather than bring them to some resolution. In "Light Becomes Darkness" Williams contemplates the transition from the cathedral to the movie house as the modern source of myth. From the perspective of, say, T. S. Eliot, the change is a terrifying one; but Williams forces us to view the shift as a natural process, inevitable and hence neutral:

> woe is translatable
> to joy if light becomes
> darkness and darkness
> light, *as it will*
>   [my emphasis]

Keeping the imagination at a more flexible, jagged resort—preventing it from settling into any fixed position—is an arduous process. Many of the poems, like "To Elsie," deal with the yearning to escape from the pressures of a full life and yield to partial solutions. The difficulties of the new mode are such that the desire for some kind of security will exert a strong and

frequent pull; but Williams continually catches the imagination as it strains after smooth progression, quick fulfillment,
and thrusts it back onto the earth. Confronted with March's
"blank fields," "The Farmer" can only dream of his later har-
vest: he is viewed ironically in the heavily weighted last word
of the poem, as an "antagonist" of nature. As "The Black
Winds" shows, to think of nature as hostile is to slip into the
old mode of pathetic fallacy.

> Hate is of the night and the day
> of flowers and rocks. Nothing
> is gained by saying the night breeds
> murder—It is the classical mistake
>
> The day

Nature for Williams is a morally neutral energy moving in cycles. The association of night with evil, day with good—like
the equation of movie houses with bad, cathedrals with good
—is simply a projection of the "I," the result of which, since it
cuts away half of nature's cycle, is to gain nothing—to establish
a form of consciousness that is abstract, empty and rigid.
What the night does breed is the day, just as winter breeds
spring, the coarse farmer his virginal daughter. Recognizing
the neutrality of nature—"there is nothing in the twist / of the
wind but—dashes of cold rain"—makes possible joyful acceptance.

> Black wind, I have poured my heart out
> to you until I am sick of it—
>
> Now I run my hand over you feeling
> the play of your body—the quiver
> of its strength—

Even here Williams is on the verge of slipping into a sentimen-
talization of the wind until he turns, across the line break,
from "quiver" to "strength." That phrase— "the quiver / of its
strength"—along with "inflated to / fifty pounds pressure" or
"the stiff curl of wildcarrot leaf"—provides one of the sequence's many images of a force coiled back on itself so

tightly that it trembles from the pressure—like an animal poised to strike. In "The Black Winds" the day is associated both with delicate beauty and with violence, the night with murder and sexual and creative energy. Images, rather than bearing fixed significances, are fluid, constantly dissolving into their opposites, just as in nature "light becomes / darkness and darkness / light." Instead of a mind that categorizes, abstracts, excludes in affirmation of the light alone, we have one that can yield to the moment, accept the generative tension of light *and* darkness.

Sometimes an hypnotic romantic voice dreaming of ascendency and perfection is played against a more prosaic voice, closer to the crude earth. In "Flight to the City," the pull is first upward, away from the physical; the speaker here gazes at the stars, traditional emblems of lofty aspiration, and muses in a lyric voice expressive of his desire to lift himself out of the cold, desolate climate of the immediate.

> The Easter stars are shining
> above lights that are flashing
> coronal of the black—

But a flat, prosaic voice breaks into this wistful lyricism and undermines the poetic awesomeness of the metropolis:

> Nobody
> to say it—
> Nobody to say: pinholes

These two voices initiate a characteristic back-and-forth movement toward a view of the city as a sham—empty and sterile.

> Thither I would carry her
> among the lights—

> Burst it asunder
> break through to the fifty words
> necessary—

> a crown for her head with
> castles upon it, skyscrapers
> filled with nut-chocolates—

          dovetame winds—
    stars of tinsel

    from the great end of a cornucopia
    of glass

The playfulness of the poem—in the fairy-tale quality of its
imagery—helps to prepare the reader for the final reversal by
distancing him slightly from the dream. The procedure is to
strip away the glamor conventionally associated with the big
city and reveal a place whose abundance cannot nourish. For a
poet residing in Rutherford, New Jersey, especially a poet
with ambitions for literary influence, the pull toward the metropolis across the river must have been a frequent one. But
Williams here purges himself of such egotistical yearnings—to
root himself more securely on native grounds.

    On the other hand, "The Sea" draws Williams into a dream
of peaceful self-obliteration, a simple surrender to the force of
nature.

    The sea that encloses her young body
    ula lu la lu
    is the sea of many arms—

    the blazing secrecy of noon is undone
    and and and
    the broken sand is the sound of love

The poem *begins* by lifting us out of ordinary reality: we are
not thrust downward with the rough, harsh music, jagged
rhythms of "By the road"; instead, we get a longer four-beat
line, a recurrence of "s" and long vowel sounds that create a
smooth, euphonious voice which lulls us into an enchanted
contemplation of the sea. It is the hypnotic song of a mermaid
inviting us to drift, easily, into transcendence. The incantatory
music urges us to yield to the poem—an urge, however, which
we finally reject. The way the poet is playfully euphonious,
mockingly incantatory, keeps us from submitting entirely to
the spell; he himself turns around to give us a less romantic
view of the sea at the end of the third stanza:

The flesh is firm that turns in the sea
O la la
the sea that is cold with dead men's tears—

Repetition of the hard "d" sound and the insistence of three
stressed words at the end of the last line break into the dreamy
music and create an awakened perception of the sea as death,
not love. Again the poem's turning on itself violates a pat
mood. The middle sections of "The Sea" swing back and forth
between these two voices. At the end we get a more direct
mockery of the flowing music of the opening—

la lu la lu
but lips too few
assume the new—marruu

and then a final image of the sea as a place where all tensions
are dissolved:

Underneath the sea where it is dark
there is no edge
so two—

A few years before this poem was written, J. Alfred Prufrock
had wandered along the beach and murmured of the mermaids,
"I do not think that they will sing to me." The ruminating
figure in Williams's poem, no man of attenuated intellect, is
sensual enough to hear the song—and resilient enough to resist
it.

With supreme confidence, the Whitman of 1855 could saun-
ter down the streets of New York City, wander along the
shores of the Atlantic, disperse himself into the crowd or the
sea and yet retain his simple, separate identity. The desire to
merge with the surging life of the city or the ocean is frequently felt by Williams; but in his neutral, broken world it is
one finally to be resisted. That is why the Atlantic and New
York City both become images of nothingness, a void in which
individual distinction disintegrates: there are no edges. In "At
the Ball Game" the crowd becomes "venomous," derisive, tyrannical; in "Light Against Darkness" it is the "dynamic mob."

"Crowds are white," the sea is dark: immersion in either gives relief, a union with a One, but halts the cyclical process of renewal. At the "edge," all can be experienced, definition achieved. Williams's geographical position in Rutherford put him at the edge of the metropolis and the sea, near enough to feel their pull but distant enough to maintain his own identity. Internally, Williams puts himself at the edge of consciousness, where "light becomes / darkness and darkness / light"—where experience becomes at once fluid and distinct; William's mockery of the "I" is not a repudiation of individuality but of that hard assertiveness which negates all sympathetic receptivity. What Williams gives us is a continual process of surrender and assertion—the way to a renewed individuality. In this way he clings "firmly to the advance."

"Why do you write?" Williams is asked in a dialogue essay. "For relaxation, relief," he answers. "To have nothing in my head—to freshen my eye by that till I see, smell, know and can reason and be" (*SE*, p. 101). By a characteristically circular process Williams empties his mind in order to fill it. Importantly, he makes clear here that creative activity, which begins by subverting rational activity, ends by renewing it. Much more often than his critics have noticed, Williams works as a special kind of reflective poet. Although nothing interested him less than systematic reasoning, he was interested in acts of what he called "understanding," quick flashes of apprehension that follow from laborious consideration, moments when darkness suddenly becomes light. "The goal," says Williams, "is to keep a beleaguered line of understanding which has movement from breaking down and becoming a hole into which we sink decoratively to rest" (*SE*, p. 118). The argument of such poems is advanced with epigrams, puns, witty turns of thought; ideas are dissolved almost as soon as they are formulated, so that we get "no ideas but in things." So eager is Williams to avoid what he calls the "managed poem," which imposes ideas on experience, that his ruminative works are sometimes broken to such an extent that they are very difficult to penetrate.[6] But at his best Williams creates the impression of a ruminating mind, quick with an elemental strength, in the *act* of generating thought. The reflective poems, like those which deal strictly with perceptions, turn slowly, disjunctively toward some jolting moment of discovery.

"The rose is obsolete," Williams muses at the beginning of one of these poems, but an act of imagination can make even this traditional symbol new. He proceeds from a consideration of the way to renew the impact of the figure to a joyous affirmation of its rediscovered power. "The Rose" appears at a point in the prose commentary of *Spring and All* when Williams is praising the Cubist painter Juan Gris for dealing with "things with which [the onlooker] is familiar, simple things—at the same time to detach them from ordinary experience to the imagination" (*SA*, p. 34). Williams is thus experimenting here with a kind of literary Cubism. He takes the familiar rose out of amorphous, ordinary contexts by making his subject inorganic, by considering a rose cut onto "metal or porcelain"; he hardens his soft subject in this way and by the mathematical language the Cubists employed: "so that to engage roses / becomes a geometry." Finally, he places the rose in a world of infinite, empty space. There, he contemplates it playfully, turning his argument on the ambiguity of the word "end." "The rose carried weight of love," he says, "but love is at an end—of roses." Just as he constantly asserts that life must be caught as it emerges out of death, so here he argues that at the end of the rose, its death and its edge, a new beginning can be found.

To see the rose anew, we must concentrate on the locus of its singularity, its edges. Raised from a flat surface, carefully worked onto china, these edges are perceived more distinctly.

> Sharper, neater, more cutting
> figured in majolica—
> the broken plate
> glazed with a rose

Only when the flower has been worked painstakingly, lovingly, onto a hard, inorganic substance will its fragile life be preserved—a paradox which gives his meditation a subtle wit; the language keeps shifting, crisply, between organic and inorganic, soft and hard, words:

> Crisp, worked to defeat
> laboredness—fragile
> plucked, moist, half-raised
> cold, precise, touching

In its abstracted realm, the realm of the imagination, the rose touches—nothing. There is a surrounding blankness which at once threatens and defines the flower, just as the white crowd and the dark sea activate the poet's individuality. In Williams, a finely wrought distinction always asserts itself at the edge of emptiness.

When he speaks of the need for objects and words to have hard edges, as he does in both poems and essays, Williams is using a phrase that can be found in the writings of a whole gamut of moderns—from Hemingway to Wittgenstein. The importance of edges for Williams is that they are the locus of maximum tension and thus of maximum life. In "The Rose" a careful, hard-edged perception of the object generates an infinite line of force.

> From the petal's edge a line starts
> that being of steel
> infinitely fine, infinitely
> rigid penetrates
> the Milky Way
> without contact—lifting
> from it—neither hanging
> nor pushing—
>
> The fragility of the flower
> unbruised
> penetrates space

The image is bold, playful, entirely characteristic: a delicate strength, a fine steel line—emerging out of the dead porcelain —triumphantly asserts its distinction through infinite space.

In the *Spring and All* sequence Williams keeps returning us to that moment, abstracted from temporal sequence, when life begins to begin. He adjusts us to a level of consciousness where historical time, and thus literary associations, do not yet exist. He pushes spring back from April to March, he deals with those weeds and wildflowers shunned as too coarse by his poetic predecessors. In short, he strips objects bare of all acquired associations and it is this neutralization of things that makes it possible for him to accept *any* thing as suitable for poetry. But Williams is not, as he is often regarded, a poet who moves simply from the object as symbol to the object as literal fact; this *is* the tendency of *Al Que Quiere!*, but *Spring and All* develops out of the pull between these two ways of apprehending things. A reader who gets to the first stanza of the last poem, "The Wildflower"—"Black eyed susan / rich orange / round the purple core"—should remember the "reddish / purplish, forked, upstanding, twiggy / stuff of bushes" from the first poem, the "horned purple" of the nineteenth and the anemones in "At the Faucet of June." The "white daisy" and the "white" "crowds" of the next two stanzas of "The Wildflower" take the reader back through the numerous references to "nothing," "without being," empty spaces, blank fields in the poems. The black-eyed susan clearly manifests that rich primitive force found in almost all of the poems—a notion reenforced by reading "core" as a pun for "Kore," as it is earlier in "to solve the core / of whirling flywheels." As always, this force tensely defines itself against a surrounding blankness. At the same time the tight sensual music (r's, long vowels) and the precisely observed detail show the poet's intense devotion to the actual flower. The point is that the serial poem genre enables Williams to create a special kind of poetic field. Williams liked to point out that poems are made of words and the spaces between them; a serial poem is then made of poems and the spaces between them. There is no articulated surface of connections that a narrative or explicit argument would provide; instead, there is a buried coherence—of recurrent words, images—which the reader himself must uncover. Literal details, in context, suddenly reverberate into mythic significance. The breaking of narrative surface, the spacing within and between poems, establish a field that is thick in texture, multidimensional. Nature and society move, according to Williams, in recurrent cycles. Movement in the serial poem, too, is circular rather than linear; the reader is constantly forced to go back before he can go on, the poem thereby becoming an *experience* of recurrence. Williams's bare, neutral objects do acquire associations, but these are developed entirely from the inside, within the poem itself. Individual poems, by their juxtaposition in a series, create a poetic field, a context; but the spaces between them enable the poet to preserve each poem's pull toward the instant. The all—the universal, the mythical—is discovered *in* the moment, not imposed upon it. Again, everything exists from the beginning.

The chief theme of Williams's critical prose, as we have seen, is that the poem is not a vehicle for thought, or for the recitation of events, but a physical object, an organization of sounds and rhythms. Williams's critics often spend a great deal of time showing that he held this belief, but they seldom take the next step and show how it informs the workings of particular poems. For the most part these writers have been concerned with establishing the underlying coherence of his work, and this has been a necessary phase in the study of a writer long dismissed as a kind of mindless eccentric. But to establish Williams's importance as an artist, we need to see how his thought pushed him into discovering new possibilities of poetic organization. So far I have been arguing for recurrence—the cyclical emergence of life out of death—as theme and as structural principle, both in particular poems and in the whole sequence; now I want to show how this jagged, circling movement extends down into the most minute workings of the poem—into the line itself.

Generalization here is difficult because poetic form for Williams is always organic, an intimate unfolding of a particular moment of experience, as if from the inside. One thing we can say is that even in the twenty-seven poems of this sequence, an extraordinary range of metrical and sonic devices can be found. This does not exclude conventional effects, although these are always used ironically. "The Right of Way" begins with two perfect lines of iambic trimeter: "In passing with my mind / on nothing in the world," the regularity appropriate to the mood of relaxed euphoria. We have also seen how he employs hypnotic rhythms and euphonious music in "Flight to the City" and "The Sea" to build moods of dreamy romanticism, which he then undermines. But the most striking thing about *Spring and All,* in contrast to Williams's preceding books, is the broken appearance of the poem on the page: short lines immediately follow long lines, single words (or in one case the diphthong "ae") constitute entire stanzas, lines begin only halfway back across the page instead of at the left-hand margin, and so on. Poetic form is shattered in order to break through the reader's protective shell, jar his relaxed euphoria, and force his attention down into an independent world of objects, solid and distinct in themselves yet fluid in their combinations.

Among the many recurrent words in the *Spring and All* series, variants of "break" and "cut" (along with related terms such as "enter," "penetrate," and "pierce") are perhaps the most frequent. They are related to the frequent images of a hard capsule—the skyscraper, the motor car, the winter casing of grief; and they are used in two opposed senses. At the ball game, the words of the tyrannical crowd "cut" their victims; the impatient J.P.M. cuts the Gordian knot instead of trying to untie it. To cut in this sense is to violate. Yet there is the edge of the rose which "cuts without cutting"; there is a breaking which liberates passion: "Clean is he alone / after whom stream / the broken pieces of the city— / flying apart at his approaches" (*CEP,* p. 255). Breaking can become a creative activity, not a violation but a release from the shell of repression. To get at the way Williams handles the line we can say that he breaks lines so as to maintain as much as possible of the energy which he finds naturally inherent in words and objects.

Generally, Williams works with short lines (four, five, or six syllables) in short stanzas (two or three lines). Among other

things these divisions serve to score the poem for speech: in
reading there should be a short pause at the end of each line, a
somewhat longer pause at the end of each stanza, a still longer
pause if there is a dash at the end of the stanza. Thus Williams's poems are made up of words and the spaces, or
rhythmic sounds and the silences, between them. The pause at
the end gives each line time to sink into the mind, gives each
line an equal weight; the reader experiences the line as an independent unit before it is merged into its syntactic relations
with the surrounding lines. This breaking of the poem into its
component lines, analogous to the splitting of mythic narrative
into a series of discrete poems, accomplishes many startling effects. "The Pot of Flowers" begins abruptly with a flash of
color—"Pink confused with white"—which only gets form in
the second line, "flowers and flowers reversed." In the more
reflective poems, the thought takes on more "point," sharper
edges, from this practice. The impact of "backed by biblical /
rigidity made into passion plays" is sharpened in the moment
we consider the second line in isolation: *rigidity* made into
passion plays (*CEP,* p. 267).

As these examples indicate, the first effect of this kind of
spacing is to split the poem into a series of discrete images, objects floating in space like the parts of a mobile. The difference
between

> The sunlight in a yellow plaque upon
> the varnished floor is full of a song

and

> The sunlight in a
> yellow plaque upon the
> varnished floor
>
> is full of a song

is that Williams's way of cutting the lines distributes emphasis
equally on all of the images. Clipped lines also point up the
thingness, the sound value of each word; and they prevent the
development of any iambic beat that might blur the scene by

lifting the words into flow. In *Al Que Quiere!* line divisions coincide with syntactic divisions: "The little sparrows / hop ingenuously / about the pavement / quarreling / with sharp voices / over those things / that interest them." But in *Spring and All*, line divisions characteristically break apart syntactic units—another source of the poems' tensed force. In the first four lines of "At the Faucet of June," Williams twice breaks the line in the middle of a prepositional phrase. Elsewhere, lines end with prepositions, adjectives, conjunctions, subjects, transitive verbs—all words we know will be followed by objects, modifiers, and so on. Quick movement through a conventional form is thus forestalled; orders become unglued, parts get space in which to define themselves distinctly, stress falling over all such parts. The "in a" and "upon the"—both of which would ordinarily be slurred over—are brought out, chiefly for their sound value; while the objects of the prepositions get stress because we must wait across the line break for our expectation of an object to be fulfilled. A Williams poem breaks cleanly through given orders, cuts experience down to its basic elements, gives a halting, disjunctive sequence of sharply defined images.

So, at least, a Williams poem begins. But the line breaks do more than isolate the parts; they also stress the novelty of their combination and make possible a fluidity, a multiplicity of combinations. The spaces between lines, subverting logical and narrative connectives, create possibilities for a more fluid kind of ordering. A pause at the end of a line which is not a complete syntactic unit creates an expectant silence—which is often filled in surprising ways. A line in "The Black Winds" reads, "That is why boxing matches and." And what? Baseball games? No—Chinese poems: "That is why boxing matches and / Chinese poems are the same." All things are the same in the sense that they constitute a neutral existential reality. But as the statement asserts identity, the line division emphasizes the tension between boxing matches and Chinese poems. Oppositions do exist; hierarchies do not—and without the line break where it is, the lines would not mean precisely that. This is the second stanza of "Death the Barber":

```
cutting my
life with
sleep to trim
my hair
```

As the reader cuts back across the page from the first line, he
expects to find "hair" but *discovers* "life"; even after this twist
he's apt to be looking for something like "scissors"—not
"sleep"—to follow "with"; and just as he's settling into this
pattern of reversals, he gets a more conventional predicate
("hair") for "to trim." Williams is highly aware of the reader's physical act of turning back and starting over again with
each line, and he often makes this gesture correspond to a turn
in the thought. At the end of "The pure products of America," the diction has led the reader to expect something uplifting, but he turns down into the terse second line, "go crazy."
"Flight to the City" ends with a similar twist:

```
from the great end of a cornucopia
of glass
```

Conversely, "Light Becomes Darkness" starts with a fall—"The
decay of cathedrals"—but then shifts upward in the second
line, "is efflorescent." "Efflorescent" means "blossoming" (the
reverse of decay) but also refers to the lights of a movie mar-
quee (the reverse of the cathedral's gloom); the pun enables
Williams to show how life issues from death, light from darkness. Or, as Williams says of the rose: "But if it ends / the
start is begun"; as it is several times in the poem, "ends" is here
a pun, meaning "if the rose dies" as we pause at the end of the
first line, but then shifting to "if the rose has an edge" as we
move through the second line. Like "everything" and "nothing," "light" and "darkness," "break" and "cut," "end" is one
of the several repeated words in the *Spring and All* sequence
which shifts back and forth between opposite senses. In Williams's world, ends are always dissolving into beginnings, as
darkness evolves into light.

   Almost as soon as any direction is established, it is dissolved,
and a new one begins. Often, this broken, circling movement is
the result of verbal or syntactic ambiguity: while critics speak

of Williams's plain style, these poems abound in puns, pronouns with more than one referent, relative clauses that dangle far away from their modifiers—all creating the possibility of multiple combinations within the poem. Ambiguities are often emphasized by the line breaks. A sentence from "The Black Winds"—"Hate is of the night and the day / of flowers and rocks"—means "hate is of *both* the night and the day" as we pause at the end of the first line, then shifts into "hate is of the night—and the day is of flowers and rocks"; Williams slips back from the new to the old mode, as he does several times in this poem. The line division gives the "cling firmly to the advance" at the end of "The Black Winds" the force of a command as well as a completion of the "how hard to" in the previous line. "Impossible // to say, impossible / to underestimate," says Williams near the end of "At the Faucet of June"; and the breaking of the second line shows us that one of the things he is saying is that it is impossible to say impossible, an anticipation of the images of unpredictable force that close the poem.

Relations are fluid. The objects in the poem are like parts of a mobile in the further sense that they are in motion. Syntactic units pull back and forth—seeming at first to go with what has come before, then shifting into relationship with what follows; both versions must be suspended in the reader's mind. In the introduction to his *Bending the Bow*, Robert Duncan (like Charles Olson and Robert Creeley, importantly influenced by Williams's handling of the line) approvingly quotes from Heraclitus: "They do not apprehend how being at variance it agrees with itself. There is a connection working in both directions." A particularly intense use of this making a phrase connect back and forth simultaneously occurs in Williams's "The Avenue of Poplars"; these are the first eight stanzas:

> The leaves embrace
> in the trees
>
> it is a wordless
> world

without personality
I do not

seek a path
I am still with

Gypsy lips pressed
to my own—

It is the kiss
of leaves

without being
poison ivy

or nettle, the kiss
of oak leaves—

Most readers, confronted with these lines and asked to produce
an oral interpretation, will look through them several times in
an effort to make certain decisions—e.g., What words get emphasis? Which parts go with what other parts? Does "without
being" mean "without existence" (as it does in the previous
poem, "Rigamarole") and go therefore with "leaves"? Or is
"being" a verb form, in which case it goes with what follows:
"without being / poison ivy"? Such an approach seeks "a
path" through the poem—which is precisely the opposite of
Williams's intent. We must yield to the poem; we must approach and read it "without personality." To read the poem in
a voice that is more flat than dramatically expressive—giving
equal weight to each of the words and observing the slight
pauses marked by lines and stanzas—is to discover a new world,
one that is open, fluid, and shifting. To give up the need for a
path through the poem is to discover the poem as a field of action.

The poem is a kind of Gordian knot; paraphrasing is cutting, in the mode of J.P.M., but does yield a sense of the
poem's tight multiplicity—a quality not usually associated with
Williams's work. It begins simply enough: "The leaves embrace / in the trees." Yet the second line cuts loose from the
first as we move into the second stanza: in the trees it is a

"wordless / world." A wordless world is a world "without
personality." That phrase, however, moves in another direction, to go with "I do not." Without personality I do not act,
as we have already seen in "To Have Done Nothing." The
next stanza converts "do" to an auxiliary verb; (without personality) I do not "seek a path"—and then, I do not seek a
path "I am still with." But "I am still with" begins as well as
ends a sentence: I am still with "Gypsy lips pressed / to my
own," a sentence which has two possible meanings, given the
ambiguity of "still." It can mean, I am quiet when Gypsy lips
are pressed to mine (a wordless world), or, I am yet kissing
Gypsy lips. Even this analysis is not exhaustive, but it is
enough to show that in Williams's work, a word retains more
of its energy, its possible connections, than any linear method
of development would allow. In fact, the edge of his line is
like the edge of the rose which "cuts without cutting"—releases rather than inhibits energy—"meets nothing"—the second
of silence at the end of the line—then "renews itself" in the
following line. Ends dissolve into beginnings. Each poem, then,
becomes a series of lines, each of which, spaced off from all
the others, pulls toward isolation, independence, at the same
time that it is pulled back by syntax, by recurrences, toward
all the other lines. At the edge of chaos, containing the pressure of its pushing and pulling, the poem trembles with force.

IV

In the American Grain

"There is a source IN AMERICA for everything we
think or do." *In the American Grain*

In 1923, at forty, Williams was at the height of his creative
achievement. In several directions he was, as he remarked of
Poe, "with amazing genius seeking to discover, and discovering, points of firmness" on which to stand—"against the slipping way they had of holding on in his locality" (p. 219). At
the same time that he was perfecting a more definite, fluid
lyric form and working out an extended prose statement of his
poetic program in *Spring and All,* Williams was also searching
the American past for points of firmness upon which he and
his bewildered contemporaries might stand—and looking for
the proper literary medium in which to embody his discoveries. Like *Spring and All, In the American Grain* begins with
Williams's perception of an agonizing split in the American
consciousness—a conflict between instinct and will, geography
and culture. In this country, the dominance of the will, burying the wilderness and stifling the instincts, has left the modern
American self-divided and dispossessed, adrift in the flux of
history. Individual development, as Williams well knew, had
become a slow and torturous process. But by tracing the
forces acting on us to their origins and by defining precisely
their qualities, we can begin to heal this split. *In the American
Grain* enacts historically Williams's central quest, the descent
to origins for renewal.

Williams's book in many respects resembles such radical reassessments of American literature and culture as Van Wyck Brooks's *America's Coming of Age* (1915), Waldo Frank's *Our America* (1919), D. H. Lawrence's *Studies in Classic American Literature* (1923), and Lewis Mumford's *The Golden Day* (1926).[1] A major tendency in these polemical works is to see American history as developing out of a Freudian conflict between repression and liberation, between will and body; and they often stress the need for a biological adjustment to place. Accordingly, the Indian emerges as the buried hero of American history, while the Puritan, sternly imposing an alien ideology on the primitive continent, becomes a kind of demonic figure. Moreover, the tone of these works is more often hortatory than "objective"; what these men were after was not just a critical analysis of the American past, but the liberation of the national psyche. As Frank grandly puts it, "We go forth all to seek America. And in the seeking we create her." [2]

In the American Grain shares both the doctrinal bias and the prophetic bent; but what makes Williams's book fundamentally different is his unique method. Williams has here invented a new kind of historical essay. Anticipating the method of later and more sophisticated attempts at American studies, Williams saw that the best way to understand his culture was by understanding its mythology; but he further believed that the best way to apprehend the specific qualities of a mythic figure was by encountering him as a created character. And so, instead of presenting an overview of American history in the form of an essay, as did Brooks and Frank, Williams worked as a literary artist as well as historian—by the recreation of such legendary characters as Red Eric, Columbus, Cortez, De Soto, Daniel Boone, Aaron Burr, and Lincoln. The result is a series of character studies somewhat like Emerson's *Representative Men*, but with the profound difference that the characters are often given a voice of their own. Thus, while the work of his contemporaries often strikes us as dated polemic—Lawrence's *Studies* is an illuminating polemic—Williams's book lives in the rich variety of its characters, moods, styles. Too often, Williams's critics, conceding a lack of historical veracity in the book, have either used it as a source of general ideas helpful in approaching his poetry, or they have tried to defend it as an avowedly "subjective" and "impressionistic" work.[3] His views certainly run counter to received opinion, sometimes defiantly so; but that makes them neither true nor false. A study of the sources he used will show, I think, that his grasp of them was often detailed, illuminating, and profound. The book has solid merits, and they are not those of a soliloquy. In fact, *In the American Grain* grows out of the tension between Williams's reverence for literal, individuating detail and his desire to discover mythic recurrences amid the welter of facts. Hence the author varies voice, intensity, perspective, length, mode of organization in order to create a series of distinct characters, and yet by placing these characters together, in a single context, he suggests historical patterns. Individuals, in context, become archetypes. At times the tension slackens from the weight of accumulated detail or, more often, the pull toward synthesis. But when Williams is at his best, American history, falling neither into dusty facts nor into empty universals, becomes at once coherent and intensely human.

Williams chose to recreate the past through characters rather than events for several reasons, the most important being his very concept of history. Like some of his more learned and conservative comtemporaries such as Joyce, Eliot, and Pound, Williams looked at history not as a linear progression of events but as a pattern of eternal recurrence. How can the man who asserted that "Nothing is good save the new" (*SE*, p. 21) think of history as the endless repetition of archetypal patterns? He does so in the following way. There are for Williams distinguishable cycles or "periods" in history; their development begins with the release of a new force, crude and physical, but ends as this power, growing more attenuated as it grows more distant from its source, finally disintegrates. The cataclysm at the beginning of *Spring and All* constitutes the beginning of such a cycle—as did the discovery of America. Yet, while the pattern of growth and decay is eternal, the par-

ticular cycles are unique—like each new spring. But the point
to be stressed for the moment is that historical periods exist in
relation to each other as a series of parallel planes—a conception that is embodied in the structure of the chapter on the
French Jesuit missionary, Père Sebastian Rasles. This chapter
takes place in the present, developing out of a conversation in
Paris between Williams and the French writer Valéry Larbaud. In January, 1924, the Rutherford poet-physician had
gone to Europe seeking relief from his twenty-year-long "brutalizing battle" (p. 105) to adjust to his locality. At this point
in his career Williams strongly felt the need, perhaps expressed
in his picture of Edgar Allan Poe, to distance himself physically from his native environment. It was while in Europe,
however, that Williams wrote several of the later chapters of
In the American Grain.

Yet his first contact with the expatriate world in Paris left
him feeling frustrated: "I felt myself with ardors not released
but beaten back, in this center of old-world culture where
everyone was tearing his own meat, *warily* conscious of a
newcomer, but wholly without inquisitiveness—No wish to
know; they were served" (p. 105). Among the cold, aloof, and
egotistical inhabitants of this cosmopolitan scene, Williams became a kind of J. Alfred Prufrock, longing for but unable to
achieve communion:

> Could I have shouted out in the midst of it, could I have loosed
> myself to embrace this turning, shouting, rustling, colored
> thing, my mind would have been relieved. I could not do
> it. . . . It infuriated my meanness. Was it not my vanity and
> impotence? We did this, we did that, we drank at the Ritz bar.
> What did I presume? (p. 106)

But when he discovers Larbaud with his keen interest in the
very documents Williams has been reading, he does let himself
go:

> Here is one at least of this world, moving to meet that other
> which is straining for release under my confining ribs—not
> wishing so much to understand it as to taste, perhaps, its
> freshness—. (p. 108)

"Valéry Larbaud," says the elated Williams, "seemed cultivating my intimate earth with his skillful hands" (p. 108). Larbaud's "gracious gesture" (p. 108) is just like the affectionate touch of Père Rasles that Williams goes on to describe. Early in their conversation Williams reflects that "he is a student while I am—the brutal thing itself" (p. 107); Williams views himself as a kind of dispossessed Indian. And so, just as the intimate touch of Père Rasles "released" (p. 121) the Indian into full consciousness, so Larbaud releases the blocked ardors of the modern American. Those remote, uprooted expatriates, "wholly without inquisitiveness" (p. 105), are the modern equivalents of the Puritan foes of Indian and Jesuit. The contemporary scene re-enacts an historical one; history moves as a pattern of eternal recurrence.

Moreover, the characters of *In the American Grain*, being mythical and eternal, are alive now, today. Still another reason that Williams rejects narrative is that a sequence of events, with beginning, middle and end, presents an action that is finished—"dead" (p. 188). But for Williams "history must stay open, it is all humanity" (p. 188). The implications of this point of view are radical, for what he is moving toward here is the disintegration of historical perspective. As many writers have observed, the idea of historical perspective developed in the Renaissance along with the use of artistic perspective.[4] Both, importantly, assume a distance between subject and object—the very distance that Williams constantly tries to dissolve. Thus for Williams all history is present, at least potentially, in the "subject," the perceiver, and the act of historical understanding is identified with an act of self-understanding. As Williams rails against Cotton Mather in the Rasles chapter, Larbaud interrupts:

> This interests me greatly because I see you brimming—you, yourself—with those three things of which you speak: a puritanical sense of order, a practical mysticism as of the Jesuits, and the sum [of] all those qualities defeated in the savage men of your country by the first two. These three things I see still battling in your heart. (p. 116)

Similarly, the Ponce de Leon chapter begins by connecting us with the Indians—"No, we are not Indians but we are men of their world. The blood means nothing; the spirit, the ghost of the land moves in the blood, moves the blood. It is we who ran to the shore naked, we who cried, 'Heavenly Man!'" (p. 39) —but then Williams abruptly turns around to equate us with their conquerors: "We are, too, the others. . . . We are the slaughterers. It is the tortured soul of our world" (p. 41). The split between a physical being shaped by geography and climate and an imperious spirit imported from abroad is the subject of both these passages; and in both cases an external conflict in the past is identified with a psychic conflict in the present. The figures Williams deals with are not locked, dead, in some self-contained historical episode; they continue to act as living forces in the contemporary field. Historical investigation is thus partly an act of introspection. Of course, study of actual historical documents is needed to draw out these hidden conflicts, but investigation of these sources is also an exploration of the intimate self. In his own aspirations for quick distinction, his pugnacious and "resistant" nature (p. 105)—in his *will*—Williams found the forces he traced back to men like Cortez and de Leon, while in his own passionate attachment to the ground—in his *body*—he felt the continuing impact of men like De Soto, Boone, and Burr. Of Burr Williams wrote: "He's in myself and so I dig through lies to resurrect him" (p. 197). The hero of will persists through cultural tradition; but the genius of place lives, too, buried in our bodies. Liberation comes by a descent that is at once historical and personal. The exhausting conflict between culture and geography still battles in Williams's heart; he *is* America and by digging into himself he hoped to resurrect the integrative spirit of place.

Williams declares "events" to be "the mere accidents of geography and climate" (p. 188)—a further instance of his hostility to the man of action and another reason for his rejection of narrative organization. Stripping away the layers of social, economic, and political causality that we usually identify with the study of history, cutting beneath the surface of chronology, Williams arrives at the core—the spirit of place. In history, too, Kora is the generative principle. If events are the mere accidents of history, she is its substantial form. Accordingly, the chief character in *In the Aemrican Grain* becomes the wilderness itself, beautiful, seductive, but dark, violent, and mysterious. At the beginning of the Columbus chapter, Williams writes:

> The New World, existing in those times beyond the sphere of all things known to history, lay in the fifteenth century as the middle of the desert or the sea lies now and must lie forever, marked with its own dark life which goes on to an immaculate fulfillment in which we have no part. (p. 7)

In Williams's imagination, America exists primarily as a violent physical force which, independent of the human will, can strip away the layers of European civilization and renew man. There exists in the New World something larger and more immaculate than the human, an otherness upon which man cannot impose his tyrannous designs. Williams wants to stir in us a passionate attachment to this feminine spirit, but without in any way sentimentalizing her. The wilderness must come to the reader as an actual, as a *savage* physical force, untamed by the artist's will. The spirit of the continent is at once shy, frail, delicate, tender, and powerful, hot, angry, cruel, often fierce in her ardors. A mythical giant like the Garrett Mountain of *Patterson*, she combines exquisite beauty with massive strength; she can tear apart all of those protective walls with which men try to secure themselves against renewal. "Rebellion, savagery," Williams writes, "a force to leap up and wrench you from your hold and force you to be part of it; the place, the absolute new without a law but the basic blood where the savage becomes brother" (p. 74). The wilderness for Williams is not merely a backdrop, against which significant human conflicts are played out. "She" is a living force, animating all of the book's male characters, who define themselves by accepting or resisting her primitive power.

The wilderness *is* source; but it is through human activity that this spirit of place is cultivated, brought to refinement. "Culture is still the effect of cultivation," Williams reminds us,

> to work with a thing until it be rare; as a golden dome among the mustard fields. It implies a solidity capable of cultivation. Its effects are marble blocks that lie perfectly fitted and aligned to express by isolate distinction the rising lusts which threw them off, regulated, in moving through the mass of impedimenta which is the world. (p. 224)

Williams again and again compares the development of a culture to the growth of a flower, stressing that a civilization must be rooted firmly in the earth before it can rise upward into distinction. On this continent, the ideal of organic civilization exists not just in utopian fantasy but, importantly for Williams, in historical fact, in the lost civilization of the Aztecs. "The Destruction of Tenochtitlan" shows how acceptance of our origins in the crude earth opens the way to an exquisite refinement of spirit. At the center of Aztec religion were the human sacrifices so shocking to the Christians.

> Here it was that the tribe's deep feeling for a reality that stems back into the permanence of remote origins had its firm hold. It was the earthward thrust of their logic; blood and earth; the realization of their primal and continuous identity with the ground itself, where everything is fixed in darkness. (p. 33)

Culture for Williams can only begin with the ritual acceptance of man's darker side, his wilder instincts and moods. But with the earth acknowledged as primal source, man's spirit can grip down and begin to awaken. And so out of the dark savagery of Aztec religion flowered the light, airy refinement of the chief, Montezuma.

> The whole waking aspirations of his people, opposed to and completing their religious sense, seemed to come off in him and in him alone: the drive upward, toward the sun and the stars. He was the very person of their ornate dreams, so delicate, so prismatically colorful, so full of tinkling sounds and rhythms, so tireless of invention. Never was such a surface

lifted above the isolate blackness of such profound savagery. (p. 35)

Williams deftly dramatizes the "suave personality" (p. 34) of the Indian in his first meeting with Cortez:

> Montezuma spoke: "They have told you that I possess houses with walls of gold and many other such things and that I am a god or make myself one. The houses you see are of stone and lime and earth."—Then opening his robe: "You see that I am composed of flesh and bone like yourselves and that I am mortal and palpable to the touch."—To this smiling sally, so full of gentleness and amused irony, Cortez could reply nothing save to demand that the man declare himself a subject of the Spanish King forthwith and that, furthermore, he should then and there announce publicly his allegiance to the new power. (p. 31)

Montezuma's subtle, dignified appeal to the humanity of the conqueror fails to penetrate; but beside the gracious sophistication of the Indian, Cortez appears as an inarticulate brute. Throughout the chapter the chief maintains an aristocratic reserve that makes him triumph even as his world falls apart. Montezuma sees from the first that his defeat is foreordained; but it is precisely this knowledge that makes him so civilized, so composed, so gracious to the conqueror. Cortez, borne along by forces he does not fathom, is as simple as he is inexorable. Montezuma, with his awareness of the ancient instincts that stir his enemy, is hospitable and magnanimous; his *qualities* dwarf the *acts* of his conqueror. Man's earthward thrust and his drive upward toward the sun—body and spirit—were integrated briefly in this seemingly primitive society; but its life was so delicate, "so completely removed from those foreign contacts which harden and protect, that at the very breath of conquest it vanished" (pp. 31–32).

Confronted with America, "the generous bulk of its animal crudity" (p. 225), most Europeans reacted with squeamish fear. Rather than submit to the painful primitive ordeal that initiation to the new place required, they sought to impose a ready-made culture upon it. In the New World, therefore, a

mythology developed which celebrated the man of will, idealized as the bearer of enlightened civilization into a primitive
environment. Williams, exemplifying the recoiling force he
identified with the New World, penetrates this facade and reveals the actual emptiness of such men. In devastating studies
he argues the hollowness of such popular legends of success as
the Voyage of the Mayflower, Benjamin Franklin, and George
Washington.

In stark contrast to the elegant, sensuous beauty of Aztec
civilization we have the harsh, frugal quality of life in Puritan
New England. Conventionally, the Puritans are praised for
their dauntless *spirit;* but in reality, they were hard, little,
empty—valuable mainly for a *physical* toughness that enabled
them to contend successfully with the climate. Here, too, qualities tell more than acts, and qualities are revealed in myth.
"The Pilgrims were mistaken not in what they did, because
they went hard to work with their hands and heads, but in
what they imagined for their warmth" (p. 65). Faced with the
bitter cold of the New England landscape, they found warmth
by imagining a disembodied spirit, a soul, a "pale negative" (p.
65)—"nothing" (p. 64). Without roots in the soil, their culture
could never rise into genuine distinction. "Their religious zeal,
mistaken for a thrust upward toward the sun"—of the sort represented by Montezuma—was really "a stroke in, in, in—not
toward germination but the confinements of a tomb" (p. 66).
The resulting "stress of spirit against flesh has produced a race
incapable of flower" (p. 66). Lacking any reverence for what
is unique in their world, the Puritans could and did "succeed
in making everything like themselves" (p. 63)—hard, little and
dead.

But idealizing this kind of imposition of the will makes any
assertion of otherness terrifying; the Puritan must be always
on guard to keep the environment tame and sterile.

> In fear and without guidance, really lost in the world, it is
> they alone who would later, at Salem, have strayed so far—
> morbidly seeking the flame,—that terrifying unknown image
> to which, like savages, they too offered sacrifices of human
> flesh. It is just such emptiness, revulsion, terror in all ages,

which in fire—a projection still of the truth—finds that which lost and desperate men have worshipped. And it is still today the Puritan who keeps his frightened grip upon the throat of the world lest it should prove him—empty. (p. 67)

Human sacrifices were for the Aztecs a ceremonial acceptance of man's baser instincts; but the persecution of witches was an instance of the return of the repressed: the flame of desire perverted into a compulsive need for destruction. Williams thus traces the landscape of violence in contemporary America not to frontier conditions but to the frightened rigidity of Puritanism, its abstraction from place, its fear of the absolute new without law. In the Puritan, striving to impose a culture from outside, Williams sees a terrified emptiness, a vindictive mediocrity that "thwarts and destroys" (p. 68) all genuine individuality. Compared to the Mexican Indian, the seventeenth-century New Englander shows a certain rude strength, but no grace, warmth, or poise. The Pilgrims created not a civilization, but a mob, the eternal "pack whom the dead drive" (p. 27).

At one point Williams bitterly reflects "how nearly all our national heroes have been driven back—and praised by reason of their shrewdness in making walls: not in bursting into flower" (p. 157). Our heroes have characteristically sacrificed themselves to the mob rather than the wilderness, and, lost themselves, they have failed to offer us guidance. In early national figures such as Washington and Franklin, Williams senses a "bulky, crude energy, something in proportion to the continent, and a colossal restraint equalizing it" (p. 153). The New World moves in their bodies as a real physical energy but, frightened, they refuse to let it rip them asunder. Of Washington Williams writes, "Here was a man of tremendous vitality buried in a massive frame and under a rather stolid and untractable exterior which the ladies somewhat feared, I fancy" (p. 140). An old story about the president provides the detail to make Williams's conception vivid.

> One can imagine him curiously alive to the need of dainty waistcoats, lace and kid gloves, in which to cover that dangerous rudeness which he must have felt about himself. His in-

terest in dress at a certain period of his career is notorious. (p. 140)

At work on a surveying contract, Washington once entered the wilderness where he must have "penetrated to the deepest parts of his nature" (p. 140). But he was no Boone: "stress he could endure but peace and regularity pleased him better" (p. 141). His basic mood was a "spirit of resignation" (p. 140) very different from the passivity of Montezuma; Washington's answer to the invitation of the New World was to "resist, be prudent, be calm—with a mad hell inside that might rise, might one day do something perhaps brilliant, perhaps joyously abandoned—but not to be thought of" (pp. 141–42). The cost of peace and regularity, both personal and civic, is an inner hell of violence and frustration. Our first president, Williams concludes, was "the typical sacrifice to the mob" (p. 143), afraid of the force that could have made him truly distinguished.

Almost every chapter in *In the American Grain* describes a fierce battle: seen in its naked reality, without idealization, life for Williams is a savage contest. What is more, characters can be quickly defined by their way of waging a battle. Whereas beleaguered rebels like Boone and Poe are quick to shoot, sure of aim, the conformist Franklin's way of dealing with the wild was less direct, "a scattering to reconnoitre" (p. 154). This slyness is his special quality. The man is epitomized in the episode with the lightning—which Williams reads in a fresh and symbolic way:

> Sure enough, he didn't dare let it go in at the top of his head and out at his toes, that's it; he *had* to fool with it. He sensed the power and knew only enough to want to run an engine with it. His fingers itched to be meddling, to do the little concrete thing—the barrier against a flood of lightning that would inundate him. (p. 155)

There is an incessant energy, right out of the New World, in Franklin; he can't keep his hands off anything—even lightning. But he refuses to let the forces he touches penetrate him. Instead, he plays with them, their sly master. Like the Puritan,

Franklin cannot tolerate otherness: "To want to touch, not to
wish anything to remain clean, aloof—comes always of a kind
of timidity, from fear" (p. 156). His "voluptuous energy" (p.
153) is dissipated in trivial projects, as he gives himself "to the
smaller, narrower, protective thing and not to the great, New
World" (p. 157). "The sweep of the force was too horrible"
for Franklin and Washington; "it would have swept them into
chaos" (p. 157).

From these beginnings the history of the New World, as
Williams reads it, proceeds mainly as a story of the slow burial
of the wilderness beneath layers of an imposed, unrelated civilization. The stroke has been not toward germination but toward
the confinements of a tomb—the result a society with a
peaceful uniformity on the surface and a buried core of violence
and frustration within. Yet this hell of repression has been lit
by occasional flickerings of genuine creativity and attachment.
True Americans, combining a fierce self-reliance with a sensitive reverence for the land, have necessarily been isolated,
often tormented into grotesque shapes in their fight for survival, and always buried by calumnies in standard histories.
They all have had "to come from under and through a dead
layer" (p. 213). Similarly, Williams's method was to cut
through established views by (in the main) ignoring secondary
sources and looking afresh at primary documents. In this way
he uncovered an underground tradition of acceptance, a series
of men who have not, in terror, held the New World by the
throat, but embraced it. At the same time that Williams strikes
out at official legends by a variety of ironic strategies, he tries
to lift these buried figures into collective consciousness. Once
again, destruction and creation are simultaneous.

The Jesuit missionary Rasles and the explorer Boone are probably Williams's most impressive recreations of this type and
mood. Faced with the massive strength of a primeval wilderness, these men answered not with Franklinian thrift, but with
a real infatuation; they boldly leapt into the chaos—to be made
new men, alive with its spirit. Both of these men, refusing to
let anything stand between them and the object of their de-

sires, disengage themselves from the "crawling mass" (p. 143),
head alone into the wilderness, die into the landscape and
thereby open the way to a distinctively American character.
The woods are not, however, represented as an idyllic alterna-
tive to the tensions of social existence. "Often suffering the
tortures of the damned" (p. 121), these men experienced harrowing frustrations and terrific violence; the wilderness is a
kind of hell—but it is the place where Kora's seed is hidden.
Struggle with this elemental world brings men close to the
sources of life; their deepest cravings are released and their
basic qualities emerge. Out of their agonizing love-battles with
nature can come regeneration.

The special quality of Père Sebastian Rasles was a selfless
ardor which brought him into intimacy with the feared inhabitants of the New World, the Indians. "Contrasted with the
Protestant *acts*, dry and splitting, those of Père Rasles were
striking in their tenderness, devotion, insight, and detail of
apprehension" (p. 121). If the early New Englanders were abstract, logical and brutal, this French Jesuit was open, sensual,
gentle: "Rasles lived thirty-four years, October 13, 1689 to
October 12, 1723, with his beloved savages, drawing their
sweet like honey, TOUCHING them every day" (p. 120). In
no way did the priest try to impose *himself* on the Indians; he
thought of himself as their servant. His deed, says Williams,
"was for humanity,—his passion held him a slave to the New
World, he strove to sound its mettle" (p. 121). One result of
this tender devotion was that Rasles could accept the Indian as
he was, without idealizing him into a Noble or Peaceful Savage.
Recognizing that "skill and courage" (p. 122) in battle are
necessary for survival in their harsh world, Rasles "speaks with
enthusiasm of the Indian as a fighter" (p. 126). This candid acceptance, in turn, makes possible an organic growth for the Indian; he is civilized but not asked to become a European: "In
Rasles one feels THE INDIAN emerging from within the pod
of his isolation from eastern understanding, he is released AN
INDIAN" (p. 121); his individual nature is cultivated and
drawn out by the priest's affectionate touch. "Père Rasles, often

suffering the tortures of the damned as the result of an early accident—fracture of both thighs, badly mended—lived with his village—alone, absorbed in them, LOST in them, swallowed, a hard yeast—" (p. 121). Yet through this act of self-loss—his descent to the ground—Rasles opened the way to the development of a native character: the release of "a spirit, rich, blossoming, generous, able to give and to receive, full of taste, a nose, a tongue, a laugh, enduring, self-forgetful in beneficence—a new spirit in the New World" (p. 120). His "living flame" contrasts vividly with the "dead ash" of Puritanism (p. 120).

In *In the American Grain*, as elsewhere, Williams's heroic ideal evolves out of a combination of fierce independence and reverent self-effacement. Here, heroic figures are always leaders, explorers, innovators, men who define themselves in lonely separation from the crowd. Yet, they are neither defiant nor imperious; their typical gesture is to turn their backs on society and head into unexplored territory—thereby opening a way out of the tormenting strife they have left behind. "Devotion" is a word that Williams uses again and again in describing the qualities of his great men—to suggest an attitude of natural piety before both the landscape and mankind. "Nothing shall be ignored. All shall be included," Williams says of Rasles's passion (p. 120). With this kind of reverence for all living things, Williams's rebel emerges as a tender and devoted servant, one who strives to sound the depths of all the objects of his desire. In Daniel Boone, Williams found an ideal combination of obstinacy and reverence needed for the emancipated individual.

"There was, thank God, a great voluptuary born to the American settlements against the niggardliness of the damming puritanical tradition," the Boone chapter begins—"one who by the single logic of his passion, which he rested on the savage life about him, destroyed at its spring that spiritually withering plague" (p. 130). While long "since buried in a miscolored legend and left for rotten," Boone, "far from dead," is still "full of a rich regenerative violence"—a power to affirm and release our blocked instincts (p. 130). Through Boone the lusty, crude spirit of the New World, at once fierce and tender, at last comes to open expression.

Sensing a wild spirit moving at the deepest levels of his being, Boone insisted upon releasing, exploring this force, tracing it to its origins in the locality he inhabited. His journey into the wilderness, a psychic as well as geographical quest, was thus "a descent to the ground of his desire" (p. 136), a refusal to let anything mediate between himself and the sources of his passions. In short, Boone enacted the archetypal descent into America, stripping away all vestiges of European civilization. While Franklin urgently felt the need to build walls around the wilderness, Boone dared to yield to the "single logic" of his passion and plunged headlong into the woods.

> As ecstasy cannot live without devotion and he who is not given to some earth of basic logic cannot enjoy, so Boone lived to enjoy ecstasy through his single devotion to the wilderness with which he was surrounded. The beauty of a lavish, primitive embrace in savage, wild beast and forest rising above the cramped life about him possessed him wholly. Passionate and thoroughly given he avoided the half logic of stealing from the immense profusion. (p. 136)

The landscape to which Boone devotes himself is decidedly not romantic or gentle; this is part of his importance. Kentucky is a "howling wilderness" (p. 134), dark, violent, and chaotic. Williams scornfully dismisses a description of Boone's time in the woods as "an uninterrupted scene of sylvan pleasures":

> Constant exposure to danger and death, a habitation which he states had been discovered by the savages, the necessity of such stratagems as the resort to the canebrake rather than to take the risk of being found in his cabin, have nothing of sylvan pleasures in them. (p. 135)

Yet, confronted with this terrifying landscape, Boone was passionate, devoted, thoroughly given; he did not seek to dominate, idealize, get rich or otherwise impose himself; he sought only to grow intimate.

Sensing a limitless fortune which daring could make his own, he sought only with primal lust to grow close to it, to understand it and to be part of its mysterious movements—like an Indian. (p. 136)

The pioneer broke out of the cramped life of the settlements and let the savage energy of the New World flow *through* him.

Boone thus submitted to a kind of primitive ordeal in which he was torn apart. Franklin and Washington sacrificed themselves, too, but in a way that was not creative; they simply vanished into an anonymous crowd. But the Boone who lost himself in the wilderness, wandering alone there for three months, emerged as a new man, different from Indian and European alike. "There must be a new wedding," he saw (p. 137)—of the sort that Whitman envisioned in the marriage of the trapper and the red girl. The white man must somehow open himself to the primitive but without simply surrendering to it: "Not for himself surely to be an Indian, though they eagerly sought to adopt him into their tribes, but the reverse: to be *himself* in a new world, Indian-like" (p. 137). And the beauty of Boone's character, as Williams imagines it, is that his acceptance of the wild results in a calm serenity of temper, comparable to the composure of Montezuma. While necessarily thrown among a "riff-raff of hunters and Indian killers," Boone himself emerges as highly civilized.

Mild and simple hearted, steady, not impulsive in courage—bold and determined, but always rather inclined to defend than attack—he stood immensely above that wretched class of men who are so often the preliminaries of civilization. (p. 131)

Williams constantly stresses the mild composure in this "great voluptuary." When members of his own family are killed by the Indians, Boone feels no rancor—expecting nothing better of the savages. Thus, the discoverer of Kentucky is important not as a pathfinder but as a man who lets certain suppressed qualities emerge.

Filled with the wild beauty of the New World to overbrimming so long as he had what he desired, to bathe in, to

explore always more deeply, to see, to feel, to touch—his
instincts were contented. (p. 136)

Immersed in the wilderness, Boone is satisfied, full; that is why
he feels no need to impress himself on his surroundings. His
content puts him in clear contrast to the restless activity of
Franklin. Hence the three months he spent in a perilous landscape became "the great ecstatic moment of his life's affirmation" (p. 136); the howling wilderness was "the land of heart's
desire" (p. 139)—a rich, solid, and independent otherness.
Through Boone the wilderness is possessed ardently; and
through his contact with the woods Boone himself is released
into an individual and a full identity. Together, they come into
new, distinct life; there *is* a new wedding.

After dealing with Boone, Williams examines several possible
loci of native vitality—John Paul Jones, the American woman,
Aaron Burr, the Negro, Sam Houston, Edgar Allan Poe and
Abraham Lincoln; but the position of the man seeking true
character becomes more and more embattled, a process that
culminates in the madness of Poe and the assassination of the
tender Lincoln. But if the struggle for individual distinction
becomes more arduous as the original landscape fades from
sight, Williams still does not think of American history as a
simple decline. Rather, he views it as developing out of the
tension between the dominant thrust toward mastery and marginal efforts at contact. This psychic and historical tension
provides structure as well as theme for his book. As in *Spring
and All*, what intrigues Williams is the confrontation of opposed forces. In *In the American Grain* the encounter may be
as dramatic as the clash between Cortez and Montezuma, the
duel between Burr and Hamilton, or it may be a more subtle
conflict between the gifted individual and the envious crowd.
But what any one chapter shares with the other twenty is this
concentration upon a kind of primitive conflict. Moreover, this
tension is generated between chapters as well as within chapters, as Williams consistently juxtaposes figures of opposite
sensibilities. The radical contrast between the Aztecs and the
New England Puritans is only the most striking instance of

this technique. The rapacious de Leon and the infatuated De Soto are dramatically placed in successive chapters. Elsewhere, elaborate relations are established among several sections. The emotionally starved Pilgrims are contrasted on the one side with the flamboyant sensuality of Raleigh and on the other with the delicate humanity of Champlain. The Mather of the witchcraft trials is similarly located between lusty Thomas Morton and the generous Père Rasles. At the same time Champlain and Morton meet in adjoining chapters and each reveals the limits of the other. Among the eighteenth-century figures, Washington's resignation and Boone's daring, the sly Franklin and the persistent Jones are paired in order to reveal basic conflicts forcefully. Such jolting shifts of character and mood make individual figures more distinct, their conflicts more dramatic. Further, the constant alternation of open and aloof character types makes recurrence a structural principle in *In the American Grain;* it is thus not just something we know abstractly, but a reality we *experience* in reading the book.

Hence the characters of *In the American Grain* have a mythical, archetypal status; but this does not mean that Williams regarded them simply as fictions. He claims an historical, individual reality for them too, and several of his rhetorical strategies have been determined by his aim of convincing us of their actuality. Certainly, if *In the American Grain* is to be free of the desire to impose self that it attacks, its characters must exist independently of the will of the author. It is exactly on this level, of course, that the book has so often been dismissed; Williams's reinterpretations of the Puritans, Aaron Burr, Edgar Allan Poe—among others—have struck many readers as more peculiar than true. Certainly, in some sense all of the book's characters are versions of William Carlos Williams, the motives and values of his heroic types are identical to his own, and the conflict that he saw in American history *was* the conflict in his own soul. Did Williams liberate his characters from conventional estimates only to impose his own tyrannous designs upon them? Was his journey into the American past a real journey of discovery—or an attempt to establish an ideological empire? The study of history, Williams well knew, requires much more than introspection; it begins with the careful study of primary documents. The best way to determine just how authentic was Williams's descent to origins for renewal is by placing his chapters alongside those documents upon which they are based.

Part of the problem is the pretentious assumption that Williams sometimes held, that he could read these documents without any assumptions. He insisted upon the actuality of his characters—that he had, for example, resurrected the "real" Aaron Burr from a grave of calumnies. To believe that, he had to assume that he could empty his mind of all personal and cultural presuppositions and come into unmediated contact with the given, even when what was given was a character from the past. Thus in reading the sources for his book, Williams says, "I wanted nothing to get between me and what they themselves had recorded" (*Auto*, p. 178); and he similarly wanted nothing, especially the idiosyncracies of his own personality, to come between his characters and his readers. By annihilating historical perspective Williams was not trying to write a merely subjective history: he thought his work would be more objective because he could get inside his historical figures. It was to this end of impersonality that he read mainly primary documents, offered his findings in the form of created characters (rather than essays) and shifted the style from chapter to chapter. At the beginning of the Burr section, Williams defends some of the peculiarities of his method:

> But history follows governments and never men. It portrays us in generic patterns, like effigies or the carvings on sarcophagi, which say nothing save, of such and such a man, that he is dead. That's history. It is concerned only with the one thing: to say everything is dead. Then it fixes up the effigy: there that's finished. Not at all. History must stay open, it is all humanity. Are lives to be twisted forcibly about events, the mere accidents of geography and climate?
>
> It is an obscenity which few escape—save at the hands of the

stylist, literature, in which alone humanity is protected against tyrannous designs. (pp. 188–89)

Historical narrative, argues Williams, maims the individual by fitting him into a larger pattern of events—a fatal error for a man more interested in qualities than in acts. Hence, still another reason for Williams's rejection of narrative is his own Rasles-like reverence for the humanity of his subjects, and he preserves the delicate living quality of his characters by a technique we have seen in *Spring and All*—abstraction. In "The Rose," for instance, Williams uncovers life hidden in an apparently dead object by abstracting the flower from historical associations and letting "nothing" come between it and the reader. He here tries to preserve the life of his characters by abstracting them from historical context and narrative sequence and letting them come to us unencumbered by the accidents of time. The variation of style from chapter to chapter thus creates the impression that the author has disappeared to let each character speak in his own voice.

In what seems to be an extreme instance of such self-effacement, Williams has included two chapters that are composed entirely of quotations from primary documents. The predicament of John Paul Jones, a gifted individual thwarted and driven off by the U.S. Navy, is reported in his letter to Benjamin Franklin about the battle between the *Bon Homme Richard* and the *Serapis*. Cotton Mather is represented by accounts of the witchcraft trials in *The Wonders of the Invisible World*.[5] Here at least, it would appear, a character from the past speaks to us in his own voice. Yet that voice is at least partly the creation of William Carlos Williams. Mather's actual position on the trials was that there was not only an urgent need to detect witches, but that there was also a responsibility to proceed cautiously. In particular, he objected to the sole reliance on so-called "spectral" evidence in the trials. But Williams has quoted only from the first two parts of "Enchantments Encountered" where Mather speaks simply of the colony's invasion by "an Army of *Devils*" (p. 84) and gives no sense of the tortured ambiguities of his real stand. This technique of simplifying the source is characteristic of Williams—and it can be defended here by his radical insistence upon judging men only by their ultimate assumptions. But it is Williams who decides which assumptions are ultimate and the voice we hear in *In the American Grain* is not the voice heard in *The Wonders of the Invisible World*—by virtue of a deliberate act of selection.

Williams wisely decided to use this technique of mere quotation in only two of the chapters: it is too simple a rhetorical trick. For the trouble with these chapters is not that they manipulate the material, but that they don't manipulate it enough. Selecting a single letter or a few pages out of the whole range of a man's work is too quick and easy a way to create the impression of objectivity while actually making him illustrate certain themes. In fact, the best chapters in *In the American Grain* are those in which Williams, discovering a kind of co-extension between himself and the source, handles the document in an original but persuasive way. He does develop his own mythology out of these readings, but he works on material with which he has become thoroughly familiar, and he leaves enough raw data in his own chapters to make his interpretations convincing. He came to know some of these documents so well that they became, like the landscape of northern New Jersey, part of his unconscious life; he was thus freed to use them creatively.[6] The effect is most like the intimate touch of Père Rasles, a sense that Williams has skillfully drawn out an hitherto hidden beauty and meaning. The triumph is not that of self-abdication, but of the kind of ardent act of *possession* that Williams constantly celebrates in his heroes; it is the triumph of the skillful but gentle hands of the literary stylist. At best, Williams does give us the feeling that he has reached out and touched something solid and new; his *is* a real journey of discovery.

Of all the characters he selected for study only two—Père Rasles and Red Eric—have fallen into real obscurity. In the case of the Jesuit, Williams's feat was mainly in the recovery of a forgotten heroic type. Once he had come upon the *Lettres Édifiantes*, all he had to do was to make a fairly simple selection of quotation and anecdote; the French missionary's qualities are quite forcefully revealed in his letters.[7] But the Red Eric chapter, opening the imaginative possibilities hidden in a text, is a beautiful example of literary invention. Williams divided this chapter into two parts: the first a monologue spoken by Eric himself, the second a third-person narrative dealing with his natural daughter Freydis. The account of Freydis is assembled by almost verbatim quotation from the sources, while Eric's monologue grows more freely out of the main events of his life related in the sagas—and the language in both cases is modeled on the prose of the translation Williams used.[8] As he does throughout *In the American Grain*, Williams draws a mythic pattern out of the facts given in the source. In the story of Eric, branded a criminal and driven first to Iceland and then to Greenland, Williams saw one of his eternal types: the strong man hounded by the pack. "Rather the ice than their way: to take what is mine by single strength, theirs by the crookedness of their law," Eric grimly begins (p. 1); and in the very first clause, which reappears in the middle of the Poe chapter, he makes a mythic gesture of rebellion, the heroic individual's insistence on his own way of doing things. Eric gives us a glimpse of primitive force, before the encroachments of Christianity, but he is not sentimentalized into the peaceful savage: his actions are violent, his manner fierce—like the spirit of the New World. Yet the force he embodies goes off in opposite directions: his wife and sons become Christians, while his natural daughter, Freydis, is violent simply out of greed. In an early expedition to the mainland, she conspires for the murder of her partners and their followers, while she herself slays the women. The narrator comments: "So, thinning out, more and more dark, it [Eric's blood] ran" (p. 5). True power splits into attenuated gentility and mindless brutality, and the chapter ends with a prediction of ill fortune for Eric's offspring—a curse that is worked out in all of what follows. The first chapter, then, presents an historical cycle, the release and decline of an elemental force, and thus establishes the mythic patterns that shape the entire book. At the same time, Williams here begins his practice of looking at the more open, alive figures from the inside (Eric in his own voice) while viewing the more domineering characters externally (Freydis in the third person). As we are distanced from the predatory figures we are pushed into intimacy with the more creative people.

Out of what historical documents offer as literal fact, then, Williams develops archetypal patterns. But confronted with his documents, he posed an even deeper question. Given the main events of a man's life, what qualities must we attribute to him? In the sagas Eric's character is hardly defined: the events of his life are reported objectively, with no attempt to penetrate to the inner world of feeling and motive. But it is precisely this world that Williams opens up by turning the point of view over to Eric himself. A man who "loves his friends, loves bed, loves food, loves the hunt, loves his sons" (p. 2), the outcast is gradually stripped of all these comforts—yet in the face of his afflictions he maintains a dignified attitude of acceptance. At times he is bitterly ironical toward his oppressors, at others he exults in his freedom, but he always possesses a kind of elemental strength; he is never outraged or defiant. These qualities come to us, moreover, in a voice which seems to grow organically out of the man and his environment.

> And so to Greenland—after bitter days fighting the ice and rough seas. Pestilence struck us. The cattle sickened. Weeks passed. The summer nearly ended before we struck land. This is my portion. I do not call it not to my liking. Hardship lives in me. What I suffer is myself that outraces the water or the wind. But that it only should be mine, cuts deep. It is the half only. And it takes it out of my taste that the choice is theirs. I have the rough of it not because I will it, but because it is all that is left, a remnant from their coatcloth. This is the gall on the meat. Let the hail beat me. It is a kind of joy I feel in such things.
>
> Greenland then. So be it. Start over again. (p. 3)

The spare diction and the impersonal tone, the slow, heavy movement of short, disjunctive sentences—these create the voice of a man who, accepting the harsh, primitive conditions around him, has absorbed a good deal of their strength and weight. By means of this voice the flat character of the sagas is brought to life and Williams, cutting beneath the level of events, reveals those qualities which are at the man's core. One feels that Williams has deeply penetrated and filled his source —like one of his own impassioned explorers.

In creating Red Eric, Williams's achievement was mainly in filling out possibilities latent in his source. But in his even more remarkable studies of Cortez and De Soto, Williams's method was to cut through a prolixity of detail in order to point up a hidden symbolic pattern. Both of these chapters are based on long, rambling firsthand accounts of conquest and exploration —narratives that under Williams's skillful hand have been brilliantly foreshortened and simplified, made at once more dramatic and symbolic. In the Tenochtitlan chapter, the technique has been, by simplification, to let basic qualities emerge—in a style that embodies those qualities. Except for a few passages of summary and comment, almost every word of the chapter has come by direct quotation or close paraphrase from Williams's source, the second and third letters of Cortez to King Ferdinand.[9] The details of the elaborate description of the Aztec city are all based solidly on facts reported by the conquistador, but these details have been artfully arranged, the narrative carefully shaped. Williams's beginning and end—the landing at Vera Cruz and the final destruction of Tenochtitlan —are not those of the letters; but even more important he has changed the pace of the action. The chapter's first paragraph ends with Cortez burning his ships at Vera Cruz before turning inland—a gesture that impressed Williams with its daring and singleness of purpose. "Montezuma immediately sent gifts," the second paragraph begins and there follows a richly detailed account of the elegant articles sent by the Indian (pp. 28–29). To this the conqueror's only reply was to dispatch a letter to his own king declaring his intention to take Monte-

zuma forthwith, dead or alive. And so at the opening of the
third paragraph Williams writes:

> The advance was like any similar military enterprise: it ac-
> complished its purpose. Surmounting every difficulty Cortez
> went his way into the country past the quiet Cempoalan maize-
> fields, past the smoking summit of Popocatepetl, until, after
> weeks of labor, he arrived upon the great lakes and the small
> cities in them adjoining Tenochtitlan itself. (p. 29)

In fact, Montezuma did not send gifts "immediately," for reasons that are at least ambiguous, and did not send the particular items listed by Williams. Moreover, "after weeks of labor"
is accurate enough but telescopes into a phrase Cortez's
lengthy account of his approach to the city, slowed down by
his frequent clashes with the natives. Williams has clearly
made these changes in order to depict the advance of Cortez as
a steady, inexorable thrust—and to set it in dramatic contrast to
the gracious hospitality of the Aztec chieftain. The complexities of motive that have so long intrigued historians are dissolved, to reveal an archetypal confrontation.

"The Tenochtitlan chapter," Williams tells us, "was written
in big, square paragraphs like Inca masonry" (*Auto*, p. 183);
the comparison is loose, but Williams is suggesting the way the
language, while often quite close to the source, has been made
to embody the qualities of the civilization described—especially
its elegant workmanship.

> Cortez now passed over his first causeway into one of the
> lesser lake cities, built of well-hewn stone sheer from the
> water. He was overcome with wonder. The houses were so
> excellently put together, so well decorated with cloths and
> carven wood, so embellished with metalwork and other marks
> of a beautiful civilization; the people were so gracious; there
> were such gardens, such trees, such conservatories of flowers
> that nothing like it had ever been seen or imagined. At the
> house where the Conqueror was entertained that day and night
> he especially noted a pool built of stone into the clear waters
> of which stone steps descended, while round it were paven
> paths lined with sweet-smelling shrubs and plants and trees of
> all sorts. Also he noted the well-stocked kitchen garden. (p. 30)

Williams normally seeks a style that is broken and spontaneous; but the most striking thing about this passage is the way
it has been so deliberately constructed. Here we find large,
square paragraphs, long, balanced sentences, a slow, measured
movement, an elegant diction, euphonious music. Everything
has been carefully worked on, artfully made smooth and sym-
metrical. There is a studied formality which is definitely not
attenuated but which lifts hard particulars into an "isolate distinction" (p. 224). The effect is a marble-like beauty, at once
solid and refined—a style that authenticates Williams's intimate
acquaintance with his subject.

Unlike Cortez, De Soto was self-divided; he internalizes the
book's basic conflict between will and instinct. So his chapter
is split into a dialogue—alternating between a factual account
of his progress across the southern portion of North America
and the oracular utterances of a "She" who is the spirit of the
new continent. Almost all of the narrative sections come directly from the history of the expedition by the Gentleman of
Elvas; much of Williams's text consists of unacknowledged direct quotation from this document.[10] Williams begins with a
substratum of literal detail, but this is amplified into a mythical journey, first of all, by the pronouncements of "She," who
gives voice to De Soto's deepest motives.

Ride upon the belly of the waters, building your boats to carry
all across. Calculate for the current; the boats move with a
force not their own, up and down, sliding upon that female
who communicates to them, across all else, herself. And still
there is that which you have not sounded, under the boats,
under the adventure—giving to all things the current, the
wave, the onwash of my passion. So cross and have done with
it, you are safe—and I am desolate.

But you are mine and I will strip you naked—jealous of
everything that touches you. Down, down to me—in and under
and down, unbeaten, the white kernel, the flame—the flame
burning under the water, that I cannot quench.

I will cause it to be known that you are a brute. Now it is
no sea-ringed island, now it is no city in a lake: Come, here is
room for search and countersearch. Come, blackbeard, tireless

> rider, with an arrow in the thigh. I wait for you—beyond the
> river. Follow me—if you can. (p. 53)

This is the prophetic tone in which she always addresses De
Soto: you may do what you wish, she tells him, but you are
mine nevertheless. Human will, purposive activity, avail nothing. She knows all, has a god's knowledge of the ancient
forces, beyond human control, that drive men. And it is she
that moves De Soto, not the supposed motive of gold or power.
But it is important to see that this prophetess is not looking
down from above, like Eliot's Tiresias; her knowledge comes
from the earth and she looks upward, fiercely seductive, at her
lover. We hear a gigantic, passionate female, a primitive goddess whose voice is low and full, heavily metaphorical, rhap-
sodically disconnected; it is a voice from deep within the
body—from the unconscious. The sensualist buried within the
warrior, the mythical journey hidden within the flat narrative
are thus opened for the modern reader.

At the same time Williams has pointed up the mythical elements in De Soto's quest by selection and arrangement of
events. Whereas the Gentleman of Elvas begins his story in
Spain, includes descriptions of numerous battles with the Indians and ends with the return of the expedition's survivors to
civilization, Williams starts with De Soto's arrival in Florida—
"turning from the sea, facing inland" (p. 45)— omits many of
the encounters with the natives, and closes with the burial of
De Soto in the Mississippi. At the start the Spaniard is rich, famous, powerful; at the end, after three years of futile search,
he is impoverished and despised. But in this apparent cutting
down of the hero Williams perceives a real expansion, a self-
destructive opening to the New World. Once again, Williams,
by pushing aside extraneous detail, makes a factual account reverberate into myth.

Among the early explorers De Soto stands alone as one who
took nothing from America; he was, in Williams's view, no
plunderer but a man who gave himself. While others sought
egotistically to make everything like themselves, De Soto had a
lover's reverence for the particulars of his new environment.

Indian place names are "to rest without definition," the voice of the continent tells him, "but to you each a thing in itself, delicate, pregnant with sudden meanings" (p. 46). De Soto and this mighty earth-goddess are lovers, but she offers him little more than violence and frustration: "And in the end you shall receive of me, nothing—save one long caress as of a great river passing forever upon your sweet corse" (p. 45). Gradually, the Spaniard is stripped of all the possessions he brought into the New World. At one point, after a fire, he and his men are forced to make clothing from the hides of local animals—a clear contrast to the Washington who was to hide his native rudeness under fine old-world dress. When De Soto obstinately pushes further inland in spite of tremendous hardships, his men begin to turn against him, as the pack always turns on the creative individual in this book. But all of De Soto's expectations in coming here are violated—and in this failure lies his greatest success; his was a voyage of *discovery*. De Soto's penetration of America was for Williams a mythic descent to origins, in several respects resembling the rites of passage of the young poet in "The Wanderer." His men are alienated, the goddess assures him, "to make you lonesome, ready for my caresses" (p. 48); alone he becomes more intimate with her. He progresses by going downward, stripping away all barriers, toward contact with the primal new and toward release of a quenchless ardor: "Down, down to me—in and under and down, unbeaten, the white kernel, the flame—the flame burning underwater, that I cannot quench" (p. 53). This descent culminates with De Soto's burial in the Mississippi: "down, down, this solitary sperm, down into the liquid, the formless, the insatiable belly of sleep" (p. 58). At the end, De Soto has gained—nothing; but it is a nothing, as in "To Have Done Nothing," that is synonymous with everything. A series of reversals, cutting away conscious egotism, have opened him, immersed him in the new environment. An "inflexible man . . . dry of word" (p. 47) is absorbed into a great river, which is both flexible and wet. The language in which this action is described suggests the act of love, defining the moment as more a beginning than an ending.

At this point, as Williams elsewhere remarks, "Europe should pass as into the New World" (*GAN*, p. 55). Now completely identified with the spirit of the place, De Soto becomes a generative power—a seed.

In these, as in the chapters dealing with Columbus, Ponce de Leon, Sir Walter Raleigh, and Daniel Boone, Williams's readings are "new," based on a personal mythology; but the mythic patterns he establishes are supported by a wealth of factual detail, and the individuality of his subjects is preserved through the qualities of the book's protean style. For the most part Williams has taken a fresh, careful look at primary documents that have been buried under a mass of often stale commentary; his solidly grounded conclusions are original but not peculiar. But this is not always the case. When Valéry Larbaud mentions Cotton Mather's *Magnalia*, Williams comments that "HE had read it. I had *seen* the book and brushed through its pages hunting for something I wished to verify" (pp. 109–10). Some of the sources were read in exactly this imperious way, particularly those dealing with the Puritans and founders on the one side, or with the satyr-like rebels, Morton and Burr, on the other.

The trouble with these sections is not that their conclusions are "wrong," not that their judgments are "simple," but that they lack the hard-edged particularity of the better chapters. This lack of definition comes, in turn, from a narrowly superficial contact with the sources. Stylistically, the special quality of Williams's study of the Pilgrims lies in the composure of its tight, epigrammatic prose.

> The Pilgrims were seed of Tudor England's lusty blossoming. The flamboyant force of that zenith, spent, became in them hard and little. Among such as they its precarious wealth of petals sank safely within bounds to lie dreaming or floating off while the Restoration throve, a sweltering seclusion of the hothouse, surrounded by winter's cold. (p. 63)

Surely and brutally, Williams strips bare their "tight-locked hearts" but he does so absolutely without rancor; his judgments seem to come passionately, implacably, but impartially from a firmly controlled center. Yet the writer's thrust seems to be grounded in a set of rigidly held ideas rather than in solid data. Seldom does the essay descend to the specific. Williams's source was Bradford's *Of Plymouth Plantation,* but quotation of two well-known incidents from the voyage to America—the abusive sailor who mysteriously dies, and the believer who is blown overboard but saved—constitute almost his only use of the document. At his best, Williams is always opening a new way into some thing outside himself; but here, in spite of the impersonal tone, he simply admits us to his own system of ideas. As Larbaud correctly remarks, "I find your interest [in the Puritans] 'très théorique' " (p. 115).

Like the pilgrims, Aaron Burr reaches us only at a mythical level; the character of the man that Williams regarded as the most distinctive figure of his age is scarcely individuated, his life rendered with little specificity. And without sharpness of detail the elemental force of Burr does not hit us with the impact of a Red Eric or De Soto. From Williams's radical position, the difference between such successful politicians as Jefferson and Hamilton could only be superficial; these sly, timid men— along with the stolid Washington—he saw arrayed almost conspiratorially against the passionate rebel Burr. As everything was rapidly becoming the same under the heavy Federalist hand, Burr dared to assert "a humanity, his own, free and independent, unyielding to the herd, practical, direct" (p. 204). It is the classic lot of the emancipated individual in Williams's mythology: a giant hounded by smaller men. But in this chapter the conflict has been dramatized not as an encounter between the historical personages involved, but as a dialogue in the present between a speaker who adopts Burr's point of view and one who takes the moralistic position of his enemies. The advantage of the dialogue form is that Williams can anticipate and undermine objections to his startling reappraisal, while locating the debate in the present affirms the persistency of such conflicts.

The difficulty is that Williams is now trying to *argue* us into a body consciousness, as he does in several of the book's later chapters; it is his voice, not that of Burr's "hidden flame" (p. 204) of desire that we hear. What is more, the progression of the argument here amounts to a parody of Williams's characteristic descent to particulars for renewal. The debate begins with a heated attack on conventional history, with Williams contending that "if a verdict be unanimous, it is sure to be a wrong one, a crude rush of the herd which has carried its object before it like a helpless condoning image" (pp. 189–90). Such rigidities Williams proposes to shatter, in order to yield up the suppressed "humanity" of Burr. Then, after some preliminary comments about Burr's nature, Williams turns to a quick characterization of his period. It was a new beginning, a tremendous force was being unleashed that might have swept all the settlers into the New World, but certain powerful men —notably Burr's foes—found it to their interest to contain this force and keep things quietly stable. Within this historical context we can recognize Burr's "profound refinement, his sense of the deeper forces working in his world that demanded freedom; things the others were beginning to stamp out, to whittle away, down to the common level" (p. 195). At this point Williams is challenged to show "how his life, in its detail, supports your roseate view of him" (p. 198); a summary account of Burr's life follows. But just the way Williams approaches his subject makes it clear that he is using Burr's life simply to vindicate his own theories. He moves not by absorbing data into a fresh viewpoint, but by establishing the viewpoint, then clamping it down upon his materials. The literary result is a remoteness about Burr's character—the very opposite of the intimacy Williams intends to establish.

In fact, the Williams who determined that nothing would get between him and what his subjects had recorded saw Burr at at least one remove, perhaps two. He claims in two places that his wife did all the reading for this chapter (*SL*, p. 187; *IW*, p. 43); this may have been an attempt to disown the work, but it may have been true. But whoever did the reading relied mainly on a secondary source. The best source for primary materials on Burr, the *Memoirs* edited by M. L. Davis, was consulted; but the chapter depends most heavily on *The Life and Times of Aaron Burr* by James Parton. The three quotes (pp. 190,192) which launch the discussion of Burr have been lifted from the epigraph to this book.[11] Out of the seven hundred pages of Parton's formal biography, Williams has assembled his ten-page defense of the politician. The trouble, however, is not that lengthy episodes in the subject's career have been omitted entirely or merely alluded to, but that the treatment always remains highly schematic. Instead of selecting particular episodes and slowly drawing out their mythic import, Williams leaps rapidly from one conclusion to the next:

> He loved and straight he went to the mark. It was an impossible plane in that world. That sort of independence was bound to bring him into disrepute with the rulers of the colonies. Never though with the people, whom he knew, lovers of the senses, as was he. Men believed in him. He tied for the presidency in spite of nearly all the upper ten against him. Jefferson succeeded. He hated Burr. Overbearing toward the Vice-President he told him—to look in the papers for the news. The Vice-Presidency was never better served, however. (p. 200)

When we read the De Soto chapter alongside the original documents, we can see how Williams slowly absorbed his material so that it became an almost physical part of his life. But the impression Williams himself creates here is of a "crude rush" through helpless data. The humanity of Burr, suppressed by Williams's theoretical pursuits, fails to rise into distinct life.

The Poe chapter, too, has struck many readers as defiantly at odds with received truth. In this case Williams has drawn his subject quite distinctly and he has recovered real, forgotten qualities in his man; the problem is with the primacy he attributes to these qualities and with what he identifies as their source. Americans customarily think of Poe as eccentric, starved, alienated, "out of Space, out of Time"; but Williams typically reverses this view, transforming the bizarre southerner into our first authentic genius of place. "His greatness," says Williams, "is that he turned his back and faced inland, to originality, with the identical gesture of a Boone" (p. 226). At the bottom of all Poe's work Williams saw a mythic gesture, the determination to be himself by finding roots in his locality. Surrounded by an "inchoate mass" (p. 221)—a sentimental literature, an imported culture, a swarming population—Poe answered with "a single gesture, not avoiding the trivial, to sweep all worthless chaff aside. It is a movement, first and last, to clear the GROUND" (p. 216). The fierce spirit of the New World speaks in the plain, implacable reasonings of Poe's essays. How then explain the abstraction of Poe's creative work? Williams ingeniously argues that Poe's very insistence on being himself left him vulnerably isolated; to avoid being overwhelmed by his time he had to distance himself from it. "He sought by stress upon construction to hold the loose-strung mass off even at the cost of an icy coldness of appearance; it was the first need of his time, an escape from the formless mass he hated" (p. 221).

But in arriving at this novel conception of Poe, Williams concentrated on a limited aspect of his work. Most of the evidence he offers comes not from the poems, the short stories or the theoretical essays, but from the fugitive criticism. In Williams's account, then, the Poe who yearned to dissolve physical reality and attain "Supernal Beauty" was a surface phenomenon; the scrupulously logical and devastatingly candid author of such essays as "Rufus Dawes" and "Longfellow and Other Plagiarists" gives us the deeper, hidden identity of Poe. In a sense, this interpretation was inevitable for Williams. Having uncovered such polemical energy, Williams could only account for it by his own "single logic" of geographical explanation; a passionate attachment to place is the only motive he can imagine for battle with the swarming population. But there were also personal pressures working on Williams. The Poe we discover here bears a marked resemblance to the neglected literary giant of *Spring and All*, the man who scornfully derides his more successful contemporaries as "THE TRADITION-ALISTS OF PLAGIARISM" (*SA*, p. 10). In fact, Williams's identification with his character is complete. When he describes Poe's style—"he wanted a lean style, rapid as a hunter, and with an aim as sure" (p. 227)—he is really talking about the quick, epigrammatic prose of his own essays. Similarly, as the author of a very peculiar, avant-garde kind of poetry and prose, Williams insisted that his literary experiments grew out of his roots in the common ground. His argument that the "bizarre designs" (p. 219) of Poe's stories and poems were surface expressions of a deep relation to place is simply an imposition of his own identity on the nineteenth-century writer.[12] Williams has dug up a lost set of qualities in Poe's criticism and he has written his chapter in a style expressive of those qualities; but he makes this "side" the core of his subject because he is finally moved here more by the need for self-justification than discovery.

It is in the later chapters that Williams most often appears to be forcing his mythology on historical fact. We feel this partly because characters such as Columbus, Montezuma, and De Soto have assumed a legendary status that enables us to accept a certain freedom in speculation about their motives that we do not tolerate in the case of a Washington or Poe. But the matter goes deeper than this. Significantly, the speaker in many of these closing sections is not the historical figure but Williams himself. The book is no longer animated by a confidence that goes back to roots—in the documents or in the place itself. Several of these chapters were written in France and it is likely that separation from Rutherford and from the New York Public Library had something to do with the decline in quality. But there are at least two things about the earlier chapters that made them congenial to Williams. His mind worked best when achieving an intense concentration within sharply defined limits. With the earlier figures there was a limited body of data, often a single document, which he could thoroughly absorb. At the same time it was the return to primitive origins, to the moment when things begin to begin, that most excited his imagination. Both of these factors were at work in his remarkable study of Columbus.

Yet, to gauge fully the impact of the Columbus study, we need to look more closely at the book's play of voice and perspective. When the Williams in Paris declares that Larbaud "is a student while I am—the brutal thing itself" (p. 107), he is defining his own point of view as the angry victim of American history; but the Williams who wrote the chapter has given us both the spontaneous outbursts of the participant and the cultivated detachment of the student. One of the most impressive things about *In the American Grain* is its multiplicity of perspectives, its dramatic shifting within chapters and from one chapter to the next between detached and involved points of view. At one end, there is a voice which can speak fatalistically of certain instinctual forces in human nature as perennial and therefore inevitable. At the other, there is a voice which speaks from inside history, as the angry product of cultural strife. This alternating point of view is behind the dialogue structure which Thomas Whitaker finds basic in the book.[13] Most important, its effect is to refuse the reader the comfort of coming to rest finally in righteousness or guilt; he is made instead to *experience* the tensions of American history.

This practice of looking at his subject from more than one angle can be seen in Williams's studies of Red Eric, de Leon, De Soto, Champlain, Rasles, Burr. But the Columbus chapter affords a particularly rich opportunity to study Williams's technique because we can compare it with an earlier and significantly different version, published in the little magazine, *Broom*.[14] Like the Mather chapter, the *Broom* version is composed almost entirely of selected quotations from a primary document, here the *Journal of the First Voyage*. Out of this lengthy document Williams cuts a compact narrative that begins on the day Columbus turns west from the Canary Islands and ends with the ecstatic discoverer walking along the shore of an island in the Carribean: "During that time I walked among the trees which was the most beautiful thing which I had ever seen" (*Broom*, p. 260). The account of the voyage is prefaced by a brief summary of Columbus's trials in finding support for his adventure and it is interrupted once by a bitter complaint written by Columbus on the fourth and last voyage, but on the whole it sticks to the first voyage, related in Columbus's own words.[15] Changes in the book version are considerable. Here, the contrast between the wondering young mariner and the frustrated old man is developed much more fully. Extracts from letters written on the last voyage are ampler, including an account of the discoverer's imprisonment, and they are inserted *before* the story of the first voyage. An episode from the first voyage concerning his return to Europe has also been added, stressing Columbus's fear that, having discovered the New World, he would not survive to bring word back to the old. This episode has been placed *before* the description of the last voyage. Finally, passages of commentary, written from a perspective high above the action, are at four points spliced into the historical documents. The book version, then, goes: commentary / return from first voyage / commentary / contracts Columbus signed with the King on his return / commentary / letters from the last voyage / commentary / lengthy account of the first voyage out.

In both versions the Columbus of the first voyage is given a purity of motive: he is tenacious, ardent, daring, wondering, detailed in his apprehension of the New World, and almost all suggestions that gold, spice, or conversion of the Indians were part of his intent have been edited out of the text.[16] But in revising the chapter Williams decided to stress the hero's betrayal of his vision, supply a point of view from which this betrayal (and thus the later suffering) would be not just intelligible but inevitable, and to move the chapter alternately forward and backward toward the key moment in Columbus's life, the discovery of America. The trouble was that his discovery stirred the Italian to dreams of personal dominion:

> . . . that henceforth I should be called Don, and should be Chief Admiral of the Ocean Sea, perpetual Viceroy and Governor of all the islands and continents that I should discover and gain in the Ocean Sea, and that my eldest son should succeed, and so from generation to generation forever. (p. 9)

"Unhappy talk," the commentator tartly remarks. "What power had such ridiculous little promises to stay man against that terrific downpour on the brink of which they were all floating? How could a king fulfill them? Yet this man, this straw in the play of the elemental giants, must go blindly on" (p. 10). A man is never so little as when he puffs himself up with ambition—like J. P. M. in *Spring and All*. The commentator here, aware of exactly those primitive powers that Columbus is blind to, views him from a detached, cosmic perspective. His role is choric; his stance analytic, impersonal, godlike in its stretching across all time and space. At the very beginning of the chapter, he identifies the discoverer's fate as a re-enactment of the fall: "For it is as the achievement of a flower, pure, white, waxlike and fragrant, that Columbus's infatuated course must be depicted, especially when compared with the acrid and poisonous apple which was later by him to be proved" (p. 7). A counterpoint is set going between the voice of Columbus himself and a voice which sees his whole career in terms of mythic recurrence, "What have I not endured?" the man complains (p. 11); the commentator views him distantly, coldly, as a straw in the play of elemental giants. Together, the two perspectives create a *total* situation. Yet, as the chapter starts with an account of Columbus's tragic end, it closes with his moment of beginning. The beauty and innocence—the purity —of the first voyage are made all the more powerful when we see them in contrast to the later betrayal and suffering. Moreover, this reversal of chronology creates the impression that, as we move through the chapter, we are stripping away the superficial layers of Columbus's personality, until we arrive at his heroic core. In the final version Williams's treatment of Columbus has cosmic scope, tragic overtones, heroic grandeur— an exact image of that ambiguous moment of our national beginning.

V

The Fiction of a Doctor

Plot is like God: the less we formulate it the closer
we are to the truth.
Selected Letters

The 1930's were in several respects a frustrating period for
Williams. At the start of the decade, now almost fifty, he had
more years of creative activity behind than ahead of him. He
could look back to the achievement of *Spring and All* and *In
the American Grain*, the *Dial* award for poetry in 1927, the
recognition of such contemporaries as Ezra Pound, Marianne
Moore, Wallace Stevens, and Kenneth Burke.[1] But Williams's
impact on the literary scene was negligible. His books did not
sell; they were not widely reviewed; he had never even been
able to establish a steady relationship with any publisher. To
make matters worse, Williams was an economic victim of the
Depression. He had planned to save enough money so that he
could retire from medicine at about fifty, but he invested his
savings and lost a great deal in the stock market crash. The
result was that at the same time he felt more and more alienated from the literary scene, he was more and more impatient
with the interruptions created by his medical practice.

Moreover, in the 1930's he produced only two rather slim
volumes of verse, *An Early Martyr* (1935) and *Adam and Eve
and the City* (1936), while he twice collected his poems in
Collected Poems, 1921–31 (1934) and *Complete Collected
Poems* (1938). Although both collections contained new

poems, and several fine individual pieces were written during
the period, the output was remarkably slender for a poet otherwise so prolific. As Thomas Whitaker points out, "Williams'
fifties were for him a time of poetic uncertainty and often of
dearth." [2] In fact, thwarted as a poet, Williams turned to prose
fiction. He had already tried a few short stories and the ironic
Great American Novel in the early 1920's, and he had written
an autobiographical novel, *A Voyage to Pagany* (1928), about
his travels in Europe. But in the next decade the bulk of his
writing was in prose: two collections of short stories, *The
Knife of the Times* (1932) and *Life Along the Passaic* (1938),
a short novel in *A Novelette and Other Prose* (1932) and two
full-length novels, *White Mule* (1937) and *In the Money*
(1940). As he wrote to Kay Boyle in 1932, "I have been working with prose, since I didn't know what to do with poetry.
Perhaps I have been in error. Maybe I should be slaving at
verse. But I don't think so. Prose can be a laboratory for met-
rics. It is lower in the literary scale. But it can throw up jew-
els which may be cleaned and grouped" (*SL*, p. 130). This descent on the literary scale had more than just metrical
consequences; it allowed Williams to deal with a kind of ordinary social and human reality missing from the intense, experimental work of the 1920's. In particular, he could explore the
material gathered in his daily experiences as a doctor. His defeat as a poet forced Williams to open a new world for his art;
his failure was liberating. And the discoveries he made give his
prose fiction a distinction in its own right.

Modern writers have acutely felt the falsity of all received
forms, the need to break them apart before filling them with
their own sense of reality. One tendency, evident in the novel
from André Gide to John Barth, has been to make this self-
conscious struggle with literary form into the fictional subject
itself. Williams appears to have been one of the first twentieth-
century writers to try this, in his ironically titled *The Great
American Novel* (1923), a novelette apparently written just
before *Spring and All* and the early chapters of *In the American Grain*. *The Great American Novel* is in no sense a finished

work; it keeps turning back on itself and beginning all over again. We are placed not in a fictional world, but in the mind of a writer as he struggles—against the dead weight of language and form—to get a novel going. At the surface we find none of the familiar properties of prose fiction: no narrative progression, no development of character, no fixed boundaries of time and space. Instead we get something like the raw materials of fiction: letters, advertisements, parodies, historical episodes, critical manifestoes, brief contemporary sketches, dialogues about the book we are reading—all coming to the reader in a swift, disjointed fashion that makes the book a zany parody of the novel form. At the beginning of his career in fiction Williams puts us at the edge—where an old form is disintegrating and new life is breaking through.

In *The Sense of an Ending* Frank Kermode remarks that "the history of the novel is the history of forms rejected or modified, by parody, manifesto, neglect, as absurd." [3] Immediately Williams announces his own aim to "progress from the mere form to the substance" (p. 10), to revitalize the novel with the shock of actuality. And Williams, who held only the moment to be real and who conceived of character as unconscious force, found plenty in the established formulas that was absurd. All of the assumptions behind his rejection of narration in *In the American Grain* apply here as well. "What is time but an impertinence?" he demands (p. 65)—and if time is an impertinence, so is plot. For to construct a plot is to abstract from the moment, losing its uniqueness and density, and shape an action that is finished, contained—with deadening effect upon character. Almost inevitably, plot moves upward toward a moment of high crisis—a scheme that establishes a hierarchy of moments that is alien to the kind of consciousness Williams is trying to create. In short, a plotted novel will release no mysteries of character, show little tolerance for the contingent, smooth over the jagged edges of raw experience and thus fail to involve the reader very deeply; he will not be drawn down and in. When Williams turns specifically to the American novel, he finds a "fixed form," "pure English" (p. 24), as dissociated from its locality as it is from the moment. *The Great American Novel* begins: "If there is progress then there is a novel. Without progress there is nothing. Everything exists from the beginning" (p. 9). All literary means are archaic, making it impossible to start the progression that would constitute a conventional novel. Like novelistic structure, language is fixed in the past: "There cannot be a novel. There can only be pyramids, pyramids of words, tombs . . . It runs backward. Words are the reverse motion. Words are the flesh of yesterday" (p. 11). Reality slips away from the writer in the very act of his grasping it; he cannot build a progression, a novel. But, as in "To Have Done Nothing," this failure does not leave the writer in a void; it leaves him in a creative confusion in which everything exists; it is the beginning.

Williams's account of the state of the American novel in the early 1920's is obviously oversimplified. It should be understood as part of his own creative activity—as a negative gesture he needs to make before he can unloose his own energies. As always, Williams needs to empty the field—just as he needs to empty his mind—before he can begin his projects. And as Kermode's remark suggests, Williams's attempt to clear fiction of all artifice is unusual only in its intensity. At the same time, Williams's view of the novel grows out of the analysis of American culture we have seen him develop in *In the American Grain. The Great American Novel* is by no means just a *literary* parody; it relates artistic problems to broader social and human concerns. In the seventh chapter Williams begins to bring in such historical figures as Columbus, Brigham Young, Aaron Burr, Red Eric, De Soto; these men, he says, give us an image of the "country with the element of time subtracted" (p. 65). Their adventures, however, are juxtaposed with contemporary episodes that document our increasing abstraction from origins: "*Nuevo Mundo,* shouted the sailors. But their cry was by now almost extinct" (p. 44). Literary forms have gone stale because the entire culture has cut itself off from the life-giving power of immediacy; in our progressive civilization we are neither in the moment nor on the ground.

Is it "too late to be Eric?" the author asks himself (p. 33). Is it possible to evolve a fictional form in which the element of time has been subtracted, one that will let through the substantial reality of the New World? Much of *The Great American Novel* is a dialogue—sometimes the author with himself, sometimes with others—on exactly these questions. Williams resolves the dilemma by giving up the aspiration for a neat progression, for a Great American Novel—and by identifying his own role as beginner. "To hell with art. To hell with literature," he declares at the end of chapter three (p. 20), and he means precisely what he says: he will "smash" the ideal of perfect beauty, forget about public recognition and "go down to hell" (p. 21). As in *Kora*, he will enter the formless moment. While some will deride this as "waste of energy," "I am far under them. I am less, far less if you will. I am a beginner. I am an American. A United Stateser" (p. 26). He is moving into a lower position, on the ground, where he releases a comic energy. The book's humor is one thing that almost all its critics have missed:

> I'm new, said she, I don't think you'll find my card here. You're new; how interesting. Can you read the letters on that chart? Open your mouth. Breathe. Do you have headaches? No. Ah, yes, you are new. I'm new said the oval moon at the bottom of the mist funnel, brightening and paling. I don't think you'll find my card there. Open your mouth—Breathe—A crater big enough to hold the land from New York to Philadelphia. New! I'm new, said the quartz crystal on the parlor table—like glass—Mr. Tiffany bought a cart load of them. Like water or white rock candy—I'm new, said the mist rising from the duck pond, rising, curling, turning under the moon—Unknown grasses asleep in the level mists, pieces of the fog. Last night it was an ocean. Tonight trees. Already it is yesterday. Turned into the wrong street seeking to pass the power house from which the hum,—sprang. Electricity has been discovered for ever. I'm new, says the great dynamo. I am progress. I make a word. Listen! UMMMMMMMMMMMM—
> UMMMMMMMMMMMM—Turned into the wrong street at three A.M. lost in the fog, listening, searching—Waaaa! said the baby. I'm new. A boy! A what? Boy. Shit, said the father

of two other sons. Listen here. This is no place to talk that
way. What a word to use. I'm new, said the sudden word.
(p. 13)

To the stuffy realism of the well-made novel Williams responds with the mockery and disarray of a kind of Dada
novel. To a prefabricated form that he finds empty and rigid,
he answers with a comic flamboyance. "America," he quotes
Vachel Lindsay, "needs the flamboyant to save her soul" (p.
51). "Flamboyance expresses faith in [creative] energy—it is a
shout of delight, a declaration of richness. It is at least the beginning of art" (p. 52). His own faith in creative energy is evident in the broken fluidity of his work, as the author records
the self-conscious twistings of his own consciousness. Williams
had clearly been reading the chapters of *Ulysses* appearing in
the *Little Review*—and Joyce helped Williams to push on from
his own stream of consciousness experiments in *Kora*. Voice,
level of intensity, mode of organization—all shift rapidly and
radically; so do time and place. Surrealistic figures abound,
often premised on a kind of animism. "Suddenly the pleiades
could be heard talking together in Phoenician" (p. 39); Williams carries on a dialogue with some white goldenrod (p. 10);
a car falls in love with a gasoline truck (pp. 22–23); a speeding auto yearns "to be a woman" (p. 41). The rigidities of ordinary perception yield and we enter a fluid primitive world;
delivered from social and literary aspiration, we laugh—with
relief.

As the novel embodies fluidity, it mocks rigidity. Whenever
the author feels he has achieved a triumph, his mood is quickly
broken down. Early on, believing he has reached "the end"
and that he has "progressed leaving the others far behind me,"
he reads the finished book to his wife:

> I have come to tell you that the book is finished.
> I have added a new chapter to the art of writing. I feel sin-
> cerely that all they say of me is true, that I am truly a great
> man and a great poet.
> What did you say dear, I have been asleep? (p. 17)

Williams frequently turns around on himself like this, showing
that the forces he's trying to negate are inside him too. But in
the state of consciousness Williams is moving toward there are
no ends, no moments of personal triumph, no progress. There
is only the arduous struggle to stay down, in the moment: everything exists from the beginning. Progress has a social as
well as a literary sense and the myth of progress, which was
supposed to provide the matter for The Great American
Novel, stimulates a desire for ascendency that is dealt with
ironically too. "Progress is dam foolishness.—It is a game"—"a
thieves' game" (p. 16). We are always speaking of evolution,
Williams notes; but who, he asks, "will write the natural history of involution?" (p. 67). His own involuted procedure
opens the way. With mock Horatio Alger stories (p. 72) and
several ironic juxtapositions of early voyages of discovery with
contemporary westward journeys, Williams redirects our attention from outward progress to inner substance. For when we
shift to an inner perspective, social progress turns out to be—
nothing. Where Williams does find signs of life in this country
is among children, Indians, mountaineers, people outside the
historical advance of American society. Similarly, when he
says that "words progress into the ground" (p. 9) or speaks of
progressing from "the mere form to the substance" (p. 10), he
is redefining progress as return, as an involution. By parody,
irony, manifesto, The Great American Novel aims to purge
certain literary forms and social myths. It takes us back to the
beginning, creating a fictional form and thus a mode of consciousness from which the element of time has been subtracted.

But The Great American Novel not only dissolves standard structures, it develops new ways of structuring. A look at
the thirteenth chapter will give us a sense of the kind of order
Williams has evolved. The chapter is composed of several
blocks, most of them a paragraph or two long, each developing a single incident. It begins with an unidentified speaker
who laments that "a most well built girl, so discrete, so
comely, so able a thing in appearance, should be so stupid";
then we move to seven boys who are "planning dire tortures

for any that should seduce or touch in any way their sisters";
to a declaration that the "real empire builders" of the colonial
period were not the "statesmen, the men of wealth, the great
planters but the unknown pioneers"; to an account of the
Mesa Verde cliff dwellers; the marriage of Abe Lincoln to "a
cultured and talented belle"; to a man who, although frightened, jumps twelve feet from a rock into the water. These dis-
parate fragments are not joined either by discursive comment
or by narrative means; they are simply juxtaposed. But as in
the *Spring and All* poems, a hidden associational logic gradually appears. The refined voice of the first part, the seven
boys, the pioneers who "fought single-handed and at once
both the primeval wilderness and the lurking savage," and Lincoln are all related by their preference for culture or virtue
over raw nature. In opposition to them are the Mesa Verde Indians, who "formed a partnership with nature." A tension of
opposites develops—what Williams was to identify in *In the
American Grain* as the tension in the American psyche—from
which we are momentarily relieved by the diver, a figure
reminiscent of the young poet in "The Wanderer." After this
man overcomes his initial timidity and leaps into the water, his
mind goes "blank," then fills with a series of memories that
ends with a similar moment when "he had dared to be happy"
and "had let his spirit go." Ordinary consciousness is shattered,
imaginative force is released; and this is exactly what happens
to the mind of the reader. As in the poems, the reader is pre-
vented from advancing in a straight line; he is forced continually to re-turn and discover the relation of the new part to
those that have preceded it; and the parts exist as equals in a
side-by-side relation, rather than in a linear sequence. All of
this goes to create a solid, three-dimensional work, in which
fiction, like the verse, has been made a "field of action."

Considered in its own right, *The Great American Novel* has
a speed, intensity, and exuberance that carry it along in spite
of its obscurities. Like *Kora in Hell* and *Spring and All*, this
book seems generated by a force that comes from deep within
the author, embattled, at the very edge of chaos, as he records

the jagged processes of his thoughts. R. P. Blackmur, not exactly an ardent admirer of Williams, paid *The Great American Novel* the tribute of including it in his *Six American Short Novels;* [4] and the book surely deserves to be read more than it has. Moreover, its quest for a new form and language, its tight, involuted structure, incorporation of historical material and the frequent comic deflation of the hero-writer make the book one of the major sources for *Paterson*. From the point of view of Williams's development as a prose writer, however, it was a beginning in only a limited sense. He did return to this work-about-itself technique in "January: A Novelette" (1932); but his mature fiction, operating at a much lower level of intensity, tends to be more literal, objective, and humane.

Williams's first full-length novel, *A Voyage to Pagany* (1928), was hardly a surer step forward. Less engaging in itself, it is even more literary and subjective than its predecessor. The playfulness about literary form and social myth disappears, to be replaced by an intense and often oppressive seriousness. Self-consciousness now grows out of the conflict between pagan Europe and moral America in the mind of Dev Evans, the doctor-writer hero. The trouble is that Europe comes across only as a mythical place in the mind of Evans; the tension is unreal. *A Voyage* "was told lyrically," Williams comments. "It turned out to be much more romantic than I had intended" (*IW*, p. 46). As another way of annihilating plot, Williams tries here to lyricize the novel, focusing mainly on Evans's rapidly shifting moods. But because the European scene never develops an actuality independent of his psyche, Evans's moods seem self-generated. The reader is never convinced that there is the slightest chance that this high-strung, defensive American will let himself go and enjoy Europe. What's more, this partiality creates an unrelievedly rapt, elevated tone in the prose; it is literally mono-tonous. Hence, in spite of all the emotional turbulence at its surface, the novel is finally static.

A Voyage to Pagany does have some moments of hard, clear prose, chiefly when Evans is studying medicine in Vienna.

And the book does mark for Williams an important advance in the art of organizing a novel—as a series of apparently self-contained episodes. Evans goes to Europe because, wearied by the stresses of his life as both doctor and poet, he decides to "let the whole works go" (p. 12). The book opens strikingly with a violent, cathartic storm at sea: "each day something of his immediate past the sea struck at and carried away—to his everlasting relief" (p. 12). At the end Evans accepts the dualities of his life and returns to America; but while in Europe he defines himself through several key relationships—to his expatriated friend, Jack, Lou, with whom he has an idyllic affair, the monumental beauty of Rome, Grace Black, for whom he feels a deep attachment, and Bess, his sister. In each case he is drawn to a person or place which he finally finds it necessary to reject. Jack's fierce independence and abandon are qualities that one side of Evans yearns for—but they make him too ruthless and cold. Lou is a timid sophisticate; Evans's ardor melts that reserve, but only temporarily. By contrast these two characters reveal Evans as a mixture of timidity and independence. But after his failure with Lou he goes off to Rome, seeking "a hard denial of despair" (p. 151) in its classic beauty. He is now pulled toward "the stonelike reality of ancient excellence" rather than the "pulpy worthlessness of every day" (p. 157): "He drank as if the purity of the source could wash away all sins in fact—and he would come out clean, clean of the world: the bone-cracking, skin-muddying impacts of his life" (p. 140). His attraction to the city and what it represents culminates before a marble Venus:

> Coming alone into the narrow chamber where this solitary bit of marble stood, it seemed to him perfection, actually, which had survived the endless defamations of the world. Actually alive she seemed, that perfect girl, in quiet pose, pure white— her fringed robe hanging from a dolphin's sculptured flukes. He looked and looked at those perfections of the breasts, the torso, the thighs—forgetting the stone, seeing a woman—young and tranquil standing by the sea—and nothing of stone, just quietness and fulfillment. (pp. 157–58)

This is the clean, perfect, timeless beauty he cannot attain in his own splintered world, and the discovery elates him. But after returning from a short trip into the country, he finds himself "quite suddenly cured, sick of the city, of museums and that white disease which makes the gods stone" (p. 169). The white disease is despair of the immediate moment as the source of life, a despair from which the writer begins to revive as he turns from the art world of Rome to the study of medicine in Vienna.

While there, however, he has an affair with an embittered expatriate, Grace Black, passionately opposed to the way democracy thwarts individual distinction. Evans relaxes her, and she him; opposites merge, and he feels delivered from the torments of self-division. Thus, after they first sleep together,

> he seemed to be sinking back through imprisoning circles of dark light as through the center of a flower, back to some dimly remembered past, Indian games—mad escapades. Back, back to a lost grace—his own early instincts, perfect and beautiful. Scale after scale dropped from him—more than he had known it to happen under any previous condition in his life before. He never felt less voluptuous, but clarified through and through, not the mind, not the spirit—but the whole body —clear, clear, clear as if he were made of some fine material strong yet permeable to every sense—opening, loosening, letting in the light. (pp. 249–50)

Miss Black represents that "lost grace," "perfect and beautiful," to which the mud-covered, inhibited American aspires. All his defenses suddenly drop away; he returns to an original pagan innocence. But her grace is hard, aristocratic: "I am a rock . . . I am cold save when the sun is on me. But you are alive, a thing of the earth" (p. 278). Her refinement is finally irreconcilable with his "need for the vulgar": "Fineness, too much of it, narcotizes me" (p. 280). They part. The last episode before Evan's return to America grows out of his affection for his sister Bess, who urges him to quit his medical practice, live with her in Europe and devote himself single-mindedly to art. America is "profusion" (p. 316); Europe, concentration—the possibility of artistic perfection and finish. In the end Evans refuses her, partly because she wants to use him to gain relief from the frustrations of her own lonely life, but more deeply because he senses the sterility of a life given purely to art. The drugged, self-absorption of this way of life Williams emphasizes by having it offered through an incestuous relation. The clean, perfect, monumental beauty of Europe draws him, but by his return to America Evans indicates his desire for an art that may be crude and profuse, yet on the ground and open to "all humanity" (*IAG*, p. 188). The gods are not stone; they are hidden in the earth, or in the flesh. The tensions of Evans's life in America *are* creative.

The novel's major episodes have been assembled into something approximating a conventional journey narrative. In the wild storm at sea, we have a clear beginning, and in the return to America, a kind of ending: both actions have obvious psychological and symbolic equivalences. And the incidents in Rome seem to mark a turning point psychically as well as geographically. Yet the important point about this organization is its looseness: there is no tight structure of events; episodes count for more than narrative continuity. In fact, these episodes exist first of all in parallel relation to each other. In each case, Evans is drawn toward some image of perfect beauty, ecstatically accepts it, then turns around and extricates himself. As we have seen elsewhere in Williams, an hypnotic, romantic mood is built up—then undercut. The entire book—going out from and returning to America—turns on itself in the same way. It closes as Evans, thinking of himself as Red Eric and gazing intently toward the North American continent, exclaims: "So this is the beginning" (p. 338). Williams was probably trying here to reverse the sense of loss developed in the similar scene at the end of *The Great Gatsby;* he was certainly affirming that it is not too late to be a discoverer like Red Eric. In any event, the episodes do generate a kind of progression; but that development is loose, allowing the parts a discrete existence. Moreover, the book's ending, which is a beginning, is formally "open." That beginning involves a rejection of the

European past and an acceptance of the present moment, so
that while *The Great American Novel* embodies a timeless
consciousness, *A Voyage to Pagany* moves backward, through
a series of reversals, to the moment when the disintegration of
historical time begins. In this way Williams reconciles a more
conventional surface with his hostility toward linear sequence,
and some such reconciliation was necessary before more ordinary reality could enter his fiction. The breaking of narrative
into episodes, their parallel relation and the use of an open
ending were to become important techniques both in Williams's mature fiction and in *Paterson*.

Yet, *A Voyage to Pagany* itself offers no reality independent
of the consciousness of its hero, who is a thinly disguised version of its author. The other characters are, as Pound remarked, impossibly "dialectical"; and they are that because
they are merely vehicles through whom Evans carries on his
inner debates. People enter his life only as extensions of himself. So, too, with the European scene. The description of the
marble Venus Evans discovers in Rome creates no sense of
what the art work actually looked like, only of the observer's
impassioned response. Here is a typical example of his feverish
meditations:

> He wrote what? that Rome filled him to overflowing with
> riotous emotions seeking intelligent expression one above the
> other. What is reality? He was too conscious of the old; to-
> day slipped too much from him or was too near. Or being
> alone, he had penetrated too far the veil of dust the gods had
> thrown up about their secrets to protect them. Thus Rome
> escaping him, he half sees it as a burning presence under the
> veneer of to-day. Panting with desire to possess it, he feels it
> slipping away nevertheless and calls it, strives to call it by a
> name, strives to fasten it in his sight—real among its everyday
> disguises. (p. 146)

There was a literal basis for this book in Williams's own travels in Europe in 1924, but, as in this passage, fact is constantly
submerged in overblown prose; "riotous emotions"—a trite and
vague phrase—are created not by the actual city but by "ideas"

about Rome, and the character strikes us as naively romantic in his impassioned preoccupation with himself. In part, the problem derived from Williams's peculiar development as a prose writer. This was his first book after *In the American Grain*, and the animistic vision—the elemental "gods" frequently enter the novel as agents—and the elevated style of the earlier work are often evident here. These techniques are suitable for creating a primitive Age of Heroes, but when they are employed with a contemporary figure, particularly when they try to show him in relation to other characters, the result is bombast. The contrast with *In the American Grain* also reminds us that while in the historical work Williams kept shifting between inner and outer perspectives he here completely turns the work over to the main character. *In the American Grain* creates a series of dialogues; *A Voyage to Pagany* is a rapt soliloquy.

The change from *A Voyage to Pagany* to *The Knife of the Times* (1932) is dramatic: we go from a novel which treats a grand theme in a confessional mode to a series of stories that treat mundane people with reportorial objectivity. Williams's devotion to experience over ideas made him resist attempts to politicize art during the 'thirties; but the Depression clearly turned his sympathetic attention to the lower class inhabitants of his native locality. Moreover, the shift from the novel to the short story was natural enough for a writer who had made the episode the basic unit of his longer fiction. The story suited his new subjects—"the briefness of their chronicles, its brokenness and heterogenity—isolation, color. A novel was 'unthinkable' " (*SE*, p. 300)—and the shorter form was structurally liberating too: "One chief advantage as against a novel—which is its nearest cousin—is that you do not have to bear in mind the complex structural paraphernalia of a novel in writing a short story and so may dwell on the manner, the writing. On the process itself. A single stroke, uncomplicated but complete. Not like a chapter or a paragraph" (*SE*, pp. 304–5). The style is no longer dense, reflexive, as in the poetry and fiction of the 1920's; instead, we get a spare, swift-moving colloquial language that has been purged of all stylistic pyrotechnics. This simplicity of manner opens Williams's fiction to the lives of the people in his locality, without the distortions any elegancies of form might impose. In fact, so casual in tone, so open to the contingent, are these stories that they strike many readers as mildly interesting vignettes of small-town life, but no more. Some of the stories in *The Knife of the Times* are slight; others depend too much on a superficial kind of shock for their effect. But before making any final estimate, we need to look at them from within the concerns of Williams's new project for fiction—to deal objectively with real characters moving in a modern locality.

One of the most memorable is the title story. Ethel and Maura, "intimates as children," separate after marriage but maintain a correspondence. Gradually, Ethel's letters become more intimate, expressing at first disappointment with her marriage and children, then openly avowing passion for Maura. At last, after twenty years, the two meet in New York City and there, in a pay toilet, Ethel presses herself on her friend, who submits. "What shall I do? thought Maura afterward on her way home, on the train alone. Ethel had begged her to visit her, to go to her, to spend a week at least with her, to sleep with her. Why not?" All this happens in three and a half pages. It is useful here, as in many of these stories, to consider what Williams has avoided doing. He has not written the story from Ethel's point of view, dwelling on the pathos of her frustrated yearning. He has not expanded a moment of moral crisis with an anguished Maura forced to choose between duty and passion; her reactions afterward on the train are deliberately played down and devoid of any moral considerations. Nor has Williams filled in any personal or social context that might make Maura's passivity more intelligible. Events are narrated objectively, yet from the "inside" in the sense that assessment of them from any external point of view is undercut. There is no cleverly executed plot, no deep probing of character, no moral critique of the issues; and these exclusions are typical of the entire collection. The reader will justly ask, what's left?

The answer is the revelation of a lower, more mysterious, more profound motive—the repository of instinctive power which, Kora-like, is buried by the pressures of everyday reality. What draws Williams to Maura is her simple acceptance of passion: "Why not?" Acceptance of these instinctual drives is the beginning of all Williams's work; but whereas the irrational entered *The Great American Novel* because the author dared to follow the associational leaps of his own consciousness, it enters his fiction now as a motive operating in other people. By sticking to the surfaces of events and people, Williams yet arrives at a deeper psychology.

The psychology here is really the physio-psychology of the doctor, and while an attitude of natural acceptance generates all of Williams's work, it is in his fiction that the relation between that point of view and his medical training become most apparent. What Williams says of Old Doc Rivers is also true of himself: "things had an absolute value for him" (*FD*, p. 103). A doctor looks at things not with an eye to their social or moral value, but simply as natural facts; his perspective is clinical—neutral. In *The Knife of the Times*, emotions are conceived physiologically: "frightened, under stress, the heart beats faster, the blood is driven to the extremities of the nerves, floods the centers of action and a man feels in a flame" (*FD*, p. 102). Characters are often defined in terms of physical presence, as is one of the subjects in "The Colored Girls of Passenack—Old and New":

> Once I went to call on a patient in a nearby suburb. As the door opened to my ring a magnificent bronze figure stood before me. She said not a word but stood there till I told her who I was, then she let me in, turned her back and walked into the kitchen. But the force of her—something, her mental alertness coupled with her erectness, muscular power, youth, seriousness—her actuality—made me want to start a new race on the spot. I had never seen anything like it. (*FD*, p. 56)

The girl says nothing, does nothing significant; she is a mysterious figure through whom a profound physical force operates. In an early crude form, the passage illustrates one of the re›

markable effects Williams achieves in his fiction: his ability
through external description to create the sense of deep contact with a character. Of course, this passage also shows that
the doctor's point of view has a value system of its own,
which determines both the kinds of people Williams treats in
his fiction and the way he treats them.

To put it another way, Williams looks at man not as a rational creature who defines himself in relation to abstract law,
but as a biological creature stirred by certain eternal and unconquerable instinctual forces. Seldom does he give us a character in the act of arriving at a conscious moral choice; he is
concerned to reveal forces working beneath this level of consciousness. Sometimes he shows us characters in the process of
pursuing preconceived ends, but these people are viewed ironically. The suffragette in "The Buffalos" who would rather ex-
pound political doctrine than make love, Belle, the kept
woman in "Pink and Blue" whose whole life is a quest for respectability, and Stewie, the banjo-strumming playboy ("A
Descendant of Kings") whose whole life is a quest for dominion over women, are all characters whose fixed purposes make
them pitifully amusing. The positive characters in *The Knife
of the Times* are the least ambitious, the least respectable—the
poor, Negroes—whose alienation from genteel society liberates
an instinctual freedom; and this boldness often enables them to
achieve momentary relief from the lonely frustration of their
ordinary lives. In any case these characters have a stoic acceptance that engages the doctor's attention. When in "The Sail-
or's Son" Manuel is caught in a homosexual act by his em-
ployer, her moral outrage is contrasted with the indifference
of his fiancée: "The boy is lonesome up here, said the woman.
Why do you keep his friends away? I am engaged to marry
him, I don't care. Why should you worry?" The woman in
"Mind and Body" is mentally and physically afflicted, but she
maintains a clinical attitude toward herself and a dignified acceptance of her life: "I am compensating for my childhood
now, she continued. I do not believe in being repressed. I am
the only one of my family that lets go. If I tire you, you must

forgive me. When I have talked it out I feel better. I have to
spit it out on someone. I do not believe in being good, in holding back." At the same time, "I do not expect people to thank
me if I do what I please." The narrators of "An Old Time
Raid" and "Pink and Blue" have been chosen for their tolerance of the eccentric and, from one point of view, cruel figures whose tales they tell. So, too, with the doctor-narrator of
"Old Doc Rivers" and with Rivers himself: "Nervous, he accepted his life at its own terms and never let it beat him—to no
matter what extremity he was driven." The "Colored Girls of
Passenack" have no real ambition to better their circumstances:
"Why don't you go on the stage, Mable? I said to her. No, I
don't want to end up in a ditch with a knife in my back, was
her reply, and anyhow it's too much work." They just accept
whatever comes along and if this doesn't make them "happy,"
it at least makes them content with their austere lives in a way
the more agitated middle class characters are not.

> I'm sorry, Mrs. R., but I gotta go, replied the laundress. I just
> had a hunch that my husband ain't alone in bed the way I left
> him this morning.
>   So the woman went away—nothing could stop her—and in
> a couple of hours she returned. Well, said my friend, did your
> hunch work out the way you thought it would? Yes, just the
> way I thought, said the laundress. I knew he was lying to me.
> What happened? asked my friend. Oh, nothin' special. When
> I got there he was sitting on the edge of the bed with one of
> those girls down there I was tellin' you about. He said they
> weren't doing nothing but I know better.
>   And what did the girl do when you arrived? asked my
> friend.
>   She? She didn't do nothing, said the laundress. She just sat
> there. I told her to git on out of my house but she just laughed
> at me.
>   What? and is she still there?
>   Yes ma'am.

But Williams was not only a doctor with an intimate knowledge of man's timeless instincts; he was also a student of culture with a sharp sense of the ways these powers are stifled in

the contemporary social environment. While many of the stories seem merely anecdotal when read in isolation, together they do define a vision of life in twentieth-century America. There is in fact further reason to believe that Williams conceived of this book as a loosely unified collection along the lines of *The Dubliners* or *Winesburg, Ohio.* All but one of the stories deal with a locality just outside New York City. Moreover, the ordering of the tales is cumulative. The first four stories treat, briefly, with the problem of sexual repression on a very personal level; but gradually a social and historical context is established—until in "Old Doc Rivers" a very rich and complex sense of the tension between individual and society is given. The narrator of that story remarks,

> This flight to the woods or something like it, is a thing we most of us have yearned for at one time or another, particularly those of us who live in the big cities. As Rivers did. For in their jumble we have lost touch with ourselves, have become indeed not authentic persons, but fantastic shapes in some gigantic fever dream.

The vision is reminiscent of Eliot's "Unreal City" in "The Waste Land"; but whereas Eliot satirically attacks the Sweeneys and Mrs. Porters of the modern city, Williams regards them clinically—as victims of an historical process that has cut them off from their most authentic selves. In "A Descendant of Kings" Stewie is a tragicomic study of the fate of natural man in urban society: he becomes impotent. Some of the stories are less tough-minded than this one; they express a definite, if low-keyed nostalgia for the past. The new colored girls of Passenack are said to be less vital than the old. Dago, the crude, defiant, rollicking battler of "An Old Time Raid," is said to belong to those bygone days "when the U.S. was a republic"; and he is appropriately killed at the end by a speeding freight train. The social identity man has created for himself is at odds with his natural being; and

> with this pressure upon us, we eventually do what all herded things do; we begin to hurry to escape it, then we break into a trot, finally into a mad run (watches in our hands), having

no idea where we are going and no time to find out. (*FD*, p. 90)

It is becoming all the time more difficult to find "those, hearing of cities and seeing trains crawling right before their eyes night and day, who remain isolated—peculiarly childish. Hot and eccentric" (*FD*, p. 99). The background for all these stories is the pressure of social, historical reality on man's passionate nature; this is the knife of the times.

Williams recalls that the title story was told to him by one of his patients (*IW*, p. 50); many of the stories contain remarks such as "she told me afterward" that suggest a similar origin. While the individual pieces are parts of a larger, imaginary world, they are not literary inventions; they are simply tales the author has heard. In addition to establishing a sense of reality, the oral tale or anecdote has a quick, loose movement, a stress on events over psychology, that make it an ideal form for Williams. But its most important feature is that it defines the writer as an impersonal recorder. Hence, on the one hand, these stories come from a vantage point inside the community, one with a doctor's access to the private lives of its citizens. The absence of careful plotting, lack of authorial comment, playing down of dramatic crises and the casual, colloquial style show the author submitting to his materials. No lofty judgments or literary ambitions intrude. But while Williams stays close to his subjects, his attention to the surfaces of things makes his viewpoint literally external. The advantages of this strategy immediately become apparent when we compare Williams with Sherwood Anderson. In its concern with repressed sexuality in small-town America and in its attempt to flatten out the short story structure, *The Knife of the Times* resembles *Winesburg, Ohio*. But Anderson writes from a universal sympathy that puts him inside the psyches of his tortured characters, while retaining an aura of mystery about their inner lives by the vagueness of the feelings described and by the incantatory repetitions of his prose. So Anderson writes of Elizabeth Willard:

Always there was something she sought blindly, passionately, some hidden wonder in life. The tall beautiful girl with the swinging stride who had walked under the trees with men was forever putting out her hand into the darkness and trying to get hold of some other hand. In all the babble of words that fell from the lips of men with whom she adventured she was trying to find what would be for her the true word.[5]

Williams feels a similar tenderness for his characters, but in these stories he is very careful to avoid this kind of emotional blur by use of a flat, neutral voice. This is how Williams begins "A Visit to the Fair":

It was a picturesque old place on a back road at the bottom of a narrow valley. The roof was sound, though, so they could move in without great cost.

Bess took it fine. She brushed all her old life aside—all but her attachment to her children and friends—and buckled down to the job.

But Fred didn't improve and while the chicken business kept them from starving outright it did that and that was about all. They lived, they even got along pretty well, but they were on their uppers and what was going to happen next?

The language takes on the very no-nonsense toughness that Williams values in his characters. Some of this comes from Hemingway: "Bess took it fine"; but the slangy speech here is much less arty, stylized, much closer to the ground. The stance of impersonal recorder enables Williams to establish proximity with his characters and yet to keep the writing clean, spare, hard.

This stance appears to be adopted somewhat self-consciously: Williams often chooses "shocking" materials and then deliberately plays them down. But the real trouble with the neutrality of the narrator is that in the process of avoiding sentimentality, it eliminates almost all involvement with individual characters; they remain types. A point of view which regards behavior in a natural rather than a moral continuum can reveal all kinds of eccentricities; but Williams seldom gets beyond these to three-dimensional people. As her letters to Maura become more intimate,

> Ethel told about her children, how she had had one after the other—to divert her mind, to distract her thoughts from their constant brooding. Each child would raise her hopes of relief, each anticipated delivery brought only renewed disappointment.

The clinical tone here can report an emotion cleanly, without surrendering to it (as Anderson would have done), but it keeps the character mysterious simply by keeping her vague. Settings too are generalized: "It was a picturesque old place on a back road at the bottom of a narrow valley." In *The Knife of the Times* Williams refreshingly turned toward a reality outside his own psyche; he really began to penetrate the America he saw at the end of *A Voyage to Pagany*. But his representation of this matter was still fairly abstract, concerned more with the conflict between social and biological "forces" than with specific human qualities. No doubt the clinical tone of the stories came from an attempt to purge the heightened passion and murky subjectivity of *A Voyage* from his writing; but the result was curiously similar—a lack of distinct character or place.

Still, in "Old Doc Rivers" Williams gets beyond these limitations, to produce at least one story with an alert specificity and genuine profundity. In this case character is complicated: Rivers is a man with "complexities and contradictions" that the narrator must struggle to define. Dealing with his patients Rivers has a way that is tough, abrupt, unsqueamishly direct—the very opposite of the courteous bedside manner of the conventional physician.

> Keep those pants buttoned. Sit down. Grab onto these arms. And don't let go until I'm through or I'll slit you in half.
> Yeow! Jesus, Mary and Joseph! Whadje do to me, Doc?
> I think your throat's cut, Jerry. Here, drink this. Go lie down over there a minute. I didn't think you were so yellow.

But Rivers is capable of real cruelty. Fed up with work, he will take off for the woods unannounced, with his patients left to fend for themselves. Even worse, he's addicted to drugs, and this leads to the deaths of several patients. But while his manner is eccentric, he is extraordinarily able as a physician, with "an uncanny sense for diagnosis." "He was not nervous but cool and painstaking—so long as he had the drug in him. His principles were sound, nor was he exhibitionistic in any sense of the word." And if he could be "cruel and crude," he could be "sentimentally tender also," treating people "with the greatest gentleness and patience" and "charging them next to nothing for his services." Rivers has a side that is aloof, aristocratic, "a little disdainful"; at one point in his career he is often drawn to the manor of a wealthy Frenchman, with its "propriety and measure," "ease and retirement":

> To play cards, to laugh, talk and partake with the Frenchman of his imported wines and liquors was good. After a snowstorm, of a Sunday morning, to sit there at ease—out of reach of patients—in a tropical environment and talk, sip wines and enjoy a good cigar—that was something. It was a quaint situation, too, in that crude environment of those days, so altogether foreign, incongruous and delightfully aloof.

Yet it was just this "civility," his "sensitivity," that made him work so hard in the first place; "it was not money." "He had the right idea, he was for humanity." With a devotion reminiscent of the heroes of *In the American Grain*, he held nothing of himself back.

> He was one of the few that ever in these parts knew the meaning of all, to give himself completely. He never asked why, never gave a damn, never thought there was anything else. He was like that, things had an absolute value for him.

Rivers was cruel and kind, aloof and devoted—a series of radical contradictions.

But the doctor is more than just a town "character"; Williams draws on his own study of the American past to amplify this figure, giving him archetypal significance. The story be-

gins, "Horses. These definitely should be taken into consideration in estimating Rivers's position, along with the bad roads,
the difficult means of communication of those times." The
speaker, a doctor who worked with Rivers as a young man, is
not drawing a character sketch; he is trying to assess the man's
social and historical "position." The entire study is framed historically: Rivers begins riding in a carriage, greeting patients
familiarly and he ends being driven silently about in a new car.
In fact, Rivers, whose career coincides with the shift in America from a rural to urban society, is a victim of history, a man
with the voluptuous energy of a Boone, condemned to the
"mad rush" of a small-town doctor's routine. At times he is
drawn back to the frontier—"He wanted to plunge into something bigger than himself. Primitive, physically sapping. Maine
gave it"—or to the pioneer type woman, "hot and eccentric,"
he finds living in an "abandoned corner of the town." But Rivers is a victim of "that awful fever of overwork that we feel
especially in the United States"; like Doctor Evans in *A Voyage to Pagany* he cannot simply let himself go to sensual release. Rivers thus acts out the basic American conflict between
sensuality and work, body and will; he is a tragic archetype.

Rivers is a distinct character; he is a significant figure—and
Williams draws brilliantly on all his technical resources to recreate him fully. The conception of the gifted physician who
turns to drugs could have led to moralistic treatment or, with a
point of view identified with the tormented doctor, to sentimental pity. Williams stresses the determining causes that
"made him, though able, the victim of the very things he
served best"; but by externalizing the point of view he tough-
ens the emotional effect of the story and keeps his complex
main character mysterious. Specifically, he turns "Old Doc
Rivers" over to a younger doctor who, with scientific detachment, tolerance, and thoroughness, examines documents, gath-
ers anecdotes, but hesitates to make conclusions. Moreover, as
the opening paragraph makes clear, we are not confronted
with a narrative, but with a speaker who is in the *process* of
getting up a case study. Instead of a finished product embody-

ing certain conclusions, we get *all* the evidence, a total picture
of Rivers. Plot, with its hierarchy of events, disappears; fictional form is flattened out, each of its parts having an absolute
value in delineating Rivers. Placing the action inside the immediate consciousness of his speaker and organizing it in a series
of parallel "blocks" looks back to *The Great American Novel;*
but the more limited subject here makes for greater precision
and impact. Most of the parts of "Old Doc Rivers" are anecdotes; but whereas earlier in *The Knife of the Times* the anecdote is the story, now a great number of them are accumulated
to create a complex reality. For these anecdotes, remembered
by people who knew Rivers, establish a multiplicity of
perspectives on him. No single point of view, from which the
contradictions of Rivers might be resolved, is allowed to dominate; we are forced, by the form, to accept him in his *total*
complexity.

Having brought the mode of *The Knife of the Times* to a
kind of perfection in "Old Doc Rivers," Williams characteristically discarded it to explore something new. In the best of
the stories collected in *Life Along the Passaic* (1938), the doctor is no longer an impersonal recorder of town gossip; he is
the narrator *and* central character, deeply involved with the
people whose lives he touches. Five of these pieces originally
appeared in *Blast: A Magazine of Proletarian Short Stories;* but
what he represents here is not the lower class character in the
act of contending with hostile circumstances, but the discovery of those *qualities* that enable him to survive. The real center of the stories is the ambivalent involvements of a doctor
with his proletarian patients; and what makes both patients and
doctor so convincing as characters is his honesty in reporting
all his feelings, revulsion *and* attraction. The clinical mode of
The Knife of the Times helped Williams to avoid sentimentality in dealing with his "low" characters; but he here moves on
to develop a form that is still clean, fast-moving, hard with detail, yet filled with vigorous feelings and vital characters. Several of these stories—"The Girl with a Pimply Face," "The
Use of Force," "A Night in June," "Jean Beicke," "A Face of

Stone"—represent Williams's best work in short fiction; "they rank," as Louis Martz says, "with the best of our time." [6]

What Williams manages to do in "Jean Beicke," "the best short story I ever wrote" (*FD*, p. xviii), is to take a subject loaded with potential sentimentality—a sick, deformed, unwanted child—and handle it in a way that is restrained, realistic and tender. He does this by the adroit use of shifting tones of voice in the narrator, a doctor in a children's ward during the Depression. A sentimental regard for children like Jean Beicke is included through the attitude of the nurses who work in the ward:

> You ought to see those nurses work. You'd think it was the brat of their best friend. They handle those kids as if they were worth a million dollars. Not that some nurses aren't better than others but in general they break their hearts over those kids, many times, when I, for one, wish they'd never get well.

The worth of these children is the question that the story keeps returning to, viewing it from several perspectives. Externally, the narrator adopts a social point of view and dismisses them as useless.

> I often kid the girls. Why not? I look at some miserable specimens they've dolled up for me when I make the rounds in the morning and I tell them: Give it an enema, maybe it will get well and grow up into a cheap prostitute or something. The country needs you, brat.

No idealist, the narrator has a fatalistic acceptance of crass actions; he feels no moral outrage against the parents who abandon their children or against the doctors who often exploit the parents. "We couldn't get it straight. We never try. What the hell? We take 'em and try to make something out of them." But Jean Beicke, by her straight look, evident intelligence, and the tenacity of her fight to live, awakens this doctor's admiration and sympathy. When she finally dies, he says,

> Somehow or other, I hated to see that kid go. Everybody felt rotten. She was such a scrawny, misshapen, worthless piece of

> humanity that I had said many times that somebody ought to
> chuck her in the garbage chute—but after a month of watch-
> ing her suck up her milk and thrive on it—and to see those
> alert blue eyes in that face—well, it wasn't pleasant.

His clinical detachment, too, can make the speaker appear cal-
lous. He answers some highly intimate revelations from Jean's
aunt—who also believes "It's better off dead—never was any
good anyway"—with a request for an autopsy, and he can regard Jean's physical deformities with a scientist's amusement
at the peculiar:

> But when the nurse took the blanket away, her legs kept on
> going for a good eight inches longer. I couldn't get used to
> it. I covered her up and asked two of the men to guess how
> long she was. Both guessed at least half a foot too short.

It is precisely this unillusioned toughness that gives such real
force to his understated admissions of feeling: "Well, it wasn't
pleasant." While the nurse refuses to aid at the autopsy, he
does go and views the operation with a technician's attention
to detail.

> The first evidence of the real trouble—for there had been
> no gross evidence of meningitis—was when the pathologist
> took the brain in his hand and made the long steady cut which
> opened up the left lateral ventricle. There was just a faint
> color of pus on the bulb of the choroid plexus there. Then
> the diagnosis cleared up quickly. The left lateral sinus was
> completely thrombosed and on going into the left temporal
> bone from the inside the mastoid process was all broken down.

The doctor's involvement does not exclude, but grows out of
an unsqueamish acceptance of all the facts about the child. As
a professional man and a member of the middle class, the narrator assesses Jean Beicke as a possibly useful citizen; but as a
doctor he is concerned with her only as a natural object, di-
vorced from all questions of "worth." For the physician people are biological things that have an absolute value: "we take
'em and try to make something out of them." The pull between social and physical perspectives that we find in all of

Williams's work is here internalized in the character of the narrator. But the important point, when we look at this story in
the context of what Williams had been doing in *The Knife of
the Times*, is that now the impersonality of medicine opens the
way to human sympathy. Clinicism leads into, deepens, and authenticates feeling.

Another thing that makes these stories so impressive is their
absolutely convincing air of reality. No affectations of structure or style creep in to suggest a self-consciously literary
treatment of the material; it comes to the reader fresh, clean,
direct—as if untouched. The key to Williams's success is in his
handling of a narrative voice which, casual and direct in its
slangy diction and clipped sentences, creates a natural line of
speech. A simple, lean, tenaciously physical, and (usually)
non-metaphorical style gives emotions a down-to-earth quality.
Beginnings and ends seem moments at which the writer has
merely cut into and out of the flow of experience, while the
middle contains no suave building of suspense, no high-pitched
moments of climax, but seems to report a rapid sequence of
events. Characters, not locked into a finished action, remain at
once more real and more mysterious. Yet if there is nothing
"of the rotten smell of the liar" (*FD*, p. 119) in these stories,
they have been put together with care and subtlety. "The Girl
with a Pimply Face" starts, "One of the local druggists sent in
the call: 50 Summer St., second floor, the door to the left" and
closes when the narrator asks the girl if she's gone back to
school: "Yeah, I had tuh." The casual beginning shows Williams opening the story to contingent detail that helps to create a sense of actuality; but the last sentence is more than just
an off-hand remark. It takes us to the core of the girl's character: the tough acceptance that Williams always values in his
characters. From the first the doctor-narrator of this story is
much more interested in this adolescent girl than in her baby
sister, the one he is sent out to examine.

> I opened the door and saw a lank haired girl of about fifteen
> standing chewing gum and eyeing me curiously from beside
> the kitchen table. The hair was coal black and one of her eye-

lids drooped a little as she spoke. Well, what do you want? she said. Boy, she was tough and no kidding but I fell for her immediately. There was that hard, straight thing about her that in itself gives an impression of excellence.

Most of the ensuing story consists of seemingly casual conversations that take place on the doctor's return visits and by means of which he finds out more about the girl and her family. But at two crucial points perspectives are introduced from which the narrator's admiration of the girl appears foolish. His wife urges him to be more worried about collecting his bills. Another doctor reveals that the family is lying about their lack of money, that they spend what they have on liquor and that the girl is the neighborhood whore. But the narrator stubbornly refuses to adopt a moralistic outlook. When he himself first notices that the mother has been drinking—this is after he finds that the baby has a bad heart: "she was no good, never would be"—he turns first to her husband,

> looking a good bit like the sun at noon day and as indifferent, then back to the woman and I felt deeply sorry for her.
>
> Then, not knowing why I said it nor of whom, precisely I was speaking, I felt myself choking inwardly with the words: Hell! God damn it. The sons of bitches. Why do these things have to be?

His outrage is directed against an indifferent world; and he compassionately regards the mother not as a reprobate but as a victim. The other physician says of the mother, "She's a liar," and the narrator responds, "Natural maternal instinct, I guess." Similarly, the girl is "that pimply faced little bitch" to his informant, while to the narrator she remains "a powerful little animal." In both cases a moralistic judgment is undercut by an acceptance of physical instinct; it is, once again, the clinical viewpoint, its moral neutrality, that enables the doctor to become humanly involved. And the story, with its careful juxtaposing of perspectives on the girl, is clearly about ways of looking at things, in particular a way that can discover in this pimply faced adolescent that hard, straight thing—that secret core of personality—that for its author means excellence.

Narrative voice, like perspective, keeps shifting to assure us that the speaker is not the kind of sentimentalist who finds a noble heart beating in every proletarian breast. In "The Girl with a Pimply Face" the doctor who says "I fell for her immediately" also says of her sister, "she was no good, never would be," just as the same man in "Jean Beicke" can say, "I, for one, wish they'd never get well" and "Everybody felt rotten." He's tough *and* sympathetic. His affirmations are not the product of a universal, mystical kind of sympathy; they are generated by a close, open-minded look at particulars. As in the poems and historical essays, we can find an underlying point of view, but one that seems to be renewed with each experience rather than imposed upon it. Moreover, acceptance does not exclude a recognition of the worst qualities in characters—the mother for whom the narrator feels sorry in "The Girl with a Pimply Face" is a hypocrite and a cheat—nor does it rule out a real antagonism between doctor and patient. Characters and narrator are complex, multi-dimensional. Contrary to the simple view of the matter propounded in the *Autobiography*, Williams felt severe conflicts about his medical practice. He managed to persuade himself in retrospect that he had always seen the practice as providing contact that refreshed him (*Auto*, p. 356); but his letters show him often furious with the time wasted on his patients, disgusted with their stupidity, and anxious to devote all his time to art. Like Old Doc Rivers, he had a side that was aloof, a little disdainful, impatient with fumbling humanity. His trip to Europe seems to have been made partly as an experiment with a life less harried and more concentrated: *A Voyage to Pagany* deals with the choice between a life devoted solely to art and one divided between art and medicine. Thus when Evans-Williams comes back to America, he is consciously choosing a life of conflict. He affirms the tender aspect of his nature that draws him to serve humanity, as well as the hard, aristocratic side that leads him to seek distinction in art. The contradictions of Rivers's life were the contradictions of Williams's. The *Autobiography* passes these over; but the short stories explore them with depth and honesty.

While the *Autobiography* beamily theorizes about "medicine and poetry," the stories document the often harrowing life of a small-town doctor, his irregular hours, conniving patients, hysterical parents, reluctant children, the unspeakable filth and vulgarity of their surroundings—a life peculiarly suited to sap the energies of a high-strung, impatient, and sensitive man such as Williams. One instance of the way these tensions develop is recorded in "The Use of Force." In this story a simple task, checking a girl's throat for signs of diphtheria, turns into a fierce and humiliating contest between adult and child. The doctor begins smoothly enough: "I smiled in my best professional manner and asking for the child's first name I said, come on, Mathlida, open your mouth and let's take a look at your throat." But the girl, who, with her "magnificent blonde hair, in profusion," looks like "one of those picture children often reproduced in advertising leaflets and the photogravure sections of the Sunday papers," turns into a "savage brat," trying to claw the doctor, knocking his glasses off, snapping a tongue depressor in bits with her teeth and generally resisting every approach with an "insane fury." As she does so, the doctor, drawn into a battle of wills, becomes infuriated too:

> But the worst of it was that I too had got beyond reason. I could have torn the child apart in my own fury and enjoyed it. It was a pleasure to attack her. My face was burning with it.

The narrator tells himself that his motives for persisting are rational and disinterested: "The damned little brat must be protected against her own idiocy, one says to one's self at such times. Others must be protected against her. It is social necessity"; but he knows that the real sources of his behavior are physical: "But a blind fury, a feeling of adult shame, bred of a longing for muscular release are the operatives. One goes on to the end." Yet even as he conducts his "unreasoning assault" on her, the doctor admires the girl. He does so not because she is beautiful or sweet or lovable, but because she reveals a certain force of character. In the struggle her "contemptible" parents "grew more and more abject, crushed, exhausted while she surely rose to magnificent heights of insane fury of effort bred of her terror of me." "The Use of Force" demonstrates that Williams's admiration for his patients is not based on any idealization of them; it is here in conflict with an almost savage rage. With the tensions between the doctor and his patients at the center, these stories reveal all sides of both narrator and characters; these tensions, as Williams suggested at the end of *A Voyage to Pagany*, are creative.

In "A Face of Stone" Williams goes even further in his willingness to reveal his ugliest feelings about people, for his initial hostility here is less clearly provoked and more cruelly expressed. But the result, again, is the impression of authenticity, a sense that we know everything about both the doctor and his patients. "He was one of those fresh Jewish types you want to kill at first sight, the presuming poor whose looks change the minute cash is mentioned," the story begins. The man, "half smiling, half insolent" to the doctor's eye, enters the office with his wife and baby.

> She, on the other hand looked Italian, a goaty slant to her eyes, a face often seen among Italian immigrants. She had a small baby tight in her arms. She stood beside her smiling husband and looked at me with no expression at all on her pointed face, unless no expression is an expression. A face of stone. It was an animal distrust, not shyness. She wasn't shy but seemed as if sensing danger, as though she were on her guard against it. She looked dirty. So did he. Her hands were definitely grimy, with black nails. And she smelled, that usual smell of sweat and dirt you find among any people who habitually do not wash or bathe.

The woman's persistent distrust is not viewed with any sympathy but merely as an inconvenience for the busy doctor in dealing with her baby, which he is asked to examine. This impatience with maternal protectiveness, the disdain for those who habitually do not wash or bathe, the open anti-Semitism, and the quick hostility toward the "insolent" poor man who connives to get something for nothing, all suggest the hard-headed ethic of a middle-class businessman. His attitude toward the two is certainly more moral than clinical: "Just dumb oxen. Why the hell do they let them into the country. Half idiots at best. Look at them." Throughout their visit the doctor's manner with them is cruelly abrupt.

> Well, put it up there on the table and take its clothes off then. Why didn't you come earlier instead of waiting here till the end of the hour. I got to live too.
> The man turned to his wife. Gimme the baby, he said.
> No. She wouldn't. Her face just took an even stupider expression of obstinacy but she clung to the child.
> Come on, come on, I said. I can't wait here all day.

His disregard for the woman's feelings makes him downright brutal:

> As I approached them the infant took one look at me and let out a wild scream. In alarm the mother clutched it to her breast and started for the door.
> I burst out laughing. The husband got red in the face but forced a smile.

Subsequently the doctor refuses to make a house call for them because of the inconvenient time (nine o'clock on a Sunday evening) and the icy roads. On their second visit to his office the doctor is similarly rude—"I want you should examine him all over, said the mother. You would, I said. Do you know what time it is?"—and when, as he's washing up afterwards, he is asked to look at the mother too, he snaps at the man: "What the hell do you think I am anyhow. You got a hell of a nerve. Don't you know. . . ." But as soon as the woman becomes his patient, his attitude toward her begins to change. He can no longer be so squeamish.

> Her lower legs were peculiarly bowed, really like Turkish simitars, flattened and somewhat rotated on themselves in an odd way that could not have come from anything but severe rickets rather late in childhood. The whole leg while not exactly weak was as ugly and misshapen as a useful leg well

could be in so young a woman. Near the knee was a large discolored area where in all probability a varicose vein had ruptured.

As he looks over the legs, "one of which I held on the palm of either hand," he learns that she grew up in Poland, that she lost all her family there during World War I. "No wonder she's built the way she is, considering what she must have been through in that invaded territory"; and no wonder she clings so obstinately to the child. Now the doctor gives her some pills to ease the pain.

> She swallows an Aspirin pill when I give it to her sometimes, said her husband, but she usually puts it in a spoonful of water first to dissolve it. His face reddened again and suddenly I understood his half shameful love for the woman and at the same time the extent of her reliance on him.
>   I was touched.

Williams at this point could have developed a moralistic tone by attributing an experience of guilt to his narrator; but guilt is a feeling notably absent from these stories that deal with a doctor who lives, simply, from moment to moment. Instead, we get a direct, open response to what *is* there: "I was touched." The tender language is unlike anything spoken by the aloof narrative voice in *The Knife of the Times;* yet by its simple, clipped, restrained manner of statement the feeling strikes us as entirely natural. Moreover, his original hostility toward these people verifies that his pity is not the sentimental outpouring of a man who has idealized the poor. If the man who speaks the first sentence of this story and who laughs at the mother's anxiety about her baby can be touched, so can we. By making the tension between himself and his patients the center of these stories Williams achieves an honest complexity—and he shows us a man like ourselves in the *act* of discovering qualities hidden in those at the lower levels of our society.

Such an act of discovery is the subject of one of Williams's most beautiful stories, "A Night in June." A pre-dawn delivery here works to strengthen and refresh rather than fatigue the doctor. As a young man he had lost a baby with this patient but had "won a friend and I found another—to admire, a sort of love for the woman." Angelina is a kind of Brueghel peasant—stolid, heavy, but full of life. She possesses "great simplicity of character—docility, patience, with a fine direct look in her grey eyes. And courageous. Devoted to her instincts and convictions and to me." The late-night atmosphere of the story is quiet, peaceful, almost serene—a tone not violated by the doctor's giving the woman an enema. Waiting for the delivery to begin, he twice falls asleep and awakens feeling "deliciously relaxed." At the beginning of the second nap, after administering a drug to speed her contractions, he begins to argue, half-asleep, "science" versus "humanity." "Our exaggerated ways will have to pull in their horns, I said. We've learned from one teacher and neglected another. Now that I'm older, I'm finding the older school." Accordingly, he stops using the drug and begins to help the woman himself:

> With my left hand steering the child's head, I used my ungloved right hand outside on her bare abdomen to press upon the fundus. The woman and I then got to work. Her two hands grabbed me at first a little timidly about the right wrist and forearm. Go ahead, I said. Pull hard. I welcomed the feel of her hands and the strong pull. It quieted me in the way the whole house had quieted me all night.
>
> This woman in her present condition would have seemed repulsive to me ten years ago—now, poor soul, I see her to be clean as a cow that calves. The flesh of my arm lay against the flesh of her knee gratefully. It was I who was being comforted and soothed.

The loving care with which Williams describes the birth, the precision with which he tells how this is done and the perfect timing established between the mother and the doctor all serve to convey his knowledge of clinical detail, his admiration for the cool, experienced mother, and his dependence on such people as a source of strength. In fact, the doctor's gesture here is one that informs all of Williams's work as a writer. Pressing down slowly, forcefully but tenderly, the artist-physician brings forth new life. Touching a woman he would once have thought repulsive, he participates in her struggle and is himself comforted and soothed; he is able to open his own consciousness, grasp something physically real, and thereby make himself new.

For if Williams often felt suspicion, anger or distrust, he was still *there*, as he said of Père Rasles, "with his beloved savages, drawing their sweet like honey, TOUCHING them every day" (*IAG*, p. 120). He had an immediate access to ordinary life that we can find in no other twentieth-century author. The tensions of this involvement were real; but so was the rough vitality he discovered in his patients, especially the young girls and women. These people, by the very want and austerity of their condition, are brought close to the sources of life; of necessity they live more inside their bodies—unlike the genteel inhabitants of the upper stratum of society. Their experiences do not make the poor beautiful, sensitive, or even likable—they are certainly not the kind of people we are accustomed to find in a work of art; but it is one of Williams's chief powers as a writer of fiction to be able to penetrate to the deeper levels of their being, without ever falsifying or disregarding the ugly surface. The girl with a pimply face, Mathilda in "The Use of Force," the woman with a face of stone, Angelina in "A Night in June," even the infant Jean Beicke—these silent, mysterious females share a natural force, a toughness that comes from their arduous struggles just to survive. They all possess an elemental consciousness, a capacity, like Red Eric's, to stand outside the progress of history. And it is the clinical perspective of the doctor—impersonal yet intimate—that has uncovered this buried world for modern fiction.

At the same time he was writing the best of the *Life Along the Passaic* stories, Williams returned to a novel he had started, then abandoned, just after *A Voyage to Pagany*. With the assurance that came from several years' experimentation with the short story, he took up *White Mule*, to be the first of three volumes dealing with the first five years in the life of his wife, Flossie.

It's a long story, "White Mule." It takes, or will take three volumes to tell it. In this volume the baby has her "pattern" set. In the next volume she learns how to dress herself, at about the age of three. In the last volume she gets as far as the first things she will remember later. That's all I want of her. While she is doing this, the family makes money and moves into the country. The third volume will end without the baby as a principle character. It has to. The social theories of yesterday finally become arthritic and Joe dies among their rigidities.[7]

Williams did not do the third volume until the early 1950's, by which time he had decided to abandon this plan and follow Flossie's life all the way up to her marriage with him. But in his original intention of ending at the point when conscious memory begins, Williams was typically attempting to uncover what is buried but crucial in the development of character. His method committed him to trace a kind of anarchic force from the moment of its birth down to the time when it is set within the pattern of a defined personality. On a personal level he was attempting to recover and celebrate the core of his wife's being—in this way to possess her more completely. More generally, early childhood offered him a dramatic image of unconscious force, mysterious and unpredictable, in conflict with the fixed purposes of the adult world. "The small prisoner," he writes, "has to be forced into the accidental mould of the life his or her parents find forced upon them in turn by their own more or less accidental economic and hereditary circumstances" (*IM*, p. 156). In the case of the young Flossie, that mold has been shaped by the aloof Puritanism of both her parents, Joe and Gurlie Stecher, and particularly by her mother's determined quest for wealth and respectability. Through these family relationships the trilogy was thus to explore the tension between natural and cultural forces that frequently informs Williams's work. The second and third volumes, *In the Money* (1940) and *The Build-up* (1952), Williams himself regarded as less than entirely successful (*IW*, pp. 67, 87). But *White Mule* (1938), combining a loving attention to domestic detail with a continuous awareness of archetypal significance, constitutes one of his major accomplishments in prose.

So painstakingly does the novel record mundane happenings, so swiftly and cleanly does it move, devoid of all conventional literary artifice, that many readers find it a pleasant but not very profound experience. Certainly the author never steps back from his material to develop its significance through explicit comment. But reportorial flatness is a risk that Williams deliberately runs, to fill his work with a fresh actuality. Structurally, the novel has been levelled out in several respects. *White Mule* begins dramatically with Flossie's delivery and the trilogy as a whole has an ending in her family's final reversals of fortune; but this loose framework still leaves a spacious middle, amplified chiefly by low-keyed incidents without any tight narrative continuity. The matter of the novel is intensely ordinary, the focus almost always domestic, with entire chapters given over to ear infections, a maid walking the baby in the park, the commonplace conversations of a Christmas or Easter dinner. If more sensational events do enter, they happen off-stage. During the strike at Joe's printing plant the narrator does not follow Joe, who is trying to break the strike, but stays with Gurlie as she worries at home. Melodrama of the sort that abounded in the proletarian novels of the 'thirties is avoided. Moreover, no attempt is made to marshall together the events of the novel into a well-articulated narrative; as in *A Voyage to Pagany*, plot has been broken into a series of discrete episodes. Often, a new character will enter, a dramatic incident take place, but neither will be developed in a conventional way. Joe's brother Oscar appears out of nowhere, provokes a great stir, seems about to become an important character, then disappears from the novel. The strike causes concern about Joe's safety for two suspenseful days, but suddenly the strike is over, with no indication of its outcome until a later passing reference in conversation. Similarly, Gurlie is constantly prodding Joe to make more money, while he derides the American way to wealth; but if the two are always sparring verbally with each other, their conflict never issues in a direct confrontation. There is in fact little sense of intimacy between the two and they work on each other like two force

fields, attracting or repelling, but never quite colliding or becoming reconciled. In particular episodes a tension will develop between them, but then will be dropped rather than
elaborated. Near the end of the book Joe is suddenly negotiat-
ing a loan to open his own printing business. Yet nowhere do
we get a scene in which Joe weighs consequences, assesses alternatives, comes to a decision. Such a scene is omitted because
the "decision" is not so much a conscious one as it is determined by external forces, and it is not any capacity for analysis but a reserved, silent acceptance of these forces that
Williams admires in Joe. Williams steers away from high-
pitched emotional scenes, even from the drama of introspection; and he refuses to subordinate some events to others in
building toward a dramatic climax. By staying raw and unfin-
ished, the novel sticks close to reality, which Williams defines
as a rapid succession of moments, each with an equal and absolute value.

Williams has thus embodied his commitment to the continuous present in novelistic form but now a form that, purged of
the pyrotechnics of *The Great American Novel*, can incorporate a recognizable human reality. For the kind of artless
chronicle Williams is writing is also the result of his refusal to
subordinate character to plot, and it is in the creation of Joe,
Gurlie, and Flossie that his novel achieves its true distinction.
The danger of sentimentality in dealing with characters whose
lives are so intimately related to his own is shown in *The
Build-up*, where Williams simply indulges himself in fond reminiscence. But success in *White Mule* comes from control of
the narrative voice, its reportorial tone. Presentation is clean,
objective, concentrated upon such externals as speech and gesture. One chapter begins:

> Oscar!
> Gott, Gurlie! You're getting good looking. Joe must be
> making money.
> Come in. Where in the world did you come from? What's
> happened to bring you here?
> Thanks. Chicago. Nothing. Give us a kiss.

He made to kiss her on the lips but she turned her cheek.
Go long wid you.
How are you anyway? he said then.
Fine. But what brings you here, insisted Gurlie.
My feet, old Gal. And the train, straight through the coun-
try. Where is everybody? Where's Lottie? And the baby!
Hey Lottie. (p. 73)

This rapid, clipped dialogue shows Williams's remarkable ear
for American speech—as well as his capacity to make the most
commonplace conversation expressive of character. Greeting
her brother-in-law after long absence, Gurlie is anything but
effusive. She shies away from physical intimacy and, worried
that Oscar may be moving in on them, insists on knowing why
he has come. Oscar, while respectful of his brother's compara-
tive success, is jolly, carefree, and open. His arrival, in fact, introduces a new force into the household that precipitates a
kind of subdued conflict; nothing earth-shattering happens but
the characters circle around each other in such a way that
their basic natures are sharply illuminated. As the chapter proceeds, we learn that Oscar, once a member of the Kaiser's Dra-
goon Guards, seduced his captain's wife and had to flee to
America. He has just quit his job in Chicago because "I got
tired of hefting their beef. Wanted a little air. Life. The big
city. You know" (p. 74). To Gurlie's sister Hilda all this
makes him appear "romantic" (p. 77) but Gurlie herself, tough
and moralistic with Oscar, calls him "a lazy good-for-nothing"
(p. 77). Oscar goes out for food and beer, a party begins and
even Gurlie, after some muttering, joins in the fun. But Joe,
when he comes home from work, never enters into the hilarity
of the others. The wandering, free spirit of Oscar provokes a
discussion of marriage, with Joe alluding to his wife's combat-
iveness and Gurlie answering: "If it wasn't for me you'd be in
the soup. I'm the one that stands behind you. I'm the one" (p.
84). There is a side of Gurlie that admires Oscar's daring, believes that "he knows how to live" (p. 85); she complains that
Joe lacks the "courage" to pursue those things they need to
enjoy life (p. 85) and taunts him with being "too serious" (p.

83). Through all this Joe soberly attempts to talk business with his brother, proposes a toast "Down with the unions" (p. 86) and urges Oscar to tear up his union card. The toast is motivated by a moral objection to Oscar and the unions, both of which Joe views as self-seeking and irresponsible; but Joe, never becoming either angry or festive, remains self-possessed, at once kindly and stern. Near the end of the chapter his reserve almost breaks down, but when Oscar proposes that they all go out to a show, Joe declines: "I've got to go to bed. I've got a big day ahead of me tomorrow" (p. 88). Again and again, it is Williams's achievement in *White Mule* to create an immaculate surface, swiftly recording domestic events in all their casualness, and yet to bring through fundamental qualities of character.

Still, the central tension of the novel is not that between Joe and Gurlie but between the infant Flossie and her parents; and this conflict is strikingly rendered in the book's first chapter, one of the tightest and most subtle pieces of writing in all of Williams's prose fiction. This is how *White Mule* begins:

> She entered, as Venus from the sea, dripping. The air enclosed her, she felt it all over her, touching, waking her. If Venus did not cry aloud after release from the pressures of that sea-womb, feeling the new and lighter flood springing in her chest, flinging out her arms—this one did. Screwing up her tiny smeared face, she let out three convulsive yells—and lay still.
> Stop that crying, said Mrs. D, you should be glad to get outa that hole.
> It's a girl. What? A girl. But I wanted a boy. Look again. It's a girl, Mam. No! Take it away. I don't want it. All this trouble for another girl.
> What is it? said Joe at the door. A little girl. That's too bad. Is it all right? Yes, a bit small though. That's all right then. Don't you think you'd better cover it up so it won't catch cold? Ah, you go on out of here now and let me manage, said Mrs. D. This appealed to him as proper so he went. Are you all right, Mama? Oh, leave me alone, what kind of a man are you? As he didn't exactly know what she meant he thought it better to close the door. So he did.

In prehistoric ooze it lay while Mrs. D wound the white
twine about its pale blue stem with kindly clumsy knuckles
and blunt fingers with black nails and with the wiped-off
scissors from the cord at her waist, cut it—while it was twist-
ing and flinging up its toes and fingers into the way—free.
(p. 1)

Williams is alluding to Botticelli's "The Birth of Venus," its
evocation of awakened sexuality and physical perfection:
Venus gracefully standing, lightly poised on one leg, her hands
covering her nakedness. The personified winds caress her from
one side, while the personified world welcomes the goddess
with a beautifully decorated cloak on the right. All is artifi-
cially perfect, with nature showering blossoms upon the deity
and the seas quietly lapping about her feet. Symmetry and
peace are found in Botticelli's painting, but Williams's Venus
enters a very different world.

The world Flossie enters is first of all a physical one. The air
which encloses the infant, "touching, waking her," is no per-
sonification but a physical fact. It is above all the *sensation* of
birth that engages the attention of Williams, the doctor—the
joyous release the infant obtains when she draws in her first
breath, her deliverance from "the *pressure* of that sea-womb."
Botticelli's maiden does not appear to be startled at her birth;
she seems passive, stoic—as if expecting life. But Williams's infant, "screwing up her tiny face," letting "out three convulsive
yells," accepts existence with a violent cry. Later on, to ac-
quaint the reader with the child, Williams has Mrs. D. carefully explore its body, making earthy comments on all her
features, anointing her as if in acknowledgment of her arrival
from another realm. This young Venus is smelly, crusted,
greasy, a scrawny, swollen and homely child: beautiful and
comically grotesque, she is both mythical and actual.

And her welcome defines a world that is anything but ideal,
artificial, perfect. The instant of birth is rendered in the author's voice, expressive of a consciousness alert both to physical reality and eternal recurrence. But his formal, reverential
tone is quickly interrupted by the tough, clinical speech of the

midwife, bringing the infant down to earth and into time: "Stop that crying, you should be glad to get outa that hole." And from there she is lowered into the mundane world of her complaining mother and her kindly but hardly overjoyed father. As soon as she has experienced her moment of pure freedom, Flossie is exposed to the determining pressures of the social environment. The first page of the novel, then, gives us a compressed image of its major characters and conflicts. But throughout the opening chapter the baby remains the center of attention. After her cord is cut, she accidentally pokes herself in the eye, wails, sleeps quietly, is washed and rubbed in oil, ludicrously dressed in crinkly new clothes, refuses several attempts to feed her, wails again, fouls a clean diaper. Though tiny, she has a rebellious strength, with her ability to foil adult purposes and with a "piercing voice so small yet so disturbing in its penetrating puniness, mastering its whole surroundings till it seemed to madden them" (p. 9). From the first the infant obstinately insists on her own way, a quality which makes the adults perceive her in different ways: a crookedly smiling little monkey to the father, a "rebellious spitting imp" to the mother (p. 8) and both a "yelling brat" (p. 9) and a "blessed little thing" (p. 10) to Mrs. D. Once again, a multiplicity of voices, tough and tender, allows Williams to achieve a complex view of his subject, here in the creation of his singular Venus.

VI

Paterson, A Pre-Epic

"a reply to Greek and Latin with the bare hands"
                                                    Paterson

His concern with the expanded moment drew Williams most often to such compact forms as the lyric poem and the short story. But the process of cutting experience down to "isolate flecks" was one that had cultural implications. *Spring and All* and *In the American Grain* are two works in which a mythopoeic intent is clear; *Paterson* is another. In fact, Williams had the project of a poem on the epic scale at the back of his mind almost from the time he started writing. The impulse "to find an image large enough to embody the whole knowable world about me" came quite "early," he says in the *Autobiography* (p. 391). In 1906, during his internship in New York City, he was working on "a monumental work, a four-book romantic poem" modeled on Keats's *Endymion* (*Auto*, p. 53). But he abandoned that grandiose project and a few years later the self-consciously anti-romantic "The Wanderer" "took its place, my first 'long' poem which in turn led to *Paterson*" (*Auto*, pp. 60–61). "The Wanderer" anticipates *Paterson* in several respects. But Williams came to hold the ancient notion that a poet, before making a total statement about his culture, had to undergo a prolonged period of preparation. And all of the experimentation with prose and verse that we have been tracing in the preceding chapters was designed to give him the range and control of language necessary "to embody the whole knowable world about me."

Williams spent some thirty years of living and writing in preparation for *Paterson,* the good part of another seven years in its composition, but reception of the poem never exactly realized his hopes for it. *Paterson* has been subjected to some stinging attacks, and while the poem has recently had some very able defenders, these still represent a minority of literary opinion.[1] Even among Williams's critics, *Paterson* is generally regarded as inferior to the poetry of his last period. From the first, looseness of organization has been the main critical issue. Typical of the kind of response a good many readers have to *Paterson* is Randall Jarrell's charge of "Organization of Irrelevance."

> Such organization is *ex post facto* organization: if something is somewhere, one can always find Some Good Reason for its being there, but if it had not been there would one reader have guessed where it should "really" have gone?[2]

Paterson does contain a good deal of accidental matter. But this is a value statement only for someone who adopts a rather extreme version of the doctrine of formal necessity. Jarrell's observation, if he had seen it as a neutral one and thus been freed to pursue it further, could have led him more deeply into the poem. Instead, we get an evaluation that only helps us to identify him. What we need now, much more than any "final" assessment, is to absorb the poem more carefully, to listen more attentively to its play of voices, to experience the poem in *its* terms, not *ours.* Admittedly, those terms are severe. *Paterson* lacks the kind of polish and continuity of surface that we find in the traditional epic; its reflexive structure makes it a work that, as Joseph Frank says of Joyce's *Ulysses,* cannot be read; it can only be reread.[3] Many readers will not want to make the extensive commitment the poem requires. That, of course, is their choice; but it is a choice that precludes them from making value statements about the poem. Again, what we need now is to open ourselves more fully to the poem.

In fact, the problems with the poem stem from its assumption of openness as the primary literary and human value. *Paterson* thus begins in self-conscious rejection of the very standards Jarrell sought to impose upon it. As Williams was starting work on his poem, he wrote a friend that he was "gradually maneuvering a mass of material I have been collecting for years into the Introduction (all there will be of it) to the impossible poem *Paterson*" (*SL*, p. 230). Williams's attempt to put the totality of his world into a single work pushed him toward the epic, the most sublime of all literary forms; yet, as he well knew, the serene tone, graceful continuity, and monumental beauty of the epic were impossible in his fragmented world. "Rigor of beauty is the quest," a voice announces at the start of the "Preface" (p. 11); but none of the poem's critics has observed that every time the aspiration for rigorous beauty comes into the poem it is dealt with ironically. At the very beginning, the poet undermines the finished elegance of the epic voice.

> Paterson lies in the valley under the Passaic Falls
> its spent waters forming the outline of his back. He
> lies on his right side, head near the thunder
> of the waters filling his dreams! Eternally asleep,
> his dreams walk about the city where he persists
> incognito. Butterflies settle on his stone ear.
> Immortal he neither moves nor rouses and is seldom
> seen, though he breathes and the subtleties of his
>   machinations
> drawing their substance from the noise of the pouring
>   river
> animate a thousand automatons. Who because they
> neither know their sources nor the sills of their
> disappointments walk outside their bodies aimlessly
>   for the most part,
> locked and forgot in their desires—unroused.   (p. 14)

As this passage shows, Williams could have written a polished, elegant poem about Paterson, but only by maintaining the kind of distance from his subject that this panoramic view of the

city requires. But just at this point a more familiar voice, blunt
and impatient, breaks in:

> —Say it, no ideas but in things—
> nothing but the blank faces of the houses
> and cylindrical trees
> bent, forked by preconception and accident—
> split, furrowed, creased, mottled, stained—
> secret—into the body of the light! (pp. 14–15)

Williams suddenly dissolves the detached perspective and
brings us down, inside the poem and inside the poet's mind, as
he writes the poem we are reading. *Paterson* is by no means a
finished work, its parts rolled up into a fixed order at several
removes from immediacy. The poem, instead, *is* the act of its
creation, recording (like *The Great American Novel*) the consciousness of its creator, whose dual fidelity to the *world* and
to the *poem* constantly forces him to turn back and start all
over again. *Paterson* is the beginning (all there can now be of
it) to the impossible poem *Paterson*.[4]

Like all of Williams's best work, *Paterson* keeps pulling its
reader—as its hero is pulled—in opposite directions. There is a
nostalgia for the beauties of given structures, but there is also
an earthward thrust, toward the flux of raw experience. Williams, again, takes an established literary genre, cuts away
much of the complicated formal apparatus that makes it feel
aloof and empty, and pushes it back toward the ground—where
it can be filled with actuality. All serious long poems since the
early nineteenth century—Wordsworth's *Prelude*, Whitman's
"Song of Myself," Eliot's "The Waste Land," Pound's *Cantos*,
Crane's *The Bridge*—have repudiated external action as an organizing method.[5] This is partly because any well-ordered sequence of events would put the poem at a level of experience
that seems unreal to these writers; they tend to be more concerned with "the growth of the poet's mind," and to view this
growth as a series of discrete moments (or episodes) rather
than as a narrative action. This we have already seen in Williams. But the inward turning itself derives from the absence of

any public mythology that would supply plot, hero, and argument for a cultural poem. The epic has been an impossible poem at least since the beginning of the last century. In the "Author's Note" to *Paterson*, Williams tells us that Book IV "will be reminiscent of episodes—all that any one man may achieve in a lifetime" (p. 9). Originally, his poem was divided into four books, each of these divided into three parts, and these in turn split into separate "blocks" of material, many of them quite self-contained.* Some of these sections were, in fact, published as separate poems. In *Paterson*, where lines of thought and feeling keep breaking down and the central character is forced to start over again, narrative has been shattered, dispersed into a series of "episodes."

In a talk given while he was still working on *Paterson*, Williams proposed that what the modern writer can achieve is a "profusion" and "accumulation" of fragmentary detail rather than the "distinction" of tight form.

> It is as though for the moment we should be profuse, we Americans; we need to build up a mass, a conglomerate maybe, containing few gems but bits of them—Brazilian brilliants— that shine of themselves, uncut as they are. (*SE*, pp. 284–85)

Disintegration of narrative deprives Williams's poem of a surface coherence that would make it more accessible to a reader, but it also permits him to open the poem in several important ways. He can shift tone rapidly and radically, he can space parts generously so that each can be weighed, experienced, for itself before being lifted into context, and he can include a profusion of detail, uncut bits of actuality. In a phrase from the "Preface," the annihilation of plot allows Williams to go "from mathematics to particulars" (p. 13).

As an avowedly primitive and experimental work, *Paterson* is a kind of pre-epic, a rough and profuse start from which some later summative genius may extract and polish: the poem

---

* Here, and throughout this chapter, I am thinking of *Paterson* as Books I–IV (1946–51). *Paterson V* (1958) can, I think, best be examined alongside the poetry of Williams's last period, which I deal with in Chapter VII.

is *"a reply to Greek and Latin with the bare hands"* (p. 10).
But *Paterson*—like the *Spring and All* poems—gets its power
from its proximity, not its surrender to chaos; it *is* a beginning.
If parts are split into discrete blocks of material, their presence,
side by side, in the poem generates a poetic field. Obviously,
the lack of explicit connections does not mean there are no
connections; it simply means that relations of parts are hidden,
rich, open, multiple. Like all of Williams's best poetry, *Paterson* has a thickness of texture, a multi-dimensional quality that
makes reading it a difficult but intense experience. What the
poem substitutes for linear plot is a cyclical structure, a buried
system of recurrences. When critics of the poem have dealt
with these motifs, it has usually been in order to arrive at the
poem's meaning. Such attempts to establish a thematic coherence in the poem are understandable enough, given its obscurities; but they necessarily make smooth and tame what is in fact
the reverse. Starting at the other end, Joel Conarroe has provided an excellent account of the range of style in *Paterson.*[6]
Yet, much more important, it seems to me, is to define how the
process of recurrence, how the montage of styles, effects our
experience of the poem—how, in short, the poem works. A
reader's movement through *Paterson*—again, like the hero's—is
often slow, torturous, hesitant: he is constantly required to go
back and relate what he has just read to all previous parts and
to revise his sense of the earlier sections in the light of what
has just been added. Not given a surface network of articulated connections, the reader is forced to suspend each block
of material in his mind until he gets to the end, when the entire poetic field has been defined. Hence, relations among parts
are fluid, and they must be uncovered by the imaginative activity of the reader. Argument has been dispersed into images,
myth buried in literal matter, like a seed. The reader is asked
to dig, and discover.

A good example of the way parts work in *Paterson* can be
found in a prose passage right near the start of Book I.

> In February 1857, David Hower, a poor shoemaker with a large
> family, out of work and money, collected a lot of mussels from

Notch Brook near the city of Paterson. He found in eating them many hard substances. At first he threw them away but at last submitted some of them to a jeweler who gave him twenty-five to thirty dollars for the lot. Later he found others. One pearl of fine lustre was sold to Tiffany for $900 and later to the Empress Eugenie for $2000 to be known thenceforth as the "Queen Pearl," the finest of its sort in the world today.

News of this sale created such excitement that search for the pearls was started throughout the country. The Unios (mussels) at Notch Brook and elsewhere were gathered by the millions and destroyed often with little or no result. A large round pearl, weighing 400 grains which would have been the finest pearl of modern times, was ruined by boiling open the shell. (p. 17)

An historical anecdote is given, the tone objective, factual. The account contains much—dates, proper names, statistics— that is purely accidental. These details do not reverberate on, or against, other details to generate metaphorical patterns; they are there simply because they are historical truth. We are assured that the poem does not just emanate from the poet's visionary imagination; it contains material, grounded in literal fact, that is entirely independent of his vision. As Ralph Nash says generally of the use of prose in *Paterson*, Williams tries to effect "a forceful marriage of his poem's world with that world of reality from which he is fearful of divorcing himself." [7] At the same time, however, critics have noted the frequency with which incidents involving the violation of nature recur throughout *Paterson*. The facts, by their recurrence in the poem, reveal an historical (and contemporary) pattern. The result is that this passage pulls in two directions simultaneously. As a self-contained unit, blocked off separately on the page, it moves toward the literal and historical, but its position as an item in an imaginative field nudges it, slightly, toward the mythical. Here, as always with the prose, the poem gives us raw material in the *process* of generating symbolic import; *Paterson*, again, gives us an act of creation, not its finished product.

Yet, these blocks of material appear in a local as well as in a total context. Most often, relation between adjoining parts will

be one of ironic counterpoint; the poem's larger pattern of antithesis between the acceptance and fear of physical experience
is realized in its smaller units. For examples, we can look at
Part I of Book I. While *Paterson* is a fragmented work, it begins with a vision of unity that is deeply romantic. The sleeping giant introduces the possibility of organic community
within the city, and shortly thereafter the poet invokes the
mountain ("female to the city"—p. 57), whose wild fecund
beauty could wake him from his dreams.

> And there, against him, stretches the low mountain.
> The Park's her head, carved, above the Falls, by the quiet
> river; Colored crystals the secret of those rocks;
> farms and ponds, laurel and the temperate wild cactus,
> yellow flowered . . facing him, his
> arm supporting her, by the *Valley of the Rocks,* asleep.
> Pearls at her ankles, her monstrous hair
> spangled with apple-blossoms is scattered about into
> the back country, waking their dreams—where the deer run
> and the wood-duck nests protecting his gallant plumage.
>
> (p. 17)

These two mythical creatures, lying face to face, are linked in
a lovers' embrace. Together, they signify, like the primitive
old chieftain with his nine wives arranged in a "descending
scale of freshness" (p. 22), a union of masculine direction with
feminine energy—an integration of mind and body. In social
terms, the giants represent a marriage of civilization with the
wilderness, the "bold association of wild and cultured life"
found in the Ramapos, as depicted in an early prose section (p.
21).

Between the two moves the Passaic River and its falls. At
the top of the Falls, the huge slabs of rock, the gnarled trees
and green bushes occasionally jutting out of stone, the water
cascading over the rocks, the thundering chaos of sound, all
confront the observer with a starkly primitive pre-historical
scene. In mythical terms, the waters of the Passaic are Paterson's subconscious thoughts, the formless experience of the
moment.

> Jostled as are the waters approaching
> the brink, his thoughts
> interlace, repel and cut under,
> rise rock-thwarted and turn aside
> but forever strain forward—or strike
> an eddy and whirl, marked by a
> leaf or curdy spume, seeming
> to forget .

Approaching the edge, "they coalesce now / glass-smooth with their swiftness," but then in the leap, they are broken, freed, scattered into the air

> as if
> floating, relieved of their weight,
> split apart, ribbons; dazed, drunk
> with the catastrophe of the descent
> floating unsupported
> to hit the rocks: to a thunder,
> as if lightning had struck

At the bottom, "weight regained," the waters "retake their course"; but final emphasis is on the Falls' "spray" and "tumult," "filling the void" with beautiful sight and sound (pp. 16–17). The water's leap over the edge, combining heavy thrust with airy lightness, force with delicacy, terror with joy, gives us that suspended moment, central to all Williams's work, in which thought is married to experience. At the center of man is no stony void but a creative force—the water out of the rock.

Yet the first Part of Book I works as a series of reductions; each time this mythical vision is developed, it is violated by modern fact. The city-giant *is* asleep, and what he draws from the falls are subtle "machinations" that "animate a thousand automatons." Its proximity to the Falls made Paterson an industrial center—a machine—whose unreal citizens "walk outside their bodies aimlessly," "unroused" (p. 14). Introduction of the mythical mountain as creative source for the city is immediately undercut by the prose anecdote of David Hower: his discovery of "pearls at her ankles" stirred no love for nature's beauty, just cold greed and more machinations—so that while the tone of that passage is not ironical, its effect, in context, is. At one point Paterson gives us a series of metaphors for his idea of an all-embracing love.

> A man like a city and a woman like a flower
> —who are in love. Two women. Three women.
> Innumerable women, each like a flower.
>   But
> only one man—like a city.   (p. 15)

But this dream is interrupted by the first letter from the poetess Cress, by the voice of an actual woman in distress accusing him of personal remoteness.

The picture of the African chief with his nine wives restates this idea of marriage as perpetual renewal; his primitive passion is juxtaposed with the sterile marriage of Mrs. Sarah Cumming.

> She had been married about two months, and was blessed with a flattering prospect of no common share of Temporal felicity and usefulness in the sphere which Providence had assigned her; but oh, how uncertain is the continuance of every earthly joy.

She and her husband visit the Falls, are "charmed with the wonderful prospect," "the sublime curiosities of the place," but as they start to leave, Mrs. Cumming slips, or jumps, over the Falls. The abstract gentility of the style of this passage, epitomized in her husband's "My dear, I believe it is time for us to set our face homeward," characterizes their relationship as decorously remote (pp. 23-24). The youngest of the chief's wives sits "erect, a proud queen, conscious of her power," fiercely beautiful and tense with life (p. 22). The Cummings' stiffness, asserted in denial of passion, makes their manner a parody of the profound dignity of the primitive. The thrust of the falls reminds Mrs. Cumming of a power that has been denied her, she is hypnotized by this force and is drawn over the edge. Book I, Part I, ends with an account of Sam Patch, whose career of diving over waterfalls, begun in Paterson, made him a "national hero" in the early nineteenth century—

until one day he tried to make a speech before jumping, found himself at a loss for words, lost his balance and drowned: "Not until the following spring was the body found frozen in an ice-cake." Diving over the Falls is designed to dramatize man's assertion over, not devotion to, natural power. The mock heroic introduction to this section, Patch's empty justification for his activity ("some things can be done as well as others"), his crucial inarticulateness, the final image of him frozen, all indicate his reduction of heroism to a sensational stunt (pp. 24–27). The pull toward immersion, the dream of mastery: woman and man are pulled in opposite directions, in a parody of the creative cycle, and so both are in the end remote, "silent, uncommunicative" (p. 31). Modern actuality keeps breaking into the poem, exploding the poet's mythic dreams.

The struggle of Paterson is to accept this kind of disintegration as part of the creative process. Criticism of the poem could have helped us much more by looking less at thematic recurrences and more at the character and conflicts of its central figure, Paterson himself. James Guimond has been alone among Williams's critics in taking up this issue.[8] Paterson is both a generic figure, all the citizens of the city of Paterson, and a particular person, who is a doctor and a poet. The identification is made possible by Williams's belief that the members of a community are the creations of its poet; they are his thoughts and their failures are finally his failures. It is perfectly permissible to identify the man Paterson with his creator, as long as we understand his creator as a man who felt strong proclivities toward a romantic visionary sense of the imagination and who at the same time possessed another earthier side, which mocked, complicated, and "grounded" the first. Williams is thus using himself here as he does in the stories—as a *literary object* (and for this reason it is misleading to label the poem a "personal epic"). Soon after the description of the Falls as Paterson's buried thoughts, we are introduced to the poet Paterson:

> Twice a month Paterson receives
> communications from the Pope and Jacques

> Barzun
> (Isocrates). His works
> have been done into French
> and Portuguese. And clerks in the post-
> office ungum rare stamps from
> his packages and steal them for their
> children's albums .
>
> Say it! No ideas but in things. Mr.
> Paterson has gone away
> to rest and write. Inside the bus one sees
> his thoughts sitting and standing. His
> thoughts alight and scatter— (pp. 17-18)

On the one hand, Paterson is pompous, cold, aloof—the great
man, less the local than the international literary figure who
goes "away / to rest and write." Many critics have noted the
frequent allusions to Eliot in *Paterson.*[9] But these are not to be
understood as attempts by Williams to define his difference
from Eliot; they are part of the creation of the character of
Paterson. In one of his aspects he is the Eliotic poet, author of
the poem's opening evocation of the "automatons" of the city,
the poet withdrawn to some distant vantage point from which
he contemplates the discrepancies between his dream of an organic community and the reality of modern chaos in a mode
of lofty irony and genteel despair. It is this Paterson who is
condemned by some of his less prestigious correspondents—like
the writer E. D. and the poetess Cress—for coldly divorcing
literature from life. At one point the poetess angrily attacks
"writers like yourself who are so sheltered from life in the raw
by the glass-walled condition of their own safe lives" (p. 106).
And it is this Paterson who is squeamishly repelled by those
gross, flagrant forms of energy he sees during his walk in the
Park in Book II. The recurrent images of glass and ice define
Paterson's hard surface—the egotism of the ambitious literary
man.

This Paterson may walk the street and ride the bus but he is
asleep and his thoughts, uprooted, "alight and scatter" in a parody of the creative leap of the Falls. But the image of the

sleeping giant cuts in two directions, illustrating the poem's basic tension on a minute verbal level. The aspiring literary giant is asleep in a metaphorical sense—torpid; but there is a true greatness which is literally sleeping within him, buried in his subconscious. From the first, a voice of genteel despair alternates with a more modest, elemental voice, one that gropes toward wakefulness.

> Only of late, late! begun to know, to
> know clearly (*as through clear ice*) whence
> I draw my breath or how to employ it
> clearly—if not well:
> > Clearly!
> speaks the red-breast his behest. Clearly!
> clearly!   (p. 31)   [my emphasis]

Soon after this, Paterson gives us a more definite image of this source.

> Which is to say, though it be poorly
> said, there is a first wife
> and a first beauty, complex, ovate—
> the woody sepals standing back under
> the stress to hold it there, innate
>
> a flower within a flower whose history
> (within the mind) crouching
> among the ferny rocks, laughs at the names
> by which they think to trap it. Escapes!
> Never by running but by lying still—
>
> A history that has, by its den in the
> rocks, bole and fangs, its own cane-brake
> whence, half hid, canes and stripes
> blending, it grins (beauty defied)
> not for the sake of the encyclopedia.
>
> Were we near enough its stinking breath
> would fell us. The temple upon
> the rock is its brother, whose majesty
> lies in jungles—made to spring,
> at the rifle-shot of learning: to kill
>
> and grind those bones: (p. 33)

This is not the decorum-seeking Paterson who goes away to rest and write. This is a figure who can accept his primitive origins, open himself to a mysterious primitive force that has much more to do with terror and defiance than with gentility and decorum. This power, of course, is that Kora-like force we have seen animating all of Williams's major work. In approaching this "first beauty," man will try to tame, study, even slay; he wants to abstract and control—afraid of mystery. Yet civilized man can never finally grasp what he reaches after, as this elusive power laughs, grins, or springs—like a savage animal—on its antagonist. The disillusionment we get from Book I, Part I, is only a partial truth; beauty is indestructible.

Hence, at the core of Paterson himself, in tension with his conscious ego, we find a seed, "a flower within a flower," a primitive physical and emotional power that, released, could shatter that "plate-glass" surface and deliver him, fully awake, onto the ground. The conflict between self-assertion and ego-loss gives us the major conflict of the poem. Paterson's problem is to accept, both in himself and in his work, disintegration as part of the creative cycle—to see in that process of "composition and decomposition" not just "despair" (p. 93) but the emergence of new life, "the radiant gist that / resists the final crystallization" (p. 133). The way to creativity, as in all of Williams, is through a process in which rigidities yield, and the unconquerable force of the imagination is let flow; this is the process of continual renewal. And *Paterson* itself, which dissolves and reforms with the addition of each new part, is a testament to that radiant gist that resists any final crystallization.

Paterson's character has clearly been conceived in terms of the tension between acceptance and resistance which Williams had apprehended historically in *In the American Grain*; the poet-doctor is representative modern man. The poem takes place in his mind; its contrapuntal movements are the formal extension of his divided consciousness. This movement can now be examined more fully. Typically, Paterson moves forward, is thwarted, starts in a new direction, is blocked again, and so on. Paterson will aspire toward mastery, drift into fantasy, build a set of metaphorical correspondences, but in each case the expansive mood is undercut and the hero forced to begin again.

> —the descent follows the ascent—to wisdom
> as to despair.
> A man is under the crassest necessity
> to break down the pinnacles of his moods
> fearlessly —
> to the bases; base! to the screaming dregs,
> to have known the clean air   .
> From that base, unabashed, to regain
> the sun kissed summits of love!   (p. 104)

No mood, of triumph or despair, can be maintained for long, if a man wants to keep in touch with the flux of reality. Moods build, break down, then turn into their opposites, as Paterson reverses direction to embrace what he has been moving away from. The way to wisdom, he asserts here at the end of Book II, is by despairing of final knowledge—by dissolving all fixed positions and returning to the base of knowledge in experience. As a result Paterson's thoughts throughout the poem, instead of moving in a linear progression, "interlace, repel and cut under, / rise rock-thwarted and turn aside / but forever strain forward "(p. 16). The form of the poem *is* the stream of his consciousness.

Once we start attending to tones of voice and stop hunting for meaning, the poem can come to life for us. For one thing, we recognize the comic nature of many of the hero's reversals. In Part II of Book I Paterson becomes impatient with his debased locality.

> The thought returns: Why have I not
> but for imagined beauty where there is none
> or none available, long since
> put myself deliberately in the way of death?
>
>   Stale as a whale's breath: breath!
>   Breath!   (pp. 30–31)

The poet draws back in disillusionment, questions himself pompously, then contemptuously turns on his own stale rheto-

ric and attitudinizing. As he does so, thought shifts from the
end (death) to the beginning (breath); comic reduction works
against egotistical rigidity, loosens energy to flow, and converts a moment of despair into its opposite. "How strange you
are, you idiot," Part III of Book I begins.

> So you think because the rose
> is red that you shall have the mastery?
> The rose is green and will bloom,
> overtopping you, green, livid
> green when you shall no more speak, or
> taste, or even be. My whole life
> has hung too long upon a partial victory.

Here, again, Paterson comes alive in the mockery of his own
literary pretensions. He yearns for artistic "mastery," but the
physical world, always "green," fresh, new, is always beginning and therefore eludes his final mastery. As his aspirations
collapse, Paterson thus turns to sense experience.

> He picked a hairpin from the floor
> and stuck it in his ear, probing
> around inside—

He listens to the dripping of "melting snow," sees a reflection
in the "linoleum at his feet," smells his hands, watches and listens as he rolls "his thumb / about the edges of his left index
finger." But Paterson characteristically gets impatient with this
kind of absorptive activity, closes the senses—"of / earth his
ears are full, there is no sound"—and lets the visionary imagination take over.

> : And his thoughts soared
> to the magnificence of imagined delights
> where he would probe
>
> as into the pupil of an eye
> as through a hoople of fire, and emerge
> sheathed in a robe
>
> streaming with light. What heroic
> dawn of desire
> is denied to his thoughts?

> They are trees
> from whose leaves streaming with rain
> his mind drinks of desire :

Some critics have misread this passage as serious affirmation,
but its tone—like that of the triumphant lyric that follows—is
plainly comic. Paterson's thoughts soar off to "imagined delights," he concedes no tension between dream and reality, he
becomes the bacchic seer, "sheathed in a robe / streaming with
light." How strange you are, you idiot. Paterson here slips into
the romantic mode, another false start (pp. 41–42).

  Paterson thus keeps turning around on itself, like all of Williams's best work. The central figure leans first in one direction, catches himself up, then starts anew. Close to the end of
Book I, revolted by the squalid vulgarity of his locality, Paterson turns to Catholicism.

> Such is the mystery of his one two, one two.
> And so among the rest he drives
> in his new car out to the suburbs, out
> by the rhubarb farm—a simple thought—
> where the convent of the Little Sisters of
> St. Ann pretends a mystery

The pull in this instance is toward a "simple thought," a decorum and beauty that provide relief from the violence, crudity
and torment of modern city life.

> It is the complement exact of vulgar streets
> a mathematic calm, controlled, the architecture
> mete, sinks there, lifts here .
> the same blank and staring eyes.
>
>   An incredible
> clumsiness of address,
> senseless rapes—caught on hands and knees
> scrubbing a greasy corridor; the blood
> boiling as though in a vat, where they soak—
>
> Plaster saints, glass jewels
> and those apt paper flowers, bafflingly

> complex—have here
> their forthright beauty, beside:
>
> Things, things unmentionable,
> the sink with the waste farina in it and
> lumps of rancid meat, milk-bottle-tops: have
> here a tranquility and loveliness
> have here (in his thoughts)
> a complement tranquil and chaste.

Those surrounded by "things unmentionable" pathetically reach after beauty and order, but the "mathematic calm" they seek, the "tranquil and chaste" thoughts they entertain, are abstracted from the unpredictabilities of raw experience; the convent merely "pretends a mystery." But suddenly, Paterson "shifts his change," a prose section records a minor earthquake, suggestive of a momentary awakening of his instinctual being. The natural catastrophe breaks the mood of tranquility—but it uncovers the real mystery, subconscious source of all beauty, thought, and speech.

> Thought clambers up,
> snail like, upon the wet rocks
> hidden from sun and sight—
> hedged in by the pouring torrent—
>
> and has its birth and death there
> in that moist chamber, shut from
> the world—and unknown to the world,
> cloaks itself in mystery—
>
> And the myth
> that holds up the rock
> that holds up the water thrives there—
> in that cavern, that profound cleft,
> a flickering green
> inspiring terror, watching   .   .
>
> And standing, shrouded there, in that din,
> Earth, the chatterer, father of all
> speech   .   .   .   .

Here at the end of Book I Paterson has, by a series of reversals, come to—the beginning. With the tremor, the poem cuts abruptly from the "mete" architecture of civilized religion to the primitive rocky cavern behind the Falls—a place strongly reminiscent of "the temple upon / the rock" where men worship the savage "majesty" of the "first beauty." Paterson rouses from an abstract calm, descends to the chamber of the unconscious where thought is mysterious, clambering, struggling—but alive. He has come to the "base"—the earth, which holds up the rock, which holds up the water—and discovers a place where "myth" "thrives." The living god, cloaked in mystery, is glimpsed, flickering green (now clearly established as the color of the life-force), inspiring terror, not tranquility (pp. 50–52). In fact, the whole of Book I, with its continued false starts, its collapsed aspirations, sinks haltingly down from the opening panoramic view of the sleeping giant to this flickering perception of his living core.

In *A Voyage to Pagany* Dr. Evans complains that "he had to discard so much to get at what he wanted that he never arrived anywhere. The whole world is built to keep it from being said" (p. 27). For Paterson, too, social, literary, and personal inhibitions are so strong that he cannot hope to arrive anywhere; all he can do is begin. Just as in "The Wanderer," "By the road," the De Soto chapter in *In the American Grain,* and *A Voyage to Pagany,* it takes to the end to get to the beginning, so in *Paterson* "the beginning is assuredly / the end" (p. 11); finalities are exactly what we, and Mr. Paterson, are asked to give up. "Virtue is wholly / in the effort to be virtuous," Paterson says in Book IV, affirming process over end (p. 221). Disintegration *is* creative, it keeps bringing the self back to formless experience; but Paterson only gradually comes to look upon his life not as a succession of defeats, but as a series of new beginnings.

One of his first conscious perceptions of this truth occurs near the end of Book II.

> The descent beckons
>   as the ascent beckoned

> Memory is a kind
> of accomplishment
> a sort of renewal
> even
> an initiation, since the spaces it opens are new
> places
> inhabited by hordes
> heretofore unrealized,
> of new kinds—
> since their movements
> are towards new objectives
> (even though formerly they were abandoned)
> No defeat is made up entirely of defeat—since
> the world it opens is always a place
> formerly
> unsuspected. A
> world lost,
> a world unsuspected
> beckons to new places
> and no whiteness (lost) is so white as the memory
> of whiteness   .   (p. 96)

Paterson here accepts failure and disintegration as necessary parts of creative activity. Successful movement is easy, quick, smooth, linear—but, without friction, it is also without discovery. Every time Paterson is blocked in his quest for beauty, he is pushed back, forced to turn around and assert a new direction. "Defeat" opens new spaces, by forcing a man to begin again, and again, and again—rather than permitting him to find a hole in which he can sink, finally, to rest. As Paterson says in Book IV, "Dissonance . . . leads to discovery" (p. 207).

The meditation on descent takes place near the end of Paterson's quest for beauty in the park in Book II, the frustrations of that search now driving him back into himself, back into memory. At the literal level Paterson is thinking of his climb down Garrett Mountain, but the generalized diction ("descent," "ascent"), along with the reader's memory of the poem's repeated images of descent—as in the leap of the Passaic Falls—suggest a primarily metaphorical sense. There is in fact a tendency in the passage toward a generality of statement and a slight elevation of manner. The speaker is at the edge of his descent, considering but not yet experiencing it. Diction is abstract and even when it seems to point toward something physical in words like "spaces" and "places," the words are really being used metaphorically. There is enough verbal repetition to create an incantatory effect, and the sense of formality is reenforced by a good deal of syntactic parallelism. Moreover, it was in this passage that Williams first used the three-stepped line which he later believed to be the solution to his lifelong search for a new metric. Each of its three parts receives an equal interval of time (regardless of syllabic count), so a relatively even measure is established.* Yet these staggered lines also create a groping, hesitant movement in the verse—a tentativeness found in phrases like "a kind // of" and "a sort of" and the concessive clause "even though." Consoling generalities, not proclaimed in a tone of rapt bardic certitude, are made by the hesitant human voice of a man who is about to make his descent. There is a lift of style and mood, but we are not allowed to forget the experience of despair. This passage has a tone of modest elevation which, unlike the elevated manner of the poem's opening passage, cannot easily be undercut. As we shall see, that is why Williams made it the source of his later style.

Yet in *Paterson* even the modest accomplishment of this section is broken down when the hero actually starts to "listen" to the falls. Paterson must go all the way down, to the base, to the primal origins of life and art—to begin all over again. He can advance only slowly, brokenly—by regression; he can begin to find himself only through frustration and defeat—in self-disintegration. At first he resists that truth; but over-all movement in the poem is a downward spiral, a series of backward somersaults. Renewal is achieved—as in "The Wanderer" —by a series of jolting reversals, a gradual stripping away of layers of egotism. At the core of Paterson—man, city, poem—

* The workings of this "new measure" will be discussed more fully in Chapter VII.

we again find "Persephone / gone to hell" (p. 151), the creative principle locked in a hell of repression. It is in the powerful Book III that Paterson sheds his fears, goes down to hell, releases the primal forces buried in him and accepts these as the sources of beauty.

At the start of the third book, Paterson turns from the suffocating summer streets, from the rebuffs and isolation of modern city life, to find relief in the rarefied world of books. "A cool of books," he says, "will sometimes lead the mind to libraries / of a hot afternoon" (p. 118). But it is typical of the poem's pattern of reversal that where Paterson goes to find "rest" (p. 119), he experiences the most terrible agonies of the entire poem. The library turns out to be even more suffocating than the streets, but its very oppressiveness stirs a profound force in Paterson, a beauty "counter to all staleness" (p. 123). He reads of the tornado, fire, and flood that wrecked the town in 1902, and these apocalyptic events are internalized as moments of violent emotional liberation in which Paterson's hard egotistical surface is profoundly shaken. The three catastrophes are dealt with separately in the three parts of Book III; each time a "lower" element is involved—air, fire, water—so that Paterson is brought further and further down, closer to that foulness in which the "first beauty" is always hidden.

Identified with these wild, unpredictable natural forces is, as always in Williams, the woman: the Beautiful Thing that haunts his imagination throughout the first two Parts of Book III.

Beautiful thing:

—a dark flame,
a wind, a flood—counter to all staleness. (p. 123)

A voice of intense lyric reverie, in counterpoint to the staleness of the dreams in books, tells of a girl in a "white lace dress," the favorite of a Paterson gang, who is taken off "drunk and bedraggled" and raped by a gang from Newark: "to release // the strictness of beauty / under a sky full of stars" (pp. 127–28).

And the guys from Paterson
    beat up
the guys from Newark and told
them to stay the hell out
of their territory and then
socked you one
        across the nose
        Beautiful Thing
for good luck and emphasis
        cracking it
till I must believe that all
desired women have had each
    in the end
    a busted nose
and live afterward marked up
    Beautiful Thing
    for memory's sake
to be credible in their deeds (p. 153)

This girl is raped, beaten, scarred, but through it all she remains wild, drunken, "indifferent"—unbeaten. She accepts her brutal treatment fatalistically, and so now does Paterson. Earlier, in his quest for rigor of beauty, Paterson turned away from the "gross," "flagrant" women in the Park (p. 88); but he now identifies beauty with abandon, a free-wheeling energy that will always be "marked," imperfect, socked across the nose. "Beautiful thing," he says, "your / vulgarity of beauty surpasses all their / perfections!" (p. 145). At this point Paterson is "conceiving / knowledge / by way of despair" (p. 121); his thoughts are now born out of a despair that gives up the struggle for "mastery" and, like the bedraggled girl, accepts experience as it comes.

The cataclysmic events of Book III are often related in the voice of a prophetic chant, with the Biblical "So be it" as a refrain, again indicating Paterson's "indifferent" acceptance of violence. One of the most striking of these passages occurs in the description of the fire in Part II:

An iron dog, eyes
aflame in a flame-filled corridor. A drunkenness

> of flames. So be it. A bottle, mauled
> by the flames, belly-bent with laughter:
> yellow, green. So be it—of drunkenness
> survived, in guffaws of flame. All fire afire!
> So be it. Swallowing the fire. So be
> it. Torqued to laughter by the fire,
> the very fire. So be it. Chortling at flames
> sucked in, a multiformity of laughter, a
> flaming gravity surpassing the sobriety of
> flames, a chastity of annihilation. Recreant,
> calling it good. Calling the fire good.
> So be it. The beauty of fire-blasted sand
> that was glass, that was a bottle: unbottled.
> Unabashed. So be it.   (p. 142)

The bottle, literally bent by the flames, is not imagined as wracked, tortured by the experience, but as letting go a howl of release, a near hysterical laughter. "Hell's fire" is not pure negation, it is a destructive / creative force which can produce the sort of primal metamorphosis it does here. The flames annihilate form—unbottle the bottle—and then, after rendering it fluid, create a new shape. Like the girl in the "white lace dress," the bottle is battered, a drunken force runs through it, but the "old bottle, mauled by the fire / gets a new glaze, the glass warped / to a new distinction, reclaiming the / undefined." Line endings here stress the unexpected turn, the creative reversal, in the process, as what is "mauled" gets a "new glaze," what is "warped" receives a "new distinction," just as the girl's busted nose marks her as "credible," a truly beautiful thing. It is through this kind of ordeal, surrender to these terrifying forces, that ultimately comes the purity Paterson has been searching for. Moreover, from Book I glass has been associated with the rigid, egotistical side of Paterson's character—as in "the regularly ordered plateglass of / his thoughts." So what happens to the bottle happens to Paterson's mind, too. He speaks of "hottest / lips lifted till no shape but a vast / molt of the news flows. Drink / of the news, fluid to the breath." Literally the "hottest lips" refer to the shape of the molten glass, but they are also the lips of the poet, burning with passion, as he drinks in the news of metamorphosis. "Molt" is a pun, referring both to "molten" and to "moulting," and as Paterson's plateglass mind is made fluid by a drunken emotion, he passes into a new phase of his life. Yet both bottle and poet finally triumph over the fire by making a transient moment of passion eternal. After the blaze the glass is "splotched with concentric rainbows / of cold fire" just as an experience of passion can be frozen, forever, in the words of a poem. The bottle is "deflowered, reflowered," "mauled / to a new distinction." At the end, the passage turns comically back on itself, with Paterson now hysterically laughing at the fire.

> Hell's fire. Fire. Sit your horny ass
> down. What's your game? Beat you
> at your own game, Fire. Outlast you:
> Poet Beats Fire at Its Own Game! The bottle!
> the bottle! the bottle! the bottle! I
> give you the bottle! What's burning
> now, Fire?

The answer to that emphatically placed "now" is, of course, the bottle—*and* the language in which the poet has caught the process of its recreation (pp. 142–43).

An advance from Paterson's state of mind in the "descent beckons" passage is quite clear, if "advance" is the right word for a step which takes him right into the process of disintegration. But in the poem's characteristic manner, even this moment of triumph—when what is deflowered, reflowers eternally—is ripped apart. From a celebration of the power of the poet to "outlast" the fire, Paterson modulates to an acknowledgment of his own inadequate responsiveness and his inability to catch the flame's mysterious movements in language. This humbler mood takes him, at the end of Book III, Part II (pp. 150–52), to memory of an episode with a black woman, another manifestation of the Beautiful Thing. Paterson encounters her below the ground, in a basement, "by the laundry tubs,"

                          in a low bed (waiting)
          under the mud plashed windows among the scabrous
          dirt of the holy sheets   .

Like the mauled bottle and the marked girl, she is "scarred"
(by whips), but indifferent and accepting—silently dignified.

               .   a docile queen, not bothered
          to stick her tongue out at the moon, indifferent,
          through loss, but   .

                              queenly,
          in bad luck, the luck of the stars, the black stars

                    .   the night of a mine

Although she is surrounded by dirt and ugliness, she does
not, as Paterson often does, lapse into despair or anxiety; she
remains loose, relaxed, "stretched out negligently on the dirty
sheet." As Paterson perceives, this dark woman in the squalid
basement is "Persephone / gone to hell"—regal in her indifference, radiant in the surrounding darkness. She gives us another
of the third book's images of hell experienced, beaten, survived.

When Paterson first remembers her in Part I, he recalls an
incident in which he had been brutally puritannical with her.

          (Then, my anger rising) TAKE OFF YOUR
          CLOTHES! I didn't ask you
          to take off your skin . I said your
          clothes, your clothes. You smell
          like a whore. I ask you to bathe in my
          opinions, the astonishing virtue of your
          lost body (I said)   .   (pp. 128–29)

This passage shows how Paterson, in his demands for a pure
beauty, is himself implicated in the maiming and violating of
natural beauty. But in Part II he recounts a subsequent episode
when he was open, receptive to the power of this woman.

                    —for I was overcome
          by amazement and could do nothing but admire
          and lean to care for you in your quietness—

> who looked at me, smiling, and we remained
> thus looking, each at the other   .   in silence   .
>
> You lethargic, waiting upon me, waiting for
> the fire and I
>   attendant upon you, shaken by your beauty
>
> Shaken by your beauty   .
>   Shaken.

Paterson is here humble, awed, "attendant," "shaken." Instead
of trying to force his righteous opinions upon her "lost body,"
he lets her physical being speak silently to him, and her care-
less, lethargic manner—a power that comes across without asserting itself—has much to teach him. At this crucial moment
of encounter between the hero and the object of his torturous
quest, we might expect a high-pitched scene of climax; but it is
the whole point of this meeting that it be quietly played
down, flattened out. The surrender of the desire for artistic
mastery and the capacity to be shaken go hand in hand for Paterson (pp. 150–52). This scene is at several levels of intensity
below the "drunken" pitch of the episode of the mauled bottle, and by the end of Part II, Paterson has dropped to a still
more modest tone.

>   I can't be half gentle enough,
>   half tender enough
>   toward you, toward you,
>   inarticulate, not half loving enough
>
> BRIGHTen
>   the cor
>   ner
>   where   you   are!
>
>   —a flame,
>   black plush, a dark flame. (p. 154)

At this key moment, words fail the inarticulate poet; not half
gentle or tender enough, they too whip and scar the Beautiful
Thing. But this admission of failure and guilt is exactly the
kind of limited triumph available to Paterson. There is so

much for him to discard, so much to be cut away, that he cannot wholly reconstitute himself; what he can do is relax, give
up the partial victories of art and open himself to the beauty
that is before him.

Searching for beauty in the refined atmosphere of the library, Paterson discovers it living in a dirty basement; as always in Williams, beauty is a flame in the underworld—the radiant gist hidden in the pitch blend. But the flood of Part III
takes Paterson down even further into the darkness and filth in
which he must begin.

>   Upon which there intervenes
> a sour stench of embers. So be it. Rain
> falls and surfeits the river's upper reaches,
> gathering slowly. So be it. Draws together,
> runnel by runnel. So be it. A broken oar
> is found by the searching waters. Loosened
> it begins to move. So be it. Old timbers
> sigh—and yield. The well that gave sweet water
> is sullied. So be it. And lilies that floated
> quiet in the shallows, anchored, tug as
> fish at a line. So be it. And are by their
> stems pulled under, drowned in the muddy flux.
> The white crane flies into the wood.
> So be it. Men stand at the bridge, silent,
> watching. So be it. So be it.

The tornado and fire are wild forces that can quickly be felt as
liberating, but the flood is heavy and oppressive, sullying clear
waters, burying all in a "muddy flux." Moreover, as soon as
the flood is introduced as natural fact, it is given a symbolic
sense—referring to the mass of books in which Paterson has
been immersing himself.

>   And there rises
> a counterpart, of reading, slowly, overwhelming
> the mind; anchors him in his chair. So be
> it. He turns   .   O Paradiso! The stream
> grows leaden within him, his lilies drag. So
> be it. Texts mount and complicate them-

> selves, lead to further texts and those
> to synopses, digests and emendations. So be it.
> Until the words break loose or—sadly
> hold, unshaken. Unshaken! So be it. For
> the made-arch holds, the water piles up debris
> against it but it is unshaken. They gather
> upon the bridge and look down, unshaken.
> So be it. So be it. So be it.   (p. 156)

Anchored to his chair in the library, Paterson at one point seems to turn away and look for relief ("O Paradiso!"), but is only turning another page. His inventive powers grow leaden, his spirit drags; he's read too much. And as books pile up, they get further and further from immediate experience—"until the words break loose"; the end of this progressive fading away from the sources of writing is sheer chaos, which is a new beginning. The alternatives for Paterson are to let this process of disintegration run its course ("So be it") or to try to build barriers against it, to get outside and above it, like the men on the bridge who watch silently, unshaken (p. 156).

Through most of Part III the waters continue to rise—"to the teeth, to the very eyes" becomes a refrain—covering all signs of life with their muddy flux. At moments Paterson wants to "*do*" something to turn against this oppressive force—

> But somehow a man must lift himself
> again—
>   again is the magic word   .
>   turning the in out   :
> Speed against the inundation (p. 162)

—but the hopelessness of this counter-thrust is suggested by the image of the fish "at full speed / stationary / in the leaping stream" (p. 163). Eventually, on page 164, words do break loose: random bits of conversation, reading, signs from a florist shop, reflections by the poet slant down the page in several directions. The poem sinks, breaks free of the regularly ordered lines of typography. On the adjacent page appears a letter from Pound, recommending more reading, more civilization. But his experience with the leaden flood of books

prompts Paterson to opt for spontaneity. At the start of Part
III, in answer to a voice urging a cautious perfectionism
("watch carefully and erase"), he declares: "write carelessly so
that nothing that is not green will survive" (p. 155). More and
more the embattled Paterson comes to identify art not with
decorum but the release of this living force.

The flood continues to rise until it reaches

> —to the teeth, to the very eyes
> .   uh,   uh
> FULL STOP
>
> —and leave the world
> to darkness
> and to
> me

But then as the waters ebb, Paterson, left in the post-alluvial
muck, falls into one of the most despairing moments of the entire poem:

> When the water has receded most things have lost their
> form. They lean in the direction the current went. Mud
> covers them
>
> —fertile(?)mud.
>
> If it were only fertile. Rather a sort of muck, a detritus,
> in this case—a pustular scum, a decay, a choking
> lifelessness—that leaves the soil clogged after it,
> that glues the sandy bottom and blackens stones—so that
> they have to be scoured three times when, because of
> an attractive brokenness, we take them up for garden uses.
> An acrid, a revolting stench comes out of them, almost one
> might say a granular stench—fouls the mind   .
>
> How to begin to find a shape—to begin to begin again,
> turning the inside out : to find one phrase that will
> lie married beside another for delight   .   ?
> —seems beyond attainment   .
>
> *American poetry is a very easy subject to discuss for the*
> *simple reason that it does not exist*   (p. 167)

As a result of the flood, Paterson the city and Paterson the man in the library are both buried in a heavy, stinking, life-choking mud; foulness covers everything. At such moments, artistic activity seems impossible. Yet, like the young poet in "The Wanderer," the man-city has gone through an immersion in foulness, a reduction to formlessness—a descent to the primal ooze which is at the start of all things. Language begins anew at the point where speech falls to an inarticulate "uh"; art begins again at the point where art ends. With the "FULL STOP" Paterson is left in a kind of graveyard—thus the allusion to Gray's "Elegy"—but left, alone and free, in the creative darkness.

So, at the bottommost point of despair, lines suddenly tighten, mood abruptly turns upward. This is exactly the kind of reversal we have seen happening again and again in the poem; it cannot be explained rationally, it results from no act of conscious will on the part of Paterson, but simply from the natural life of feelings, a process in which moods build, disintegrate, generate their opposites. By now we are prepared to accept this as the "logic" of Paterson's mind, and thus of the poem—and so is Paterson. In fact, the rise of feeling here is equated with his acceptance of natural processes: now that the flood has run its course, Paterson is willing to turn the task of renewal over to the digestive processes of the earth.

> Degraded. The leaf torn from
> the calendar. All forgot. Give
> it over to the woman, let her
> begin again—with insects
> and decay, decay and then insects :
> the leaves—that were varnished
> with sediment, fallen, the clutter
> made piecemeal by decay, a
> digestion takes place   .
>
> —of this, make it of *this*, this
> this, this, this, this   .   (pp. 167–68)

This is a crucial moment in the poem, for Paterson, having experienced a series of agonizing and humiliating ordeals, never-

theless asserts a faith that creation issues from destruction. The
degradation has ripped away the accumulations of calendar
time and actually cleaned his mind: "all forgot." Antithetical
to his own immersion in these painful processes is the detachment of the men who coldly watch from the bridge—a remoteness that Paterson identifies with T. S. Eliot. "Who was it
spoke of April?" he asks. "Some / insane engineer." The
bridge is a metaphor for technical mastery of any kind, including a poetic one, that is achieved by abstraction from the processes of nature. "Loosen the flesh / from the machine," Paterson proclaims, "build no more / bridges." Instead of seeking
technical perfection, "let the words / fall any way at all—that
they may / hit love aslant"—as they do on the chaotic page
164. "They want to rescue too much, / the flood," annihilating
the works of engineers, "has done its work" (p. 169).

As Paterson now recognizes, the marriage of form and energy he envisioned at the start of the poem could be realized
"in a hundred years, perhaps," but at the moment a rough, flagrant vitality is all he can hope for. Rather than the attainment
of formal mastery, the writer must begin by breaking apart
fixed modes; but the collapse of his artistic aspirations takes Paterson back to the origins of art in the formless moment. And
so at the end of Book III, he abandons the library and returns
to the Falls.

> The past above, the future below
> and the present pouring down: the roar,
> the roar of the present, a speech—
> is, of necessity, my sole concern .
>
> They plunged, they fell in a swoon .
> or by intention, to make an end—the
> roar, unrelenting, witnessing   .
> Neither the past nor the future
>
> Neither to stare, amnesic—forgetting.
> The language cascades into the
> invisible, beyond and above : the falls
> of which it is the visible part—

Not until I had made of it a replica
will my sins be forgiven and my
disease cured—in wax: *la capella di S. Rocco*
on the sandstone crest above the old

copper mines—where I used to see
the images of arms and knees
hung on nails (de Montpellier)   .
No meaning. And yet, unless I find a place

apart from it, I am its slave,
its sleeper, bewildered—dazzled
by distance   .   I cannot stay here
to spend my life looking into the past:

the future's no answer. I must
find my meaning and lay it, white,
beside the sliding water: myself—
comb out the language—or succumb

—whatever the complexion. Let
me out!   (Well, go!) this rhetoric
is real!   (pp. 172–73)

Paterson reflects on the dilemmas that have beset him through-out the poem. Meaning, he here decides, cannot be found in li-brary or church, past or future, but must be combed out of the undifferentiated chaos of the present. Whatever its com-plexion, the physical world must be the source of any common language or mythology. Yet man cannot simply lose himself in the "roar" of immediacy: he can not stare amnesic, like Mrs. Cumming, forgetting the self in yearning for union with na-ture. The self is here identified in terms of a tension between mind and matter, form and actuality—but with most emphasis on the present need for the mind to refresh its contact with physical experience. The Falls, again, stands for the core of creative energy shared by all the citizens of Paterson, but for-gotten in the ambitions, distractions of modern industrial life. To redeem himself and his city, the poet must create a replica of this forgotten power, a verbal object that is different from the Falls but preserving its beauty and force. Earlier in Book III Paterson claims that "the writing is nothing, the being / in a position to write (that's // where they get you) is nine tenths / of the difficulty . . ." (p. 137). Most of his energy goes into breaking forms down, getting back to the sources of art; mastery seems beyond attainment. But by the end of Book III he has maneuvered himself into a position to write, and that position, characteristic for Williams, is at the *edge* of the Falls, place of maximum exposure to the risks, and to the power, of raw experience. At last Paterson has begun.

Book IV takes us down into some of the poem's most hellish experiences in the ironic "An Idyll" of Part I, only to lift us into its most visionary mood in Part II's celebration of Madame Curie as the creative principle. This descent/ascent pattern is also exemplified in Part III, originally intended to be *Paterson's* final episode. The title for Book IV is "The Run to the Sea," and in this last section Paterson follows the Passaic down past Manhattan to its end, and its origin, in the Atlantic. Here the sea is anything but the gentle, buoyant element we find in a writer like Emerson; it is brute nature, unordered and shark-infested. At moments the sea becomes "our nostalgic / mother in whom the dead, enwombed again / cry out to us to return . / the blood dark sea" (p. 236). This pull toward nostalgia becomes especially strong as Paterson, now quite old, engages in extensive reminiscences of old friends, lovers, his mother, a visit to Haiti and the history of his town. The blood dark sea is death, and Paterson appears to be slowly, helplessly, sinking into it. He stutters hopelessly at one point: "—you cannot believe / that it can begin again, again, here / again . here" (p. 234).

Yet, if the sea is death, it is also birth, the origin of life. Among "the scum / and wrack . among the brown fronds / and limp starfish," says Paterson, "seeds float in" (p. 235); the sea is another hell he must endure to recover the seeds of Persephone. For this reason both voices in the debate near the close of the poem—"the sea is not our home," "you must come to it"—are right. The debate precedes a swim Paterson takes in the Atlantic. He goes so far out that he is no longer recognizably human—he dies into the scene. Yet the episode ends not with the swimmer being swept helplessly out to sea, but with his return to the beach where he naps briefly, rises, puts on a pair of faded overalls and a shirt with its sleeves still rolled up, picks some beach plums and heads inland accompanied by his dog (pp. 236–38). He has come to the sea, but it is not his home. The seeds turned up by this process of renewal must be planted in the earth. Moreover, this solitary and carefree rough is headed, Williams tells us, "toward Camden where Walt Whitman, much traduced, lived the latter years of his life and died" (*Auto*, p. 392). This figure is identified with Whitman, Paterson, and the younger poet A. G. (Allen Ginsberg) whose work shows, as he tells Paterson in a letter, that "at least one actual citizen of your community has inherited your experience in his struggle to love and know his world-city, through your work, which is an accomplishment you almost cannot have hoped to achieve" (p. 205). The seed of creativity persists through time; the wanderer heading inland is an archetypal figure. At its close, the poem affirms that the quest for beginnings is an eternal one.

Shortly before finishing the fourth book Williams wrote to a friend,

> A man wonders why he bothers to continue to write. And yet it is precisely then that to write is most imperative for us. That, if I can do it, will be the end of *Paterson*, Book IV. The ocean of savage lusts in which the wounded shark gnashes at his own tail is not our home. It is the seed that floats to shore, one word, one tiny even microscopic word, is that which can alone save us. (*SL*, p. 292)

At the end of "The Waste Land" Tiresias makes a similarly modest claim: "These fragments I have shored against my ruins." But the difference between these two poems is basic. "The Waste Land" is a kind of anti-epic, a poem in which the quest for meaning is entirely thwarted and we are left, at the end, waiting for the collapse of western civilization. *Paterson* is a pre-epic, showing that the process of disintegration releases forces that can build a new world. It confronts, again and again, the savagery of contemporary society, but still affirms a creative seed. Eliot's end is Williams's beginning.

VII

A Celebration of the Light

"The serpent // has its tail in its mouth / AGAIN!"
                                                    Paterson V

In 1954 Williams published *The Desert Music and Other Poems,* a book that announced a new departure in his career. To the author himself the book was "special" because it contained the first poems in which he employed his new "variable foot" (*IW,* pp. 88–89). But a reader coming to these poems across the whole course of Williams's development will recognize that the new line is simply one manifestation of a pervasive shift of style and point of view. The earlier poems are remarkable for their toughness and spontaneity, their intensity and fluidity, their disciplined objectification of personal feeling. But in the poetry of *The Desert Music, Journey to Love* (1955), *Paterson* V (1958) and *Pictures from Brueghel* (1962) we discover an easy, measured grace, a tone of relaxed assurance, tenderness and benignity of feeling, a manner that is openly discursive and personal. The need to break things apart has gone; the aging poet, content with his long and productive life, speaks out in a tone of sagacity and pulls the diverse parts of his experience into unity.

As Williams writes in *Paterson* V, "The (self) direction has been changed" (*P,* p. 271). His use of the passive voice is exact: the new direction his work took in the 1950's was not the result of any act of volition, it grew out of a new set of circumstances that were thrust on him. In March, 1951—as he was finishing his *Autobiography*—Williams suffered a severe apoplectic stroke.[1] He almost died, temporarily lost the power of speech, was forced into a prolonged period of recuperation and, eventually, into retirement from his medical practice. Suddenly, Williams had been cut off from those contacts which had always been the source of his creativity. Yet, by May he was already emphasizing the positive consequences of his setback in a letter to Louis Martz. "This is the second time I have been knocked out"—he had had a less serious stroke in 1948—"But this time I seem to have come out of it with a clearer head. Perhaps it derived from a feeling that I might have died, or, worse, have been left with a mind permanently incapacitated." Williams goes on to speak optimistically of the "opportunity for thought" and reading afforded by his new idleness. He had been reading a translation of Homer's *Iliad*, and this has enabled him "to 'place' the new in relation to the past much more accurately. . . . We have been looking for too big, too spectacular a divergence from the old. The 'new measure' is much more particular, much more related to the remote past than I, for one, believed. It was a natural blunder from the excess of our own feelings, but one that must now be corrected" and so, he declares, "we are through with the crude 'fight' we have had to wage. Our position is now established, the approach must be more an inversion upon ourselves . . . a thing we didn't have time for formerly." Williams chastizes himself for the failure to "make myself clear" and directs himself toward "a final summary" (*SL*, pp. 298–99).

The tone and substance of this letter reveal much about the mood in which Williams's later poems were written. Now willing to acknowledge continuities between his work and that of the past, Williams no longer conceives of himself as the combative revolutionary, cutting through the dried husks of dead forms in order to begin anew. That crude fight is over. In particular he now feels no need to contend against the pressure of historical time; it is as if, having come so close to death and having retired from the rushed life of a physician, Williams's life became a prolonged instant, completely outside the passage of time—an eternal moment. Williams had always sought to find the all in the momentary; but while the early work suggests the presence of the archetypal hidden in the instant, the last poems emphasize the eternal over the immediate and bring the universalizing process very much to the surface of the poetry. The poet turns increasingly inward, often into personal memory, an inversion upon himself made possible by the new leisurely pace of his life, and his manner becomes more obviously symbolic and even elegant. Williams's whole above-the-battle stance in the letter to Prof. Martz suggests the kind of eternal perspective from which the later poems are written, and it is a perspective which emphasizes unities rather than distinctions. The crude, earthy aspect of Williams's personality falls away; we see the emergence of a much more relaxed and sagacious figure, close to the humble and kindly spirit of St. Francis of Assisi Williams describes in "The Mental Hospital Garden." His illness and retirement brought a new season into Williams's life, and he met it by advancing an entirely new style of verse—a remarkable achievement for a man in his seventies.

It is in the context of this shift in Williams's position that we should approach *Paterson* V. The publication of this book, seven years after the apparent completion of the poem, revived the critical debate about the nature and even the existence of the poem's unity. Addition of the fifth book has been defended by several critics who cite Williams's belief in "open form." Walter Sutton argues,

> The addition of another part or an indefinite number of parts is in accord with Dr. Williams's theory of the poem. For to him the whole of *Paterson*, or of any poem, can be construed as a search for adequate form, a search that is always advancing, as it must advance, in time, but that is never completed.[2]

Prof. Sutton's article is an important early attempt to explore *Paterson's* form from the inside. Books I–IV do enact a process of creation and disintegration which *is* the poem's form, and the close of Book IV, its image of the explorer heading inland with his dog, is certainly an instance of the open ending: the image suggests a search that is continuing rather than finished. Presumably, further episodes, illustrating this never-ending quest from new angles of vision, could be added. The trouble with this line of argument is that while it could be used to justify the inclusion of a fifth or even an "indefinite number of parts," it does not quite apply to the fifth book we do have. For the Paterson of this book is not the kind of explorer we see at the end of Book IV. He is no longer struggling to get into the position in which to write; he now occupies that position. Instead of splitting things down to their elementary particles, his aim is now to pull them together, easily, into unity. In fact, it was clearly to incorporate this new perspective into his major work that Williams wrote Book V.

Hence Louis Martz comes much closer to the truth when he calls *Paterson* V "an epilogue or coda." [3] Its relation to Books I–IV is different from the relations of the original four books to each other. In his working notes for Book V Williams speaks of one incident as "the same as in Book II *but in a different key*"; [4] Book V is a coda in which the author reviews earlier episodes and motifs, their discordancies now resolved in a new mood of harmonious affirmation. In Book II Paterson walks up Garrett Mountain in a frustrating search for beauty; in Book V Audubon walks through the wilderness "across three states" to discover "a horned beast among the trees" (p. 245), the mythical unicorn which becomes the book's recurrent symbol for beauty. In Book III Paterson can only release his creative powers by purging his mind of the art of the past, but he can now speak of The Cloisters, the New York City museum where he saw a series of medieval tapestries describing the hunt of the unicorn, as "real" (p. 244); again, his crude fight with the past is over. At the end of Book I Paterson quotes John Addington Symond's defense of the Greeks' use of "deformed and mutilated verses" as appropriate to "the distorted subjects with which they dealt" (p. 53), the quote serving to justify the mutilated form of his own poem. But in Book V "all the deformities take wing" (p. 238) and Paterson translates a lyric by Sappho who, we are told, "wrote for a clear gentle tinkling voice. She avoided all roughness" (p. 253). In *Paterson* V the poet does not keep breaking through form to get at the substance; he celebrates the marriage of contemporary matter with eternal form.

The seven Unicorn Tapestries at The Cloisters serve Williams as both an instance of and a means to this kind of artistic unity. They combine painstaking devotion to detail with an awareness of archetypal pattern in a way that makes them an ideal union of the literal and the mythical.[5] Moreover, just as Williams now conceives of himself as part of a community of artists, rather than as the isolated rebel, the tapestries were woven by a group of men and women, young and old, "all together, working together" (p. 270); they define art as a collective enterprise. At one point Williams refers to the tapestries as a "living fiction" (p. 272), a paradox that self-consciously concedes their status as art works but still insists on their continuing vitality. In fact, this paradox also suggests how the tapestries can work as an organizing device in the poem itself: since they are recurrent, the same patterns we find there can be found in contemporary experience. In the middle ages the hunt of the unicorn was usually allegorized into the story of Christ, with the captured animal in the final tapestry standing for the resurrected saviour. In Williams's work, the unicorn stands for the artist or the imagination, their transcendence of time, suffering, and death: the beast in the final tapestry is wounded, penned in, but regal and indifferent and thus unconquerable. The unicorn becomes a more elegant and more universal symbol for that beauty Paterson had found in the girl in the basement in Book III. In these tapestries he finds a rich set of equivalents for his own quest, a symbolic legend that amplifies, elevates and pulls together the details of his own poem; they *are* a living fiction.

But it is important to see exactly the kind of unity Williams is after here. *Paterson* V is also broken into discrete blocks of material, individual parts are still kept separate; their joining occurs as an imaginative process, not as a static fusion. Instead of creating, for example, a finished symbolic narrative, Williams gives us both the raw material and the symbolic tapestries—allowing their combination to occur as a process in the mind of the reader. Modern and ancient, literal and symbolic, wind in and out of the poem "contrapuntally" (p. 278), in an imaginative dance. A look at a passage near the end of Part III of Book V will show us how this process works in the poem.

```
            —the aging body
                    with the deformed great-toe nail
        makes itself known
                    coming
                            to search me out—with a
                            rare smile
        among the thronging flowers of that field
                    where the Unicorn
                            is penned by a low
        wooden fence
                    in April!
                            the same month
        when at the foot of the post
                    he saw the man dig up
        the red snake and kill it with a spade
                    Godwin told me
                            its tail
        would not stop wriggling till
                    after the sun
                            goes down—
        he knew everything
                    or nothing
                            and died insane
        when he was still a young man      (pp. 270–71)
```

The passage begins with a backyard scene in the present, equates it with a scene from the Unicorn Tapestries, then shifts back from this metaphorization of experience to a specific memory of boyhood trauma. The three parts, placed side by side in a loosely associative fashion, are kept discrete, their relations left unstated, open. The reader is therefore asked to circle around within this unit and discover, not a single unify-

ing idea, but a complex network of relations. One motif is the
sense of a tenacious holding onto life. There is the poet's wife
who, in spite of old age's deformities, still asserts a physical
presence (it is her body, not, say, her voice that makes her
known) as well as an undying love ("rare smile") for him.
There is Paterson himself who, unlike Godwin, has been
penned in by old age, the roles of husband and father, but
who, like the unicorn, has nevertheless maintained a kind of
sexual and imaginative potency. There is finally the tenacity of
the snake which, with its head crushed, wriggles violently until
sundown. Yet the emphasis in this last episode is less on persistence than on the place of death in the cycles of nature and on
Godwin's knowledge of these mysterious processes. In fact,
Godwin's wisdom is like the awareness of the artist who can
equate his domestic affairs with the symbolic patterns of a medieval tapestry; both are forms of knowing which, staying
close to physical experience, involve a sense of what is recurrent in such experience. And it is this sense that his own life is
simply one manifestation of an eternally recurrent pattern that
frees Paterson from all fear of death.

What is most striking about this passage to any reader of the
first four books of *Paterson* is its stress on the harmonies,
rather than the tensions, among its parts. The use of the poetic
fiction, the unicorn as analogue for the poet, would earlier have
been broken down ironically, but it here serves to amplify the
significance of the contemporary material. In the passage following the one we have just been looking at, Paterson turns
self-consciously around to meditate about the movement of his
own thoughts; but the result, again, is no reversal but an expansion of idea and mood.

> The (self) direction has been changed
>   the serpent
>   its tail in its mouth
> "the river has returned to its beginnings"
>   and backward
>   (and forward)
> it tortures itself within me

until time has been washed finally under:
and "I knew all (or enough)
it became me   .   "
—the times are not heroic
since then
but they are cleaner
and freer of disease
the mind rotted within them   .
we'll say
the serpent
has its tail in its mouth
AGAIN!
the all-wise serpent   (p. 271)

Paterson steps back to view his present situation in the context of his entire career. In old age, he says, the self is forced to take up new directions—specifically, those opened by personal memory. The kind of reminiscence he is talking about, however, is not just an old man's mind drifting into random recollection. The snake with its tail in its mouth, the river returning to its beginnings: both of these images remind us that the act of memory, in its circularity, achieves a transcendence of time. What is remembered is, after all, what has persisted through time; and it has persisted because, like the memory of Godwin that suddenly surfaces from the subconscious, it has an archetypal status. The quoted lines in the passage are taken from "The Wanderer"; they serve as an instance as well as a definition of memory. Paterson, circling back from the end to the beginning of his career, then bringing himself up to the present again, moves backward and forward so that time *is* finally washed under. Old age may be less heroic, its tone is certainly more modest, it entails a lessening of perceptual powers but, through memory, "the serpent // has its tail in its mouth / AGAIN!"; the process of renewal goes on.

Most of the later poems share the impulse in *Paterson* V to pull things together into this easygoing, circling process. Williams himself regarded the work of this period as the summit of his art; and the general tendency among his critics has been to echo this judgment.[6] Certainly the image the poems project

—a benevolent old man, recovering from some near fatal illness, now filled with love, blessing all he sees, humbly dispensing wisdom—is a touching one. Moreover, the changed circumstances of Williams's life resulted in a more personal and discursive medium while this very step back from immediate experience made possible a greater degree of artistic finish. All this has made the Williams of the 1950's a figure hard to resist; but our admiration for his tenacity in developing a new mode, our engagement with the figure in the poems, must be separated from our estimate of the poetry. For in his later years Williams more and more found himself irresistible and, his self-divisions resolved, lost much of his capacity for self-criticism. This is already evident in the *Autobiography* (1951) where Williams tries to persuade us of his essential innocence, honesty and tenderness and, in the process, tells us everything but how this simple, rustic figure could have produced the tough, involuted verse and prose of William Carlos Williams. In the more reminiscent of the poems there is a similar proclivity to project present equanimity onto the past. The new looseness of manner and tenderness of feeling can sometimes sink into the sort of soggy, uplifting didacticism that had prompted Imagism in the first place. At the very least, it seems to me an open question whether the divisions of Williams's character did not generate an intense, multi-dimensional language in *Spring and All* that makes that book superior to the works of the middle 'fifties. Williams, of course, continued to write some fine poems: "To Daphne and Virginia," "The Orchestra," "The Yellow Flower," "The Mental Hospital Garden," "The Desert Music," "The Pink Locust," "Shadows" and "Asphodel, That Greeny Flower." [7] But even among these, the best tend to be the more self-conscious, notably the "Asphodel" poem.

"Asphodel, That Greeny Flower" is a rather long meditative poem, divided into three books and a coda. The poet is addressing his wife, whom he has abused through his sexual and artistic pursuits. He is approaching her one last time, reviewing their life together and asking her forgiveness. Here Williams is

no longer dispersing himself into a set of objects; the "I,"
slowly purged from his verse in the teens, now returns in the
figure of a wise old man who, while aware of loss and suffering, offers advice, hope and consolation. Old age has always
held its right to its opinions and Williams is now not reluctant
to state his explicitly.

> So we come to watch time's flight
>   as we might watch
> summer lightning
>   or fireflies, secure
>   by grace of the imagination,
>   safe in its care.   (pp. 179–80)

Time is finally powerless to affect us, Williams tells us in a
voice of grandfatherly solicitude. Yet, he can also discourse
somberly, and again explicitly, about its effects on our physical
powers.

> Approaching death
>   as we think, the death of love,
>   no distinction
> any more suffices to differentiate
>   the particulars
>   of place and condition
>   with which we have been long
>   familiar.   (p. 162)

The outlines of things are not so distinct any more. And so,
instead of cutting things down to "isolate flecks" and juxtaposing them in empty space, he supplies many transitional links,
fills in the spaces between images.

> The sea! The sea!
>   Always
>   when I think of the sea
> there comes to mind
>   the *Iliad*
>   and Helen's public fault
>   that bred it.   (p. 158)

Not all transitions are made so explicitly, but even when they
are not, the shifts are never violent; there is never the tension

of opposed forces that we find in *Spring and All*. Moreover, in "Asphodel" Williams often explains the significances of his images. After describing "the statue / of Colleoni's horse / with the thickset little man // on top / in armor / presenting a naked sword" and "the horse rampant / roused by the mare in / the Venus and Adonis," Williams comments that "these are pictures / of crude force" (p. 171). "Of love, abiding love // it will be telling," he says of the asphodel (p. 153). As we shall see, the images in this poem are rich, fluid, complex; his comments by no means exhaust their significance. But the effect of this discursive quality is to ease the reader's movement through the verse. "It is not // a flute note either, it is the relation / of a flute note / to a drum," Williams writes in "The Orchestra" (*PB*, p. 81). Relations here emerge as more important than discrete objects, and these relations are often articulated at the surface of the poetry. Creative activity now takes place at a "higher" level of consciousness; Williams does not take us to the edge of unconscious chaos but to a place in the mind where form and continuity become more predominant.

Williams's poetry of the 1950's thus has a more accessible surface—a fact that accounts for its greater critical popularity. Other manifestations of this loosening up are his unequivocal acceptance of romantic feeling and his dependence on personal, biographical material. In "Asphodel," emotions, like ideas, are often stated: "with fear in my heart" (p. 154), "I regret" (p. 169), "I adore" (p. 169), "I am tortured // and cannot rest" (p. 170). Moreover, these feelings are much tenderer than any Williams had previously been willing to admit to his verse; emotion ranges from "every drill / driven into the earth // for oil enters my side / also" (p. 168) through "our eyes fill / with tears" (p. 153) to "Sweet, creep into my arms!" (p. 175). He is embarrassed neither by uplifting sentiments—"the palm goes // always to the light" (p. 180)—nor by poignancy:

> At the altar
> so intent was I
> before my vows
> so moved by your presence
> a girl so pale

> and ready to faint
>   that I pitied
>   and wanted to protect you. (p. 181)

A sad, tender, consoling mood is evoked, one that is never violently undercut by a tougher voice uttering "pah!" or "pinholes" or the like. The mood *is* complex, including the torture of oil drills as well as the celebration of the light; but whereas in *Spring and All* light and darkness were left in a kind of agonizing tension, we now get a resolution of conflict: "the palm goes // always to the light."

The quality of the feeling stems, of course, from the poem's origin in a specific personal situation: Williams's ambivalent relation with his wife, Flossie. In *The Build-up*, the last novel in the *White Mule* trilogy, Williams describes his rather peculiar courtship of Flossie. He proposed to her, it appears, a few days after her older sister, with whom he was in love, was engaged to his younger brother. He defines the love between them as "not romantic love" but "a dark sort of passion . . . a passion of despair, as all life is despair" (p. 262). He is evading a good deal here, but the feeling he speaks of—an acceptance of what imperfectly exists—is exactly that dark passion we have seen animating all of his creative work; Flossie is its ultimate source. But even if she was "the rock on which I have built" (*Auto*, p. 55), Williams frequently wandered off. In the *Autobiography* she remains a rather dim figure, given a few vague tributes, but essentially in the background; and in some respects that must have seemed to her her place in his life. Medicine, poetry, and other women occupied much more of his time than domestic pursuits. As early as the "Prologue" to *Kora in Hell*, Williams had argued that love, like literary style, had periodically to be broken down in order to come to new life (*SE*, p. 20). Love had to be constantly reborn out of its own despair. Yet it would be surprising if Flossie did not occasionally feel that her husband's affairs were more a form of self-indulgence than a rather strange way of renewing their marriage; and being the ultimate source of the poet's work is a fairly abstract role for his wife to adopt. The tensions that developed in their marriage were first explored in Williams's best play, *A Dream of Love* (1948)—and they provide the background for "Asphodel."

In the poem, Williams now turns to address his wife directly and remorsefully. Old, nearing death, he approaches her "perhaps for the last time" (p. 154). The time is winter, but this is more an internal state than a season in Rutherford—defined by the strong sense of loss, fading, and mutability with which the poem begins. "Today // I'm filled with the fading memory of those flowers / that we both loved," Williams says (p. 153). He recalls first the "poor // colorless" (p. 153) asphodel, a flower that grows in the meadows of New Jersey, but also (he had read in Homer) along the fields in the underworld. In fact, Williams speaks at the start as if from among the dead, identifying with their groping recollection as they gaze at the asphodel: "What do I remember / that was shaped / as this thing is shaped?" (p. 153). "There is something / something urgent" (p. 154) which he *must* say, but he does not want to rush it—"while I drink in / the joy of your approach, / perhaps for the last time" (p. 154)—and fading powers of memory make it hard to begin. There is an urgency about the very act of speech: "I dare not stop. / Listen while I talk on // against time." "Only give me time," he asks,

> time to recall them
> > before I shall speak out
> Give me time,
> > time.   (p. 154)

He gropes for memory, for speech, for his wife's love—the three will become identified in the course of the poem—for these have the power to save him from time's push toward oblivion; they can bring him back from the realm of the dead.

At the end of Book III of "Asphodel" Williams does gain the forgiveness he seeks: "You have forgiven me / making me new again" (p. 177). And the asphodel becomes the appropriate symbol for this renewal of love in the poet's old age: though colorless and odorless, "little prized among the living"

(p. 153), it is a sturdy perennial: "I have invoked the flower /
in that // frail as it is / after winter's harshness / it comes
again" (pp. 169–70). The basic pattern of "Asphodel," the
transition from death to life, is a familiar one in Williams's
work. But one important difference from the earlier treatment
of this process is the change in the length and pace of the
poem—that is, in the poet's sense of time. The poem is strongly
reminiscent, but it is located in a now: the line breaks give the
isolated word "today" equal weight with "I'm filled with the
fading memory of those flowers." Memory soon begins to
flow, but Williams keeps turning back from recollection of
their long life together to their present situation. "Inseparable
from the fire / its light / takes precedence over it," Williams
writes in the Coda.

> In the huge gap
> > between the flash
> and the thunderstroke
> > spring has come in
> > > or a deep snow fallen.
> Call it old age.
> > In that stretch
> > > we have lived to see
> a colt kick up his heels.
> > Do not hasten
> > > laugh and play
> in an eternity
> > the heat will not overtake the light.
> > > (pp. 178–79)

The urgency felt at the start of the poem has vanished. Precedence of the light over the fire guarantees that death is not,
as we think, the death of love. Old age need not be merely an
experience of loss and emptiness. If youth can be filled with a
multiplicity of physical sensations, old age can achieve a fullness of the imagination. In fact, variants of the word "fill"
echo and re-echo through this poem. The life of the poet and
his wife has been "filled" with flowers, their eyes "fill" with

tears, Williams's mind is now "filled" with the fading memory of those flowers. At one point speech almost lapses into silence, emptiness.

> Silence can be complex too,
>   but you do not get far
>   with silence.
> Begin again.
>   It is like Homer's
>   catalogue of ships:
> it fills up the time.   (p. 159)

Context, aided by the isolation of the phrase in its own line, gives a cynical slang expression ("well, it fills up the time") a poetic and a more positive force. Silence is emptiness, death; speech makes the time full, and this is one of the ways in which poetic speech and love are identified. "Do not hasten / laugh and play // in an eternity." At the brink of death, in that instant between the flash and the thunderstroke, Williams opens a "huge gap" and fills it with the unhurried recollections and discursive wisdom of this poem. The suspended moment he had always sought is now stretched out, expanded into "an eternity"; the heat will not overtake the light.

This sense of the eternal moment, however, importantly qualifies any sense in which the poem can be called personal. The "I" is there, and the events of the speaker's life are clearly those of Williams's. Yet, the stress here is on the metaphorization of experience; the author sees his life as a living fiction. Past events are frequently rendered figuratively. The time of youthful passion is a "garden" (p. 156), while the later trials of marriage are a "storm" (p. 157). Williams compares his own leisurely manner of discourse with "Homer's / catalogue of ships," then takes a step back to comment on his technique.

> I speak in figures,
>   well enough, the dresses
> you wear are figures also,
>   we could not meet
>   otherwise.   (p. 159)

Emphasis has shifted from a kind of naked utterance—the bare object—to a more figurative style, and the figures themselves—like the comparison between metaphor and clothing—are deliberately more conventional than startling. All of the poem's central metaphors—flower, garden, sea, storm, fire, light—are commonplace in literature. What is more, they are not given any novel twist, of the sort spring receives in "By the road," to give them the fresh impact of literal experience.

Even more important than their commonplace quality is the way the figures work in this poem. In *Spring and All* Williams pushed away from conventional symbolism, down into the literal, there to discover a new symbolic world. But in "Asphodel," his main tendency is to move through the literal toward the symbolic, though he is self-conscious about speaking in figures and keeps coming back to the literal to verify his hardmindedness. In Book III Williams recalls "waiting at a station / with a friend," "a distinguished artist," when "a fast freight / thundered through." "That's what we'd all like to be, Bill," the friend commented—showing exactly that sense of the all in the momentary that made him a distinguished artist (p. 171). Throughout "Asphodel" Williams himself keeps discovering the archetypal in the particular. Just after the episode with his artist friend, Williams recalls a man seen "yesterday / in the subway." A detailed account of the man's mixture of crudity and refinement follows; then Williams suddenly realizes why he is so intrigued by this person.

> This man
>   reminds me of my father.
> I am looking
>   into my father's
>   face!

The image of the man expands still further; he becomes the universal father: "With him // went all men / and all women too / were in his loins."

> And so, by chance,
>   how should it be otherwise?

                              from what came to me
          in a subway train
                  I build a picture
                      of all men. (pp. 172–74)

It is memory that, re-awakened, enables the older poet to transcend time: as he moves back, first through personal and then
the racial past, he gets to the eternal, the archetypal. Moreover, mythic vision has not been dispersed into scattered details in the verse, to be perceived in sudden flashes; the process
of its recovery has been brought up to the surface of the poetry.

   This universalizing process is going on constantly in "Asphodel." The speaker may be the particular person "Bill" Williams, but he is also the (timeless) father of all poets,
Homer—with strong suggestions of his difference from the
weary, death-longing Tiresias of "The Waste Land."

                          Death is no answer,
          no answer—
                      to a blind old man
                          whose bones
          have the movement
                      of the sea,
                          a sexless old man
          for whom it is a sea
                      of which his verses
                          are made up. (p. 166)

Williams is highly self-conscious about this kind of poetic
speech, and his tentativeness makes it easier for the reader to
accept the process of metaphorization. "Fanciful or not," he
says of his thoughts about the old man in the subway (p. 174).
At the very beginning of the poem he is hesitant about asserting a metaphor too boldly:

          We lived long together
                      a life filled,
                          if you will,
          with flowers. [my emphasis] (p. 153)

He is aware that his reader is apt to take "lightly" what is said
in poems, that poems in his world are "despised poems" (p.
161). He has to turn around on, and gently defend, himself: "I
speak in figures." All of this helps to define the speaker as one
who is not blindly, arrogantly, pushing experience into forms,
unities. The poem does not simply proclaim a synthesis—it
gives us a process, a process in which images are constantly ex-
panding toward the archetypical, contracting to the literal, ex-
panding again, and so on. This process can best be seen in Williams's handling of the figure of Flossie.

It is important to see that, while Williams is sorry for the
pain he has caused his wife, he does not try to revoke his past
life. "I do not come to you / abjectly // with confessions of
my faults" (p. 170). Instead, he tries to "give the steps" "by
which you shall mount, / again to think well of me" (p. 171).
Her forgiveness is to come from her understanding of the peculiar nature of his love for her. From the first, the love she
awoke in him was expansive, all-embracing:

> Endless wealth,
>   I thought,
>   held out its arms to me.
> A thousand topics
>   in an apple blossom.
>   The generous earth itself
> gave us lief.
>   The whole world
>   became my garden! (pp. 155–56)

Accordingly, Flossie is not just Flossie; she is a "single image"
running through all things (p. 169). This figure freed Williams to pluck many other flowers of the field and created
some of the main tensions of their marriage. Williams knows
that this argument will not seem "wholly credible" (p. 154),
but he insists that love should not be a limiting thing:

>   Love is something else,
>   or so I thought it,
> a garden which expands,
>   though I knew you as a woman

                and never thought otherwise,
        until the whole sea
                has been taken up
                        and all its gardens. (p. 160)

Love at first vaguely expands, then turns back to the literal
"you," then reaches out toward the all, the whole sea. In the
following lines Williams fills in our sense of the all, but comes
back again at the end to the "you" which is love's source.

    It was the love of love
                the love that swallows up all else
                        a grateful love,
        a love of nature, of people
                animals,
                        a love engendering
        gentleness and goodness
                that moved me
                        and *that* I saw in you. (p. 160).

Shifts of direction like this have always been characteristic of
Williams's work, though they are now less rapid and startling.
Their importance here, however, is that they enact the notion
of love as a force that expands to the all, then returns to its origin, in the movement of the verse; in the poem Flossie *is* the
single image that generates all the others.

    Near the end of Book III, after he has invoked some of the
flowers that counted most for them, Williams says,

    You were like those,
                though I quickly
                        correct myself
        for you were a woman
                and no flower
                        and had to face
        the problems which confront a woman.
                But you were for all that
                        flowerlike
        and I say this to you now
                and it is a thing
                        which compounded

my torment
            that I never
                    forgot it. (p. 177)

Again, the poet self-consciously asserts, takes back, then reasserts a poetic figure. And when the comparison is finally made,
it is stated carefully—as a simile. Williams had once declared
that "the coining of similes is a pastime of very low order"
(*SE*, p. 16); but explicit comparisons frequently enter his later
poetry. They are ideally suited for creating the kind of loose
unity Williams was after in these poems: they establish a relation between, but not a fusion of, the two items compared.
Flossie is "a woman" and "no flower"; but she is also "flower-
like" [my emphasis].

The literal presence of Flossie is extremely important; she is
the "rock" on which the rest of the poem is built. As in *Spring
and All* and *Paterson*, Williams creates a poetic field by means
of recurrent words, images. Crucial figures in "Asphodel" are
the flower, garden, sea. At the very beginning asphodel, "that
greeny flower," is formally announced as the poetic subject.
The poet reflects on a "long" life "filled" "with flowers" and is
thus "cheered" "to know / that there were flowers also / in
hell" (p. 153). Book I is filled with flowers. There are a variety of specific flowers, memories of youthful passion: butter-
cup, honeysuckle, lily, rose hedges, pink mallow, orchid, lil-
ies-of-the-valley; the word "flower(s)" appears fourteen times.
Yet images in this poem quickly move toward the symbolic.
When Williams tells us that the "storm" "is a flower" (p.
157), we read "marital turbulence" for storm and "love" for
flower. Similarly, when he uses the word "garden," he is not
pointing toward "this garden," he is invoking the *idea* of gar-
dens. But those equivalences are not static; for the way the recurrences in this poem work is to take a traditional literary figure—like the garden—and make it more open, fluid, expansive.
In its multiplicity the flower becomes a garden; with the
awakening of his love for Flossie, says Williams, "The whole
world / became my garden!" At this point the writer, as if
questioning his hyperbole, self-consciously interrupts himself

and remembers the garden's opposite: "But the sea / which no one tends. . . ." Yet this turn—in a manner characteristic of this poem—does not undercut the garden image but extends it:

> But the sea
>   which no one tends
>   is also a garden

The thought does not stop here, however; the comparison is qualified: the sea is a garden "when the sun strikes it / and the waves / are wakened." At such moments "it puts all flowers / to shame." Yet, from this affirmation of the sea's beauty, Williams can turn around to concede its death and ugliness:

> Too, there are the starfish
>   stiffened by the sun
>   and other sea wrack
>   and weeds.   (p. 156)

The sea is a garden; the sea is not a garden. As in *Paterson*, the sea is recognized as death; but "the sea alone // with its multiplicity / holds any hope" (p. 158). Niggardliness, the fear of that "love that swallows up all else" (p. 160), the single-minded thrust through the world, ends in death, silence, despair—a desert. But surrender to multiplicity—as with the old man "whose bones // have the movement / of the sea," "for whom it is a sea / of which his verses / are made up" (p. 166)—cures "the mind" and "the will becomes again / a garden" (p. 159). The way Williams keeps turning back before going on, but keeps moving forward, defines the similarity to and difference from his earlier work. The motion of this poem is through a recognition of the fact of death, toward an affirmation of the transcendent power of love—symbolized by the asphodel, the flower that grows "in hell." This circling movement keeps going throughout the poem, through the elaborate dissection of "the deaths I suffered" (p. 164) in Book II, to culminate in the affirmations at the end of III:

> Don't think
> that because I say this

```
              in a poem
                   it can be treated lightly
         or that the facts will not uphold it.
              Are facts not flowers
                   and flowers facts
         or poems flowers
                   or all works of the imagination
                        interchangeable?
         Which proves
              that love
                   rules them all, for then
         you will be my queen,
              my queen of love
                   forever more.  (p. 178)
```

At this climactic point the poet's self-conscious awareness of
the frivolousness that most men associate with figurative
speech is absorbed into a firm instructional tone, "Don't think"
—while his own counter-assertion of the identity of fact and
figure is made gently, as a rhetorical question. Earlier, Williams had spoken of "the free interchange // of light" on the
sea's surface (p. 165). All things are works of the imagination,
and they are all interchangeable—like the images of this poem
—because they are all manifestations of a single principle, the
light. These things are not fused; but they are joined. It was
this all-pervading light that "was wakened / and shone" at
"our wedding" (p. 181). Whether we accept Williams's argument of a "single image" running through the multiplicity of
his loves as credible or not, the important point is that his argument is made good in the structure of his poem. The way its
images split and join, split and join—their fluidity and openness
—shows that love does rule them all.

"Asphodel" is written in the triadic stanza pattern which,
taken over from the "descent beckons" passage in *Paterson* II,
Williams employed in all but one of the poems in *The Desert
Music* and *Journey to Love*. In theorizing about the poem
Williams always dwelt on its basic structural unit—the line.
The iambic pentameter line, or any line measured by counting
stresses or syllables, seemed to him too rigid to express the
modern sense of reality. Poems, he argues,

cannot any longer be made following a Euclidian measure, "beautiful" as this may make them. The very grounds for our beliefs have altered. We do not live that way any more; nothing in our lives, at bottom, is ordered according to that measure; our social concepts, our schools, our very religious ideas, certainly our understanding of mathematics are greatly altered. . . . Only the construction of our poems—and at best the construction of a poem must engage the tips of our intellectual awareness—is left shamefully to the past. (*SE*, p. 337)

At the same time Williams was just as opposed to free verse as he was to more archaic ways of ordering. If the second pushes down too hard from the outside, the first lifts not at all and creates no tension in the poem; both, by blurring experience, fail to bring its distinct elements into the kind of proximity that will create an imaginative field. Only invention can do that; "poetry is creation of new form—" (*SL*, p. 134); and the rhythmical sources of that form will be found not in the literature of the past but in the spoken language of today, the American idiom. Hence, what Williams was after was a new way of measuring, one more consonant with the speech, with the realities of our time. As he told Kay Boyle in 1932, this new measure "must be large enough, free enough, elastic enough, new enough yet firm enough to hold the new well, without spilling. It must have a form" (*SL*, p. 133). How to uncover this new form? "Relativity gives us the cue," says Williams, directing us to a "*relatively* stable foot, not a rigid one" (*SE*, p. 340). His lifelong search for such a new measure culminated, he believed, in the triadic stanza, its use of a "variable foot."

A relative stability? A variable foot? Williams is well aware that these phrases will strike a certain kind of mind as contradictory; he is trying to dissolve what he takes to be a false antithesis in such minds. The real question is, what do these notions mean when applied to a specific passage of verse? In public discussions of this new measure Williams stays tantalizingly abstract, abundant on theory but wary of examples. But in a letter to Richard Eberhart he reveals that "by measure I mean musical pace" and that he counts one for each of the three feet in a stanza (*SL*, pp. 326–27). The practice, it appears, is rather easily understood and much less radical than the theory would lead us to expect: uniform intervals of lapsed time (musical pace) establish a regularity in the poem; but the syllable count, ranging from one to thirteen in "Asphodel," is variable, with pauses used to fill out the intervals in the shorter lines. Whether or not this line will, as Williams believed, open the way for poets to come, only the future can tell. But it is perfectly suited to the mood and point of view of the poems of his own old age.

In the triadic stanza, the line begins to move across the page, turns slightly back, begins again, goes through another short turn, then begins once more—before turning all the way back to the left hand margin. The medium itself suggests the kind of halting progression, self-conscious affirmation, that we find in a poem like "Asphodel." This quality can be best epitomized by a passage in which Williams simultaneously quotes Spenser's "Prothalamion" and alludes to "The Waste Land."

> All pomp and ceremony
> of weddings,
> "Sweet Thames, run softly
> till I end
> my song,"—
> are of an equal sort.   (p. 181)

Williams's three-stepped stanza does take away much of the flow of Spenser's line. But while in Eliot's shattered world this mellifluousness can only be used ironically, Williams's breaking of the line does not undercut—it prolongs, deepens, extends; it makes possible a tentative acceptance of the whole mood and manner implied by Spenser's line. Williams is still spacing things out carefully, isolating them in rather short lines; but he now does this much more gently and builds a halting but genuine rhythmic flow. The lines, while momentarily suspended as individual units, do move across the page in a fairly regular pattern: if there is not the flow possible in a line of iambic pentameter, there is not the tensed, jagged quality of Wil-

liams's earlier work either. "Asphodel" has more the ease of a
matured craftsmanship.

The freedom of the "variable foot" still requires its own
kind of discipline: since the syllable count is variable, each line
break must still carry its own justification. Hence, in spite of
the regular pace, each line must be filled subtly, attentively.
To begin with, the line divisions (as always in Williams) slow
down movement of the verse, momentarily isolate syntactic
units—giving each an interval of its own, time to sink into the
mind. Under Williams's careful hand, parts we might otherwise glide past are given emphatic weight and more exact
meaning. There is a delicate but significant difference between
this line from "Asphodel"

> The end
>   will come
>   in its time.   (p. 165)

and these two of many possible variants:

> The end will come in its time.

>   The end will come
> in its time.

The first variant rushes, as if eager to dismiss thoughts of the
end; the second, by cutting the sentence across a stanza break,
stresses that the end will come *when it comes.* Williams's version, descending deliberately across the page, gives equal stress
to "end," "come" and "time" and is thus the only one of the
three which defines a full and measured acceptance of death
over which we have no control.

Similarly, at the beginning of the "Coda" Williams writes,

> Inseparable from the fire,
>   its light
>   takes percedence over it.

Light takes precedence not just by assertion of the poet but by
its fulfillment of syntactic expectations raised by "inseparable,"

its short, closed sound, its near isolation in a line that is surrounded by longer, quicker lines. Williams goes on:

> Then follows
> > what we have dreaded—
> > > but it can never
> overcome what has gone before.   (p. 178)

"Then follows" puts us into the dimension of temporal sequence; we wait, expectantly, for what follows to be named.
Instead, the next line tells us more about our attitude (dread)
toward that thing than what that thing actually is. The dash at
the end of the line suggests that the object of dread may be
named in the following one, but the speaker turns away from
direct confrontation, toward assurance: "but it can never //
overcome what has gone before." Dividing auxiliary from
main verb across a stanza break gives great weight to both
"never" and "overcome." Both of these are time words—although "overcome," like "precedence," has connotations of
value too—and the turn back across the page shifts us out of
time as a forward-moving, irretrievable progression, and into
the eternal moment. An experience of the "light" does not
fade into the past and die; it is an experience of eternity and
stays alive forever—like the memory of his own wedding
which, Williams says at the end of the "Coda," has the power
to revive him *now*. This groping turn through the temporal
and into the eternal—typical of the entire poem—could not be
rendered in any other but the verse form Williams has employed.

The opening passage of the "Coda" shows that Williams still
suspends a grammatical expectation across a line or stanza division as a means of distributing emphasis exactly. But these divisions are much less striking than in *Spring and All*. Williams
will cut a line between subject and verb, verb and object, main
clause and subordinate clause, parts of a compound sentence.
He will even let "logic" words such as "and so" or "but if"
stand alone in a line. But he does not end lines strikingly with
prepositions, articles or (for the most part) adjectives. There is

less antagonism towards the conventional units of syntax, a
fact also evident in the elimination of sentence fragments. Even
more important, our expectations are not dealt with so violently: "what we have dreaded" may not be exactly what we
anticipated, but it is not a reversal either. At the start of Book
III Williams writes,

> What power has love but forgiveness?
> > In other words
> > > by its intervention
> what has been done
> > can be undone.   (p. 169)

Argument has been distributed easily across these stanzas: lines
mark off a sentence, a phrase, a phrase, a subject-clause, a verb.
Reversal *is* the idea advanced—the denial of time via love—but
the last line comes as the unraveling of a logical consequence
of what has been stated in the first line. There is more the
sense of a deliberate building toward a triumphant climax than
the experience of a series of swift, startling turns of thought.

   In "Asphodel" relations are more defined; ambiguities are
cleaned away. Argument does not proceed remorselessly forward in a straight line; it circles, winds into progression, but
its turning has been spread out more—like the lines across the
page—making movement easier, more relaxed. Occasionally
punctuation has been omitted to create alternate readings:

> > Do not hasten
> > > laugh and play
> in an eternity
> > the heat will not overtake the light.
> > > > (p. 179)

"In an eternity" can either go with what comes before ("laugh
and play // in an eternity") or with what follows ("in an eternity / the heat will not overtake the light"). But the two
senses work to fill out, amplify—not contradict—each other.
As before, line breaks serve to point up turns in the thought.
But now directions are not abruptly established by a shift of
tone; they are eased by use of such logic words as "but,"

"save" and the like. Williams is especially given to shifting the
direction of thought across the long turn from the third line
of one stanza to the first line of the next. He does this twice in
the concluding passage of "Asphodel":

As I think of it now,
            after a lifetime,
                        it is as if
a sweet-scented flower
            were poised
                        and for me did open.
Asphodel
            has no odor
                        save to the imagination
but it too
            celebrates the light.
                        It is late
but an odor
            as from our wedding
                        has revived for me
and begun again to penetrate
            into all crevices
                        of my world.   (p. 182)

At first Williams expresses a strong sense of loss through the
passage of time. The old man modestly asserts a common-place
figure—the bride seemed "as if" a "sweet-scented flower"—but
the distance between "now" and then ("did open") is stressed.
The flower of old age, the asphodel, "has no odor"; and "it is
late." Yet each time Williams falls into this feeling of loss, the
imagination delivers an upward turn—one that occurs as the
lines move back across the page to the left margin: "but it
too," "but an odor." A strong line begins the final stanza too:
"and begun again to penetrate." At this point the imagination
has dissolved temporal progression; the imaginary odor has
begun *now* to fill *all* the dark and empty spaces of the poet's
world.

   Another aspect of Williams's relaxed craftsmanship in this
poem is his willingness to draw on iambic rhythms as a technical resource.

        Of asphodel, that greeny flower,
                like a buttercup
                        upon its branching stem
        save that it's green and wooden—
                I come, my sweet,
                        to sing to you,   (p. 153)

the poem begins. Syllabic count ranges from four to nine in
these lines; but a strong iambic beat has been established by the
third line. Then, as Williams pulls back across the page to start
a new stanza, as he pulls back from the simile to give the literal
truth of the asphodel as well, a trochaic (reverse) beat is introduced. Then, with the asphodel established as both fact and
figure, Williams tightens into a regular two foot iambic beat
and the invocation comes to a formal close.

   Iambic meter, inverted word order, poetic epithet and peri-
odic sentence structure all contribute to create a stylistic elevation. This is partly the deliberate heightening of a formal beginning; but it is not as atypical as we might at first suppose.
Williams has probably confused more readers than he has
helped by suggesting that these later poems employ the
"American idiom," the speech we hear spoken about us every
day. It is exceedingly difficult to establish norms that enable us
to distinguish spoken use of the language from other uses. But
it becomes pretty clear, when we write some of his sentences
out as prose, that Williams's utterance is more elevated than
common speech.

    Begin again. It is like Homer's catalogue of ships: it fills up
    the time. I speak in figures, well enough, the dresses you wear
    are figures also, we could not meet otherwise. When I speak
    of flowers it is to recall that at one time we were young. All
    women are not Helen, I know that, but have Helen in their
    hearts. My sweet, you have it also, therefore I love you and
    could not love you otherwise. (p. 159)

The personal pronouns "I" and "you," direct address to "my
sweet," an interrupter like "I know that," create a conversational tone. Accordingly, the diction stays simple, containing
only two words of more than two syllables. There *is* a flat,

loose, prosaic quality to the style, but no one in Rutherford ever spoke sentences like these. The passage, for one thing, has a slight incantatory effect. The words "time," "figures," "otherwise," "speak," "flowers," "Helen," "also," "love" are all repeated; some of these, along with "meet" and "sweet" and "know," have appeared several times earlier in the poem. In fact, not only are these sentences unlike natural speech, but the self-conscious use of poetic figures and the subdued incantation suggest that the intended effect is one of deliberate rather than spontaneous utterance. Rather than simply recording American speech, Williams's style operates at a level where a flat, discursive, conversational language has been gently pushed, one step upward, toward ritual expression. Like the asphodel, this style is mainly colorless, abstract; but it too celebrates the light and it does so in a way that has both ease *and* a formal elegance.

As a result, the style embodies that value of decorum which the poet argues for; we could not meet him otherwise. Formality, ritual, decorum—all these were values that the younger Williams had heaped contempt on. Now, that crude fight is over. In "Asphodel" Williams can quote Spenser, identify with Homer, use the language of courtly love, speak of the "*grace* of the imagination" (p. 180; my emphasis), extol "medieval pageantry," "the reading of Chaucer," a priest's (or a savage chieftain's) "raiment," celebrate "all the pomp and ceremony / of weddings" (p. 181). *All* are works of the imagination. Like his own poetic figures, these are all manifestations of that "single image," first opened by Flossie, to which, he now says, he had devoted his entire life. His earlier work had put us at that edge of consciousness where light becomes darkness, and darkness light. At the end, in "Asphodel," "it is all // a celebration of the light" (p. 181).

Notes

Most of the references to Williams's work have been made in my text. But in order to keep the text as clean as possible, I have given no specific references when the work is short (a lyric poem or short story) and the title is mentioned. In addition, where a single work is dealt with extensively, I give page numbers without repeating the title. The following abbreviations are used:

Poems (Rutherford, N.J.: privately printed, 1909) *Poems*

Kora in Hell: Improvisations (San Francisco: City Lights, 1957) *Kora*

Spring and All (Dijon: Contact, 1923) *SA*

The Great American Novel (Paris: Contact, 1923) *GAN*

In the American Grain (Norfolk, Conn.: New Directions, 1956) *IAG*

A Voyage to Pagany (New York: The Macaulay Co., 1928) *A Voyage*

A Novelette and Other Prose, 1921–31 (Toulon: TO, Publishers, 1932) *A Novelette*

White Mule (Norfolk, Conn.: New Directions, 1938) *WM*

In the Money (Norfolk, Conn.: New Directions, 1940) *IM*

The Collected Earlier Poems (Norfolk, Conn.: New Directions, 1951) *CEP*

The Autobiography of William Carlos Williams (New York: Random House, 1951) *Auto*

Selected Essays (New York: Random House, 1954) *SE*

Selected Letters, ed. John C. Thirlwall (New York: McDowell Obolensky, 1957) *SL*

I Wanted To Write a Poem, ed. Edith Heal (Bos-   IW
ton: Beacon Press, 1958)
The Farmers' Daughters: The Collected Stories of   FD
William Carlos Williams (Norfolk, Conn.: New
Directions, 1961)
Pictures from Brueghel and Other Poems (Norfolk,   PB
Conn.: New Directions, 1962)
The Collected Later Poems (Norfolk, Conn.: New   CLP
Directions, 1963)
Paterson (Norfolk, Conn.: New Directions, 1963)   P

CHAPTER I

1. Water Sutton, "A Visit with William Carlos Williams," *The Minnesota Review,* I (April 1961), 312.

2. See Erik Erikson's *Young Man Luther* (New York, 1958).

3. There is an excellent study of the relations between medicine and art in Williams by Kenneth Burke, "William Carlos Williams, 1883–1963," in *Language as Symbolic Action* (Berkeley and Los Angeles, 1966), pp. 282–91.

4. *The Letters of Ezra Pound, 1907–1941,* ed. D. D. Paige (New York, 1950), p. 8.

5. "America, Whitman, and the Art of Poetry," *The Poetry Journal* (November 1917), 31.

6. "An Essay on *Leaves of Grass*" first appeared in *Leaves of Grass: One Hundred Years After,* ed. Milton Hindus (Stanford, 1955), pp. 22–31.

7. Walter Sutton, "A Visit with William Carlos Willams," 312.

8. William Carlos Williams, "An Approach to the Poem," *English Institute Essays* (New York, 1948), pp. 67–68.

9. J. Hillis Miller, *Poets of Reality* (Cambridge, Mass., 1965), p. 288. Later on, discussing the descent/ascent pattern in Williams's work (pp. 336–39), Professor Miller himself implies that there is a kind of subject-object tension in Williams's work; but he does not relate these perceptions to his main thesis.

CHAPTER II

1. Henry Adams, *The Life of George Cabot Lodge,* in *The Shock of Recognition,* ed. Edmund Wilson (New York, 1955), p. 751.

2. Walt Whitman, "In Paths Untrodden," *Complete Poetry and Selected Prose*, ed. James E. Miller, Jr. (Boston, 1959), p. 84.

3. This theme is developed at length in Larzer Ziff, *The American 1890s* (New York, 1966).

4. Ezra Pound, *Gaudier-Brzeska, A Memoir* (Norfolk, Conn., 1960), p. 102.

5. Quoted in Robert Buttel, *Wallace Stevens, The Making of Harmonium* (Princeton, N.J., 1967), p. 47.

6. Such is the main thesis of Pound's *Patria Mia* (Chicago, 1960).

7. "Rebellion in Art," in *America in Crisis*, ed. Daniel Aaron (New York, 1952), pp. 205–6.

8. Unpublished letter in the poetry collection at the Lockwood Memorial Library, State University of New York at Buffalo.

9. An unpublished letter to Horace Gregory, May 9, 1944, in the Beinecke Library, Yale University, gives an account by Williams of a performance by Miss Graham; the biography project is mentioned in *SL*, p. 171.

10. William Carlos Williams, "An Essay on *Leaves of Grass*," 23.

11. Quoted in Constance Rourke, *Charles Sheeler* (New York, 1938), p. 49.

12. The subject of Williams's relation to modern painting has been perceptively explored by Abraham Jan Dijkstra, in "William Carlos Williams and Painting: The Hieroglyphics of a New Speech," unpublished dissertation (University of California, Berkeley, 1967).

13. *The New Age*, X (Feb. 15, 1912), 370.

14. George Santayana, *Winds of Doctrine* (New York, 1913), pp. 1–24. Subsequent references are made in the text.

15. T. E. Hulme, *Speculations* (New York, 1924), p. 97.

16. Ibid. p. 101.

17. T. E. Hulme, *Further Speculations* (Lincoln, 1962), p. 90.

18. J. Hillis Miller, *Poets of Reality*, pp. 309–10.

19. William Carlos Williams, "How To Write," *New Directions in Prose and Poetry*, No. 1 (Norfolk, Conn., 1936), n.p.

20. Ibid.

21. William Carlos Williams, *Briarcliff Quarterly*, III (October 1946), 205, 208.

CHAPTER III

1. For convenience, however, I will make reference to the titles Williams later provided, rather than to the original numbers. The *CEP* has twenty-eight poems in the sequence but its XXVII ("The Hermaphroditic Telephones") was not in the original version.

2. Quoted by Williams in the "Prologue" to *Kora in Hell* (*SE*, p. 12).

3. See Dijkstra, "William Carlos Williams and Painting," pp. 84–89.

4. Quoted by John C. Thirwall, "William Carlos Williams' 'Paterson,'" *New Directions in Prose and Poetry*, No. 17 (Norfolk, Conn., 1961), p. 253.

5. *Leaves of Grass: One Hundred Years After*, ed. Milton Hindus, p. 24.

6. William Carlos Williams, "An Approach to the Poem," pp. 58–59.

CHAPTER IV

1. I am using these writers only to establish a context in which to define and assess Williams. Other critics have suggested direct influence. James Guimond relates *In the American Grain* to Lawrence's *Studies* and the critics connected with the *Seven Arts* magazine in *The Art of William Carlos Williams* (Urbana, Ill., 1968), pp. 65–71; Abraham Dijkstra relates the book to the so-called "American Group" around Alfred Stieglitz in "William Carlos Williams and Painting," pp. 193–225.

2. Waldo Frank, *Our America* (New York, 1919), p. 10.

3. In "William Carlos Williams: On the Road to *Paterson*" and "The Unicorn in *Paterson*: William Carlos Williams"—both collected in *The Poem of the Mind* (New York, 1966), pp. 125–61; Louis Martz uses *In the American Grain* to introduce a discussion of *Paterson*; his student Walter Scott Peterson follows this practice in *An Approach to Paterson* (New Haven, Conn., 1967). Mr. Martz's pieces are important generative studies of Williams, and the Peterson book is an exhaustive study of *Paterson*'s themes, but their format implies a secondary status for *In the American Grain*. In "*In the American Grain:* William Carlos Williams on the Amer-

ican Past," *American Quarterly*, XIX (Fall 1967), 499–515, Alan Holder argues that Williams's book is "a highly selective, impressionistic account of our history, the product of his imagination playing over the documents. As might be expected of such a work, it is not committed to a single, monolithic thesis, but has several central concerns . . ." (500–1). Mr. Holder thus does not see either the coherence or the profundity of Williams's book. In the struggle between will and the land the book does have a unifying center, and "playing over," as we shall see, is an entirely inaccurate characterization of Williams's grasp of the documents, which is often deep and firm. Mr. Holder does attempt to establish Williams's sources, but his study is incomplete—not all available sources have been cited—and inexact—sometimes wrong translations are cited.

4. See the discussion in Phillip Damon, "History and Idea in Renaissance Criticism," in *Literary Criticism and Historical Understanding*, ed. Phillip Damon (New York, 1967), pp. 25–51.

5. The Mather quotations are from *The Wonders of the Invisible World* (London, 1862), pp. 9–14, 129–48, 159–63. Since he associates the trials with the suppression of natural energy, Williams quotes only accounts of the trials of women, although Mather also includes the trial of a minister (pp. 149–58).

6. References to Tenochtitlan (*Kora*, p. 40) and Columbus (*Kora*, p. 34) in *Kora in Hell* indicate that Williams began looking at these documents as early as 1917, six years before these early chapters appeared in *Broom*.

7. Alan Holder cites the translation of Rasles's second letter which appears in Rev. William Ingraham Kip's *The Early Jesuit Missions in North America* (New York, 1946); but Williams himself cites the original *Lettres Édifiantes* (p. 120), uses both letters printed there and always quotes the French of the source. Williams may have discovered Rasles through Kip, but this was one of the few cases in which he refused to rely on a translation.

8. Sources for the Red Eric chapter are "The Saga of Eric the Red" and "The Vinland History of the Flat Island Book" in the translation by Arthur Middleton Reeves. Williams probably found these documents in *The Northmen, Columbus and Cabot, 985–1503*, eds. Julius Olson and Edward G. Bourne (New York, 1906), since this is clearly the book he used for the Columbus chapter. The first three paragraphs of the Freydis episode are taken from

"The Saga of Eric the Red," pp. 31, 37–38, while the rest is drawn
from "The Vinland History," pp. 62–65. In both cases he sticks
close to the language of the Reeves translation, but he often
edits it in small ways that make the language more economical and
forceful.

9. *Conquest: Dispatches of Cortez from the New World*, eds.
Irwin Blacker and Harry Rosen (New York, 1962), is cited by
Professor Holder. The book reprints a 1906 translation by Francis
A. MacNutt, but Williams used the translation by George Folsom
(New York, 1843), whose wording he often follows very closely
and from whose introduction he has taken the list of artifacts on
pp. 28–29.

10. The main source for the De Soto chapter is the "Relation"
of the journey by the unidentified Hidalgo of Elvas, translated by
Edward G. Bourne in *Narratives of the Career of Hernando
De Soto* (New York, 1904), I, 3–223. Williams also read "Relation"
by De Biedma (ibid. II, 3–40) from which he took a few quotes,
such as "which seemed like a thousand years" (p. 45), "obscure
and intricate parts" (p. 46), and "He went about for the road and
returned to us desperate" (p. 47).

11. A few details—Jefferson's suggestion that Burr get the news
from the papers, Hamilton's confession that he might have been
misinformed of Burr's intentions—are not in Parton and seem to
come from the *Memoirs* (New York, 1837), II, 320, and II, 139,
respectively. But in speaking about Burr's feats in the Revolutionary War, his clash with Washington, his courtship and marriage,
Williams comes close to Parton's wording often enough to show
that he, or his wife, mainly relied on *The Life and Times* (New
York, 1858). The "they say" anecdote with which he concludes
(p. 207) comes directly from Parton, p. 637. It is an index of how
hotheaded Williams's handling of this source was that in the debates over who fired first in the duel with Hamilton, he does not
accept Parton's judicious reconstruction (p. 350), but the one
offered by Burr's seconds, quoted by Parton (p. 617).

12. Benjamin Spencer shows how Williams shifts the meaning
of "local" in order to push his argument; see "Doctor Williams'
American Grain," *Tennessee Studies in Literature*, VIII (1963), 4.

13. Thomas Whitaker, *William Carlos Williams* (New York,
1968), pp. 77–91. I agree with his contention that "in theme and
style, *In the American Grain* is a dialogical encounter with the

New World" (p. 78) but I have extensive disagreement with his
application of it.

14. *Broom*, IV (March 1923), 252–60.

15. Williams read the *Journal of the First Voyage*, translated
by Sir Clements R. Markham, in *The Northmen, Columbus and
Cabot*, eds. Julius Olson and Edward G. Bourne, pp. 89–258. For
the fourth voyage he relied on the *Letter of Columbus to the Nurse
of Prince John*, translated by George F. Barwick (ibid. pp. 371–
83) and the *Letter of Columbus on his Fourth Voyage*, translated
by R. H. Major (ibid. pp. 389–418).

16. See, for example, the last four paragraphs of Williams's text
(pp. 25–26) which appear to give exact quotation of the *Journal;*
but there actually has been a good deal of elision, designed to draw
out the basic motive, the true voice, of the young Columbus.

CHAPTER V

1. All of their early critical assessments of Williams have been
collected in *William Carlos Williams, A Collection of Critical
Essays*, ed. J. Hillis Miller (Englewood Cliffs, N. J., 1966).

2. Thomas Whitaker, *William Carlos Williams*, p. 119.

3. Frank Kermode, *The Sense of an Ending* (New York, 1967),
pp. 129–30.

4. *Six American Short Novels*, ed. R. P. Blackmur (New York,
1960).

5. Sherwood Anderson, *Winesburg, Ohio* (New York, 1946),
p. 144.

6. Louis Martz, *The Poem of the Mind*, p. 132.

7. William Carlos Williams, "'White Mule' versus Poetry,"
The Writer, L (August 1937), 243–45.

CHAPTER VI

1. Much more has been written about *Paterson* than Williams's
earlier work. Among defenders of the poem are Louis Martz in
the two articles already referred to; Sister M. Bernetta Quinn, *The
Metamorphic Tradition in Modern Poetry* (New Brunswick, N.J.,
1955), pp. 89–129; Walter Sutton, "Dr. Williams' 'Paterson' and the
Quest for Form," *Criticism*, II (Summer 1960), 242–59; Roy Har-
vey Pearce, *The Continuity of American Poetry* (Princeton, N.J.,

1961), pp. 111–30; Walter Scott Peterson, *An Approach to Paterson* (New Haven, Conn., 1967); A. Kingsley Weatherhead, *The Edge of the Image* (Seattle, 1967), pp. 121–36 and *passim;* James Guimond, *The Art of William Carlos Williams,* pp. 153–200; Thomas Whitaker, *William Carlos Williams,* pp. 129–51; Joel Osborne Conarroe, "A Local Pride: The Poetry of *Paterson,*" *PMLA,* LXXXIV (May 1969), 547–58.

2. Randall Jarrell, *Poetry and the Age* (New York, 1955), pp. 238–39.

3. Joseph Frank, *The Widening Gyre* (New Brunswick, 1963), p. 19.

4. My discussion of the modern epic here is indebted to Richard Hutson, "The Word Dimensional," unpublished dissertation (University of Illinois, 1967), pp. 33–46.

5. The relationships between Williams and some of his predecessors in the modern long poem is incisively discussed by Joel Conarroe, "A Local Pride: The Poetry of *Paterson,*" 548–52.

6. Ibid., 552–58.

7. Ralph Nash, "The Use of Prose in 'Paterson,' " *Perspective,* VI (Autumn–Winter 1953), 194.

8. James Guimond, *The Art of William Carlos Williams,* pp. 175–200.

9. These allusions are discussed most extensively by Walter Scott Peterson, *An Approach to Paterson,* pp. 16, 36n, 62–64, 68–70, 85–86, 95f., 110, 178, 179, 191.

CHAPTER VII

1. This crisis in Williams's career has been examined at length in Sherman Paul's excellent *The Music of Survival* (Urbana, Ill., 1968).

2. Walter Sutton, "Dr. Williams' 'Paterson' and the Quest for Form," 242.

3. Louis Martz, *The Poem of the Mind,* p. 155. Professor Martz himself, however, stresses the "wholeness" of the entire work, Books I–V (p. 156).

4. Quoted in Linda W. Wagner, *The Poems of William Carlos Williams* (Middletown, Conn., 1964), p. 110.

5. For elaboration of this point, see *The Poem of the Mind,* pp. 156f.

6. J. Hillis Miller, *Poets of Reality*, p. 355; Sherman Paul, *The Music of Survival*, p. 1.

7. Because these poems have been more widely accepted, they have been the subject of some perceptive criticism. See *The Music of Survival*, pp. 62–109; *Poets of Reality*, pp. 355–59; A. Kingsley Weatherhead, *The Edge of the Image*, pp. 136–52, 162–69; and Thomas Whitaker, *William Carlos Williams*, pp. 152–63.

Index

WILLIAM CARLOS WILLIAMS